The Long Way to Europe

The Long Way to Europe

*Historical Observations
from a Contemporary View*

Edited by Wolfgang J. Mommsen
With a Foreword by Walter Laqueur

 edition q, inc.
Chicago, Berlin, Tokyo, and Moscow

Also available in German as *Der lange Weg nach Europa: Historische Betrachtungen aus gegenwärtiger Sicht*, by edition q Verlags-GmbH, Berlin.

Library of Congress Cataloging-In-Publication Data:

Lange Weg nach Europa. English.
    The long way to Europe : historical observations from a contemporary view / edited by Wolfgang J. Mommsen ; foreword by Walter Laqueur.
      p. cm.
    Includes bibliographical references.
    ISBN 0-86715-270-2
    1. European federation.   2. Europe—Politics and government—20th century. I. Mommsen, Wolfgang J., 1930–   . II. Title.
d1060.L326 1994
940.55—dc20   93-36819
                                                            CIP

Contents

Foreword

Walter Laqueur

Americans have watched Europe's long road to unity with attention and sympathy but also with considerable irritation; it has taken very long and no end is in sight. When the essays by Prof. Mommsen were written, there was more optimism than now; full unity seemed to be just around the corner. Now it appears much further ahead. In most European countries, the Eurosceptics and Europessimists have uttered dire warnings and succeeded in watering down the Maastricht blueprints. The obstacle race to European unity resembles that famous pilgrimage somewhere in northwest Germany where three steps forward are invariably followed by two steps back— sometimes even three.

Americans tend to believe in continents; they are impatient with small countries. Quite often, after a return from Europe to Washington, I was asked what Europe thought of a new president or a new political or intellectual fashion. My answer that such generalizations were impossible because there was no Europe, and certainly no European consensus, was always met with disbelief or even dismay: When would the Europeans at long last get their act (in their opinion) together? Americans tend to forget that their country, too, was quite small at one time; it took a long time to unite Italy and Germany (three wars, Bismarck and many decades), and even the United States, like Rome, was not built in a day. Secessionism is not unknown in American history.

Once upon a time Europe was united and it was a beautiful, brilliant time, as Novalis pointed out in a famous essay. But then division prevailed and it was only in the eighteenth century that the European idea found new advocates among some philosophers, writers and, of course, Napoleon. At that time it was generally thought, at least by the intellectuals, that only Christianity could unit Europe; even Victor Hugo, a Republican, shared this belief (which was somewhat unreal), for how could Protestant Europe accept the leadership of the Pope? But there was also the beginning of a new vision of Europe, of common interest, best expressed by Saint-Simon and Thierry in 1814 in a book about the reconstruction of a community of European states in which even a European parliament was envisaged. In contrast to Novalis, they thought that the golden age of Europe did not belong to the distant past—it was yet to come.

To what extent was America an idol for those in Europe dreaming about unity? There were a few looking with interest and even enthusiasm to America; Goethe *(Amerika, du hast es besser)* was one of them, so was Chateaubriand, and Victor Hugo expected an infusion of warmth, vitality and youthful spirit from the new continent to the old.[1]

But, on the whole, America was a very distant and savage country about which even the educated knew very little and which hardly intrigued them.

Curiously, simple people, the huddled masses, were far more attracted, and millions of them emigrated to the country of freedom and economic opportunity. There was as intriguing a disparity between elite attitudes and mass culture in the nineteenth century as in the twentieth. The year George Bernard Shaw wrote that a 100 percent American was a 99 percent idiot, European immigrants were queuing up in European ports to get a place even in the most miserable conditions to cross the Atlantic. In the second half of the twentieth century, when cultural anti-Americanism was the great fashion in Western Europe, American culture was winning hands-down the battle for the hearts and minds of Europe. It became difficult to watch any movie in Berlin, Paris or London that was not of American origin.

Among the European countries most interested in America at the time was Russia, and the first Russian to provide a detailed and systematic account of how the American system of government worked (the term democracy was used at the time with some hesitation) was a distant relative of mine, Alexander Borisovich Lakier.[2] He was sanguine about America's future.

"Young, active, practical, happy in their enterprises, the American people will have an influence on Europe, but it will use neither arms, nor swords nor fire, nor death and destruction. They will spread their influence by the strength of their own inventions, their trade and their industry. And this influence will be more durable than any conquest."

Lakier's prediction was correct as far as it went, but incomplete. On two occasions America did have to intervene in Europe with sword and fire to redress the political balance, and for many years after the Second World War the American presence in Europe was taken for granted.

Some Europeans and many Americans reached the conclusion years ago that America had outstayed its welcome in Europe, and the slogan "Yankee Go Home" was heard on both sides of the Atlantic. At the same time, there has been a tendency in Europe to exaggerate America's vital interests in the old continent. America could not possibly surrender its position in Europe, it was frequently argued in the sixties and seventies, because of its massive investments, but those investments in Canada and Mexico were even more substantial. In any case, foreign trade was less important for the U.S. than for the major European nations. But America could not possibly surrender Western Europe to Soviet pressure, it was argued. This, too, was not quite convincing, for whatever the Soviet Union might have done in Europe, America was not in the front line, whereas Germany and the other European nations were. Cultural ties and ethnic kinship were invoked as the cement of the alliance. This, too, was correct as far as it went, but no massive American military presence in Europe was needed to preserve these ties; in any case, New York had become the world's most important art market and musical center.

Many Europeans are not wholly familiar with the depth of the American isolationist tradition and American ambivalence toward Europe. They seem to have forgotten that the early settlers in North America did not come because life was so good in Europe, to paraphrase a Russian saying. They came because of religious persecution, famine and lack of prospects. The very first major American literary document, William Bradford's *History of Plymouth Plantation*, written between 1630 and 1651, included dire comments on that "gross darkness of popery" which the pilgrims escaped. George Washington admonished his fellow countrymen to evade at any cost entanglement in the quarrels and intrigues of Europe, "The Federalist" wrote about the arrogant pretensions of a Europe that claimed everything was degenerate in America — even the dogs were said to stop barking, having breathed American air.

Through American intellectual life in the nineteenth century, suspicion of Europe runs like a red thread. If European visitors from Trollope to Dickens were shocked by the uncivilized American natives, American writers also portrayed the country with bitterness and sarcasm as in James Kirke Paulding's *John Bull in America (1825)*: Every third American was drunk by nine in the morning, pigs were about to be given the right to vote, and the inhabitants of New York consisted of three classes—beggars, thieves and those who made debts. Ferdinand Kürnberger, a liberal German novelist, wrote a book (*Der Amerikamüde*, 1855) that was very famous at the time; it contained all the stereotypes of anti-Americanism prevailing to this day, above all the basic tenet that Americans had only one god—Mammon. Heine, who had never been to America, subscribed to that idea, so did Knut Hamsun and Maxim Gorky, who made their way to God's own country in later years and came to regret it. There is the famous exchange between Oswald Spengler and Harvard University, which had invited him to attend a celebration. Spengler, who had never been to the United States, declined with thanks; he feared that the shock would be too great and that he might be compelled to revise some of his views as a result of the exposure to American realities.

American judgment on Europe, despite all suspicions and reservations, was less disdainful. Americans continued to attend Europe's leading univer-sities because they were superior to their own, and a few settled in Europe, having found Britain's aristocratic society more congenial, or the social and cultural freedom of Paris in the 1920s more attractive. But, like Sam Dodsworth, they did not feel at ease in Europe; the snobbery and arrogance of the aristocracy made them uncomfortable. While they were often pain-fully aware of their own lack of sophistication, they decried the insincerity and the frivolity of the upper-class Europeans they met.

There were knowledgeable and sensible people on both sides of the Atlantic concentrating on the admirable rather than the negative features of the American and the European ways of life. But there was little love lost between the continents.[3] In retrospect, it still is not quite clear why America entered the First World War. Economic interest was certainly not a decisive factor; if economic rivalry had been the main motive, America should have made war against Britain, not Germany. Ethnic and cultural kinship did play a role, but it cannot account for everything. Pro-British sentiments were counterbalanced by anti-Russian (or rather anti-Tsarist) feelings. In the final analysis, American idealism was indeed important—the belief that the Kaiser was up to no good, and that he might win unless the Yanks were coming.

The role of idealism in American foreign policy has seldom been fully appreciated in Europe perhaps because it has been so long since important decisions in the foreign policy of the major European states had been motivated by idealistic consideration—or at least disinterest. Everyone knew that in foreign affairs there was no room for friendship, only for interests and ambitions. Why should America be different? American preoccupation with human rights in the 1970s again caused considerable annoyance in European foreign ministries; this surely was not the right way to promote peace between nations and further international coordination. Aside from a few exceptions such as Holland and (within limits) the Scandinavian countries, the foreign policies of the major European countries kept human rights far from the top of the political agenda.

American policy makers, on the other hand, complained about European reluctance to resist aggression, whether it came from the Soviet Union or in the Middle East. Part of the explanation was, as Henry Kissinger said on more than one occasion, that only America was thinking in global terms, of *Weltpolitik*, whereas the horizon of even the major European countries was continental, regional. European statesmen did not like Kissinger's observation, but in retrospect it cannot be seriously contested.

America's involvement in European affairs was quite limited prior to the First World War. True, American presidents helped to make peace between Russia and Japan (1905), and they were prominently involved in the establishment of an International Court at Hague and the peace conferences around the turn of the century (1899 and 1907). But primarily, America's impact on Europe was through economic power and the most advanced technology, the country of central heating and the best dentists, of incandescent lamps, the telephone, moving pictures and, of course, aircraft. The fact that America also emerged in the 1870s as the world's leading agricultural producer, and subsequently as the strongest industrial power, did not fail to impress the Europeans. But economic power did not translate into political influence, as far as the European leaders were concerned: America's business was business, not world politics—American imperial conquests came as an afterthought. They were small and did not last long.

The great change came with the First World War. In 1919 there was no world statesman more popular in Europe than President Wilson. But Congress did not ratify American participation in the League of Nations, and for all one knows the League would have failed even if America had joined. There still were some major American initiatives in Europe in the interwar years, such as the Kellogg-Briand pact to outlaw war, and the Dawes and Young plans to reduce the amount of reparations to be paid by Germany. These were not successful. The Kellogg-Briand pact was signed by the major powers (except Japan and the Soviet Union), but helped in no way to stem the tide of war in the 1930s. It is now of interest mainly because many of its provisions became part of the United Nations Charter. The Dawes and Young plans were not of decisive importance either. Germany prospered in the middle twenties despite reparations, and like the rest of the world it

underwent a major crisis after 1929, which was not caused by the reparations. The political damage had been done at the Versailles peace conference,
and the German nationalists did the most to make capital of it.

President Roosevelt's attempts to prevent the outbreak of the war in
Europe, and later on to limit it, were ineffectual, and it was only after Pearl
Harbor and America's entry into the war that the last chapter began of
America's involvement in Europe's affairs, which continues to this day.
During the war all sorts of declarations were passed by the leaders of the
United Nations, but they referred to a new world order rather than European
unity. After the war, the tendency in America was to demobilize the armed
force as quickly as possible and to withdraw from Europe, as it did in 1919.
But it was not to be. The threat of economic ruin in Western Europe and the
danger of a Soviet invasion, or at least the imposition of a Soviet zone of
influence in Europe, led to the Truman Doctrine and the Marshall Plan. The
idea of close European cooperation began to figure prominently in American strategy. The Marshall Plan led by necessity to steps toward integration—the liberalization of trade, a European Payments Union, the Organization for European Economic Cooperation (EEC) and, eventually, the idea of
a common market. American thinking at the time was that Europe would be
able to overcome its difficulties only in close cooperation; this was a radical
new departure, which not everyone in Europe liked. It is interesting in
retrospect that these American initiatives, even if not quite specific, predated
European initiatives for greater unity, such as the Coal and Steel Community, the Monnet Plan and, eventually, the Treaty of Rome.

Moves toward common defense followed a similar pattern, even though
the resistance in this respect was stronger still. American policy makers had
no wish to deploy forces in Europe without a commensurate European
effort. Washington was looking not for a dozen partners but one partner;
after the French parliament had defeated the initiative to bring about a
European Defense Community (and after WEU—the West European
Union—remained stillborn) NATO was the only realistic alternative.

The makers of American foreign policy in the early postwar period all
believed in a united Europe, if only because such collaboration was bound to
reduce the burden on America. This was true up to the time of President
Kennedy, who said in 1962 that a strong and united Europe, which he
regarded as a partner and not as a rival, was part of the American grand
design, the main task of American foreign policy. In the years that followed,
American enthusiasm diminished. France had virtually withdrawn from
NATO, and de Gaulle and some of his successors, such as Jobert, did their
best to reduce European cooperation with America (and to prevent the
extension of the European Community). America complained that the

European countries did not pull their weight in NATO, and felt let down by her European allies in critical situations. As they saw it, the alliance had become a one-sided affair or, to be precise, had never moved beyond this initial stage. This situation was further complicated by economic conflicts that persist to this day. Once the main problem in U.S.–European relations had been the "dollar gap" and the (technological) *défi américain*. But then the various economic miracles took place in Europe, while the value of the dollar declined. Europe became more and more reluctant to support a world financial system (Bretton Woods), which had been designed by the Americans in their own best interest, and which after 1970 seemed outdated. This attitude strengthened those in America who had argued all along that Europe was not so much an ally as a competitor, and if America was treated as an adversary, why not retaliate in kind? It ought be recalled that certain initiatives in Congress to reduce U.S. forces in Europe were defeated only by the narrowest of margins (the Mansfield amendment). If Europeans were arguing that America was a spent force, a growing number of Americans maintained that the Far East was much more important for America economically, and in the long run also politically.

But this orientation toward the Pacific as replacement for the Atlantic Alliance never became U.S. foreign policy. Nixon and Kissinger had their misgivings about European steadfastness, but they still declared 1973 the "Year of Europe." It was not a great success, but since expectations had not only been unduly high in the beginning, disappointment was not that acute. Early on during his presidency, Nixon had stated that a united Europe had to be built by the Europeans — no one else. He thought that if America had been an eager advocate of European unity earlier, it might have done more harm than good. America would have to follow the process from the sidelines as a sympathetic spectator. In the meantime, the emphasis would have to be on bilateral relations with the various states of Europe.[4]

The recent history of European unity has a certain resemblance to the case history of a manic-depressive. After the dejection of the early 1980s about the lack of progress, a new initiative began, and by 1989–90 real unity seemed just around the corner, giving way to overconfidence. Well in advance, 1992 was declared to be a historical milestone. America was virtually written off by European statesmen such as François Mitterrand; looking a mere few years ahead, these prophets did not see a major role for the U.S. to play — economically weak and declining, its commitments far exceeding its real power. (Only five years earlier, Mitterrand had compared Europe with a deserted building site.) The future clearly belonged to a united Europe, the greatest common market in the world. Such optimism was greatly enhanced by the collapse of communism and the disintegration of the Soviet empire. The attitude towards America in influential circles in France, Germany and other European countries became one not so much of antagonism but of pity — poor America, its shrinking political and economic power was reason for commiseration rather than jubilation.

But 1992 came and went, and unkind critics were reminded of the famous verse in Horace's *Ars Poetica* — "mountains being in labor and a ridiculous mouse being born." Denmark voted against Maastricht,[5] France approved it with a microscopic majority, and if there had been a plebiscite in Britain, it would probably have been defeated. As Margaret Thatcher told her listeners, the people of the Magna Carta would never surrender its liberties to the malevolent and faceless bureaucrats in Brussels.

By the summer of 1993 there was near despair with regard to the stalled momentum of European unity, and even more with regard to the economic and political crises afflicting virtually all countries of the continent. (Some of the contributors to this volume had been aware of the coming of the crisis, but they could not envisage its full extent.) Mitterand's party suffered a crushing defeat in the French elections of 1993, the German economy faced its severest crisis since the Second World War, Italy and Britain were in deep political trouble, and even such models of prosperity and stability as Sweden and Finland were facing unprecedented economic difficulties. Industrial output declined all over Europe (by almost 10 percent in the case of Germany), the unemployment rate exceeded 10 percent in most European countries. Ironically, the only Western economy to show modest progress was America's. (The British economic indicators were also slightly better than those of their European neighbors, but Britain's economic performance had been so dismal in other respects that this hardly mattered.)

Seen against this background, European fears about the future, coming after years of overconfidence, were not entirely groundless. It was also true that conditions in America gave rise to apprehension, domestically and in foreign affairs: Bush's foreign policy with all its shortcomings seemed, in retrospect, a model of vision and competence in comparison with the amateurishness displayed by the Clinton administration in its early phase.

Europe did, of course, face serious economic and political problems. The resistance against European unity had been underrated: What had seemed reasonable to a political elite was taken as self-evident truth, and no serious attempt had been made to explain to the public at large that many of the fears connected with the reduction of sovereignty were unfounded. Norway would not have to converse in Sicilian dialect, nor would they become a German colony. It should have been frankly conceded that unification did involve risks and threats, but that none of these were fatal. Shortcomings could be put right as a new Europe was built, the advantages outweighed the losses, and a united Europe would be in everyone's overall interest.

But the original political impetus seemed to have faded. In the beginning, and for many years after, the two main *raison d'êtres* of a united Europe were the conviction that another war in Europe (most likely between France and Germany) had to be prevented at any cost, and that a counterweight was needed against the Russian colossus.

By 1992, the danger of another European civil war had disappeared and so had the danger from the East. In the circumstances, the urgency for making some major steps towards unity had vanished. The European nation-states had existed for centuries; why make radical new departures if the old system worked reasonably well? No one in Europe opposed economic cooperation, but in the absence of a clear and present danger, a considerable number of Europeans were reluctant to give up time-honored traditions and customs, fearful of challenges from within and without that would confront Europe in the years to come — which the individual countries will not be able to solve in isolation. The Eurosceptics will have to learn the hard way; the learning process could be protracted and costly. But it is pointless to exert pressure from the outside; recognition that a united Europe is needed must come from within to be lasting. Whenever the nations of Europe were forced to unite, the endeavor ended in disaster. All indications show that a free and reasonably prosperous Europe will survive only in unity, but it seems equally obvious that the long road to Europe is not finished yet, that the nation-states will fight tooth and nail against any surrender of their sovereignty. Some further shocks are probably needed to provide fresh impetus to the movement toward unity. Jean Monnet once said that crises are the great federators; Europe is in a state of crisis, but it might not be severe enough to generate the momentum that is needed.

But what is Europe, where are its frontiers? It was easy enough to answer this question while the Cold War lasted. Europe was the countries this side of the iron curtain. With the disappearance of the iron curtain there are no such certainties anymore. The "return to Europe" was an essential part of the vision of the East European nations and also the Baltic countries. The situation in Russia was more complicated; Slavophilism may be in a state of agony, but the "Eurasians" have had a field day among the Russian right. This refers to the school of thought that first appeared among the Russian emigres in the 1920s, according to which Russia's future was in Asia. It had never truly belonged to Europe, and the Europeans had always treated it (according to this doctrine) with contempt as an alien body. It is certainly true that Russia's history points to a *Sonderweg* from the Middle Ages on; what has been said about Germany is *a fortiori* true with regard to Russia, whose traditions differ in important respects from those of Europe. But there is no future for Russia in the East, for the Asia the Eurasians invoke is imaginary. They have no wish to convert to Islamic fundamentalism, and the Chinese and Indian cultures are infinitely more remote than that of Europe.

The westernization of Russia is by no means over. It could well be a long process and there will be disappointments and setbacks in the years and decades ahead. The hopes concerning Western assistance will certainly not be fulfilled, and in Eastern Europe and Russia there is the growing realization that certain aspects of the European way of life cannot be copied in conditions differing greatly from those prevailing in the western part of the continent.

The disappearance of the iron curtain has removed a threat and made an opening to the East possible. This is a great chance that no one could have envisaged even a few years ago. But it is a chance for the distant, not the immediate, future. Eastern Europe and Russia should, of course, eventually be part of a united Europe. But in view of the enormous economic and social disparities between West and East, a common market cannot possibly soon become a reality; all kinds of special arrangements will be needed to prepare the way for a gradual rapprochement. And it is not even certain that in its present sorry state Europe has the necessary political will to make use of a chance which, if neglected, may not occur again in the near future. A leading European statesman once said that Europe half-finished was like a house that the building workers failed to complete: Exposed to the elements, it will deteriorate and eventually collapse.

One day Americans may lose patience with Europe. The slow uphill struggle for unity has been exasperating, and if many Europeans believe that no closer collaboration is needed than exists at present, it is not up to Americans to act as advisors and advocates. The unending and frustrating talks about the liberalization of world trade have certainly not enhanced pro–united Europe sentiment in America.

A more detached attitude has much to recommend itself. But it should also be accepted that unless America will withdraw altogether from world politics, it will need allies; if so, Europe is bound to be its most important ally for the foreseeable future. American trade with the Far East may increase more quickly in the years to come, but as far as commercial relations are concerned, there is bound to be as much, if not more, rivalry with the Far East as with Europe.

Apart from the various written agreements with Europe with regard to defense, commerce and political cooperation, there has been an unwritten understanding underlying the alliance. This understanding has been sorely tried at times, and as alliances are not eternal, the one between North America and Europe may one day come to an end. But this moment has not yet come. Even the most inveterate critics of America in Europe know in their innermost hearts that they still need America even more than America needs Europe. The present state of Europe is not conducive to sanguine optimism, but it is useful to remember that this is not the first time that the idea of Europe seemed to have run out of steam. The European mood tends to change every few years. Measured by the dreams of the early architects of a united Europe, the achievements of the last four decades have been disappointing. Again, as in the 1970s and early 1980s, Europe seems to be struck by *aboulia*, that strange paralysis of political will. Measured by less exacting standards, the achievements are quite impressive; many steps toward closer cooperation seem irreversible, and, for all one knows, one day a fresh start might be made. In his *magnum opus*, Alfred Marshall wrote that progress in the economic world must be slow for *natura not facit saltum*. This is even more true with regard to political progress, except, of course, in time of war.

Notes

1. Quoted in P.M. Lützeler, *Europa, Analysen und Visionen der Romantik*, Frankfurt, 1982, p. 24.

2. Alexander Borisovich Lakier, *Puteshevstvie . . .* (1859). An English, abridged version, *A Russian Looks at America* (eds. A. Schrier and J. Story), was published by the University of Chicago Press in 1979.

3. This refers much more to Western than to Eastern Europe, where attitudes toward America were traditionally more positive than in Britain, France and Germany.

4. Richard M. Nixon, *U.S. Foreign Policy for the 1970s*. Washington, 1970, p. 32.

5. After a revision of the draft treaty, the Danish electorate reversed its vote and came out in favor of Maastricht in 1993 — but not by an overwhelming majority.

Introduction

Wolfgang J. Mommsen

With the establishment of a common market and the Maastricht treaty's call for a common currency within five years, the European Community is taking another step toward still-greater integration of the European economy. The integration of the national economies will in all likelihood forge closer ties among the member states of the Community, bringing the great idea of a unified Europe a good deal closer to reality. This moves the debate over the future structure of a new Europe from the realm of theoretical discussion onto a stage of concrete inquiry. At its center is the question of whether the future Europe is to be a European nation-state with a sovereign parliament and central institutions authorized to act independently taking the place of the current nation-states, or whether the future Europe will be a European federal state whose member states retain their individual national identities. Even if the choice turns out to be the latter model—although this would be a great disappointment to the pioneers of the European idea of the fifties and sixties—how power is to be shared between the central authorities of this European federal state and the nation-state governments would remain a subject of dispute. There is good reason to think that the future European state will have to rely on the governments and parliaments of the existing European nation-states to legitimize its policies. Still, nation-states will have to do without many of the sovereignty rights they still possess *de jure*, if not more often *de facto*. They will have to align their national identities with Europe to a much stronger degree than they do today, even if, at least in Western Europe, we have come a long way from the classic principle of the autonomous nation-state. In general, the signs for progress toward a unified Europe, all obstacles aside, are good, despite some thunder in the distance. Other states with considerable economic power, especially Austria and Sweden, are expected to join the European Community in the foreseeable future. Even Switzerland, committed to everlasting neutrality since its founding and always proud of its independence within the European system in good times and bad, considers joining. But with the expansion of the Club of Twelve, the problems of economic and political integration may become considerably larger, and so will the need to find a way of harmonizing the still strongly opposing national identities, particularly as there is no external opponent to force unification after the collapse of the communist world system.

Moreover, the coordinates of European unification were fundamentally changed by the democratic revolution in East-Central and in Eastern Europe. With the collapse of the "Wall" or, more precisely, the Iron Curtain, which had stretched diagonally across Europe, the road to Europe, firmly closed to the Eastern nations for a long time by Soviet policies, has now been opened and all are determined to take it. It will not be possible simply to leave them standing at the doorstep of a unified Europe forever. Even now the economies of the European Community have been significantly affected by the unification of the two German states. The German government quite properly never allowed any doubt about its determination not to let the process of a unified Europe be slowed down by the reunification of the two German states. The French government, especially, saw in German re-unification a compelling reason for forging ahead with European unification to prevent a German hegemony in East-Central Europe. However, the need to rebuild the desolate economy left behind by the SED regime in the new German states makes considerable demands on the financial resources of Germany, and the economic problems this entails cannot be ignored. Interest rates have risen enormously, bringing economy injury to the other member states in the European community, some already clearly beyond the pain threshold.

It is, however, crucial that a closer merger of the Western European states, or even the formation of a supranational European federal state, cannot be envisioned in the long run unless the East-Central European states are included in this system. Nor will the "associate" model be enough in the long run. The enduring stability of political and social relations in Central Europe can be secured only when the political and economic conditions in the East-Central European states are elevated to a level comparable to those of Western Europe, and if they are included in the family of the new Europe.

The income scales alone as they presently exist would have a destabilizing effect in the long run. An increasing East-West emigration of work force into the rich countries of the Community would be just as difficult to prevent as a flow of trade that would find ways of circumventing the customs barriers of the Community. (Unless a "wall" were to be erected again, this time by the West but placed further to the East.) Above all, Eastern Europe, provided it did not achieve long-term improvement of economic conditions, would become a virulent political trouble spot inevitably contagious to the countries of the new Europe. Democratic conditions and a pure free market economy *à la* Western Europe will be achieved only with the unstinting help of the West; it would certainly come to a halt if the door to the united European Community remains closed to the East-Central states, which now so bravely reach out for Europe.

Once before, at the end of World War I, Europe and the world confronted the great task of building a new political and economic order for East-Central Europe after the collapse of the Hapsburg monarchy and the czarist empire. In 1917 American President Woodrow Wilson proclaimed it as his objective "to make the world safe for democracy." This great goal was a complete failure at that time, mostly because the European nations, West and East, failed to repudiate an aggressive nationalism, which had risen to unprecedented heights in World War I, rather than seek common solutions for Europe. Instead, these aggressive nationalists, after an interlude of Left-radical revolutionary attempts right after the war, went on an uncontrolled rampage between the two wars. This was encouraged by oppressive economic conditions in most of the European states, made even worse by narrow-minded, selfish policies.

For this reason, conditions were favorable for the rise of the fascist movement or the proto-fascist regimes, founded on a policy of native nationalism and contemptuous of the efforts of the League of Nations to ensure appropriate protection for the national minorities in the newly created national states. In turn, ethnic minorities joined the predominantly radical nationalist parties, which rejected any compromise between the ethnic groups, advocating instead the breakup of the respective native state and the homecoming to one's own national state, like the Sudeten Germans in Czechoslovakia, the Hungarians in Rumania and the Poles in the Ukraine and in Lithuania. The great undertaking to give Europe a stable new order based on the foundations of the democratic right of self-determination failed, with far-reaching consequences obvious to us all, particularly the world catastrophe of World War II, which brought about the physical annihilation of more than 25 million people. It is good to remember this today, because we stand at a similar point of historical development as that of 1920, a point at which even Soviet policies under the NEP temporarily considered departing from the course of forced collectivization of its economy and opening its own society toward Europe. It is as if Europe is given a chance to put its own house in order for the second time in history. But today, in view of the advanced unification of West European nations and their economic affluence, conditions are far more favorable.

These are the considerations that underlie this collection of essays commenting on the "long road to Europe" principally from the point of view of individual European nations. It allows authors not only from the member states of the European Community, but also from the Eastern states to have a word. Complete representation of the individual countries was never intended; this would have been beyond the bounds of such a publication. The contributions included here deal first with the great intellectual, political and social issues, which determined the positions of the respective countries or regions vis-à-vis Europe in the past and which even today hold considerable sway over attitudes to the ideas of European unification. They are, as a rule, historical views, or at least views which arose historically, which are responsible for the degree to which the different peoples have an inner relationship to the larger unity of Europe, regardless of their roots in a particular national identity.

The idea of a federation of European states appears relatively early in Europe's history of ideas: It is already fully developed in thought during the epoch of enlightenment. Much time was required, however, and many obstacles had to be overcome before it could gain wide acceptance. The European idea was always in the shadow of hegemonic power politics, especially during the epoch of the national power states, and never more so than in the era of the fascist movement that followed. Especially the National Socialists misused the idea of a unified Europe to give their claims to power ideological legitimacy. Only as a democratic Europe was rebuilt after World War II did the idea of a unified Europe win a secure place in the political consciousness of the European nations. Along with it came the hope for a new political order in Europe to end the division of the European peoples and simultaneously lay the foundations for a speedy economic recovery. In retrospect, however, it was indeed a "long road" to that point, and the political realization of this great ideal is even now only partially completed. The obstacles standing in the way of Europe's unification were many, and the setbacks, especially those of an economic nature, sometimes considerable. Nevertheless, Europe was guided on the right path by a relatively small group of statesmen and politicians, as well as some leaders of industry and culture, all deeply committed to a policy of a united Europe. We may expect this to be true in the future as well.

In Western Europe, it appears the course has been set irrevocably on the establishment of a unified Europe, even if there remain many differences about how the European house should be furnished in its details. The reservations of a large number of people in individual states, especially Great Britain, about giving up national sovereign rights too quickly or too completely should be taken seriously; they are not only the results of special interests, but rather go back, as some of the present contributions show, to attitudes rooted in history, which cannot easily be changed by bureaucratic decree or parliamentary or plebiscite decisions. The best way to bring a unified Europe about is to listen to their objections and patiently answer them one by one, instead of impatiently shoving them aside, as sometimes — understandably — happens.

The more difficult situation is that of the East-Central European nations. Under the rule of the Soviet communist system, they were forced to orient their policies to the East in order to build the so-called "real socialism," which cut them off from participation in most developments in Western Europe. They have largely succeeded in shaking off the yoke of Marxism-Leninism, not least under the influence and trust of the West and the expected help only it can give. But they must first refashion their intellectual and political orientation. The problem is portrayed most dramatically by Russia, the center of the former Soviet empire. The politics of Perestroika led to a decisive opening to Europe and the West of the states of the former USSR that made the central political values and ideals of the Western democratic system their own. But the old debate about whether Russia is a European nation or a nation with its own culture and social tradition in complete contrast to Europe has remained unresolved. The question is now being argued anew in the successor states of the USSR with great passion.

The first chapters are those of authors who speak for the nations that played a decisive role in the process of European unity since its beginning. François Bédarida, in his contribution "France and Europe — From Yesterday to Today," impressively demonstrates that the idea of a "United States of Europe" throughout French history has stood in opposition to the idea of the sovereign French nation as the premier cultural nation of the world. Nevertheless, numerous French philosophers predicted as early as the eighteenth and nineteenth centuries that the nation-states would dissolve into a unified Europe. Ernest Renan, for example, in 1882 when the influence of European national states was at its peak, believed nations were not an "eternal affair" and probably would be replaced by a European confederation. This was a view held by a minority at that time. Only among groups of the resistance during World War II did the idea arise — in opposition to the fraudulent European ideology of the National Socialists — that a precondition of postwar reconstruction would be the unification of Europe. Bédarida then reviews the stages of French-European politics since the early fifties. The German-French understanding formed the backbone of the policies France pursued with determination. Charles de Gaulle's words about the "Europe of the Fatherland," crudely misinterpreted by the public as rejecting the idea of a unified Europe, are given a far more differentiated and welcome reading. However, Bédarida leaves no doubt that the unified Europe will be realized only as a community of national states, each with its own individual, unmistakable identity.

In his article "The Germans and European Unification," Wilfried Loth describes the various stages European policy has undergone in the Federal Republic of Germany since its beginnings. The idea of a unified Europe has always been fraught with difficulty in the German political tradition; most often it was bound to the idea of a Central Europe strongly influenced by Germany, with which more or less open hegemonic goals were connected. The unique political constellation after World War II permitted the idea that the renewed rise of Germany would be possible only in the framework of a unified Europe. In the beginning, the idea of a "unified Europe" as a "third force" between the two superpowers was welcomed in the most diverse camps. It was then replaced, not without considerable internal objections, by the policy of Western integration, which sought close ties between Germany and the West.

In the sixties, the idea of a unified Europe won new appeal as a substitute for the conventional German national idea, as Ralf Dahrendorf, among others, has explained. Of course, pragmatic reasons also played a role, especially with the chance of making Germany more easily acceptable in the international community under the cover of a unified Europe. The postnational fundamental political ideas of the Germans, as Loth calls them, made a consistent European policy easier. All governments since Adenauer have supported it, with barely varying accents. Loth particularly portrays the latest developments following reunification. He refers as well to the different political mentality of the citizens of the former GDR who, unlike the West Germans, did and still do sympathize with the autonomous national state and who are not uniformly in favor of European unification.

The chapter by Valerio Castronovo, "Italian Europeanism in the Twentieth Century," makes it clear that Italy may well be called the true pioneer of European unification, which had its foundations in the Rome agreements of 1956. Italian political thought has looked longingly toward Europe since the Risorgimento, always inclined to argue in favor of the concerns of Europe as a whole. Guiseppe Mazzini, in the first half of the nineteenth century, proclaimed the idea of a free democratic Europe of national states that no longer wage war against each other, instead seeking peaceful economic competition. This was the credo of the free emancipatory national state, which set itself against the obsolete rule of the principalities, at the same time striving to respect the national efforts of their European neighbors. This great idea was then distorted in the course of time to support first the power of the nation-state and, finally, imperialism. So it was not coincidental that the idea of a European federation as a foundation of a new political order of Europe was openly propagated by Giovanni Agnelli and Attilio Cabiati at the end of World War I, which was to a large extent the result of uncontrolled eruption of aggressive nationalism among European peoples. Luigi Einaudi declared in 1919 that nationalism is the greatest scourge of humanity, which must be overcome if the new European order is to exist.

All these beginnings of fundamentally new orientation, however, were subsequently swept away by fascism. Just as in France, the idea of a "united Europe" originally re-emerged in Italy in the circles of the anti-fascist resistance in opposition to the European ideology of the Nazis. After the end of World War II, Luigi Einaudi, in particular, made himself the spokesman of the idea of a unified Europe, and he was successful in converting the leadership of Italian politics to this cause. Castronovo's account of how purposefully and tenaciously Italian diplomacy and the leaders of Italian industry and commerce have since pursued the creation of European unity is remarkable and demands our respect for the statesmen and their unwavering determination, despite disappointments and setbacks. Even at the risk of creating potential economic competition for itself, Italy initiated Spain and Portugal, and finally Greece, into the European community. It acted in the conviction that the long-term advantage of political merger of Europe outweighed the short-term economic disadvantages.

William Wallace, in his study "The British Approach to Europe," discusses a painful area in the history of the "long road to Europe"; the ambivalent and hesitant attitude of the English toward the idea of a European federation. He reaches back into the distant past in order to highlight the special characteristics of the British national identity, which never felt it belonged to Europe. Great Britain, as Wallace points out, more than the other European nations, is in danger of losing its identity by joining the West European community — an identity influenced considerably during the nineteenth and early twentieth centuries by its political and economic struggle with France and later with the German Reich. In both world wars, Great Britain fought with much energy and commitment to keep alive a Europe of diverse independent national states against the hegemonic demands of individual continental powers, but it did this from the other side of the English Channel, as a power that was "only half European," whose strength derived from its overseas ties as the center of the Commonwealth. That is one reason for the distrust British politics and the British public feel toward the efforts of the European community to extend its role from cooperation to that of a true state. Decisive in the reservations of British politics and the public toward the European community, however, were ties to the British Commonwealth of nations and the overseas orientation not only of British economy, but also its diplomacy. For a long time, the Commonwealth and the Near East appeared more important than the European problem. In addition, there was the often-repeated "special relationship" with the United States, which Downing Street was not ready to sacrifice on the altar of a European pact. Only with the fiasco of the Suez intervention of 1956 and the subsequent disillusionment about the economic potential of the shrinking British Commonwealth in the wake of decolonization came a turn toward Europe. But readiness to cooperate with the European Community remained far from enthusiastic because of what seemed to London like corporate or mandated policies of EEC agencies in violation of the principles of free trade. This confirmed the deep-seated mistrust rooted in national prejudices against far-reaching European unification, particularly on the part of Margaret Thatcher. Instead, London favored a strictly neoliberal economic policy modeled on that of the United States under the presidency of Ronald Reagan. This all makes clear why Britain was stalling European unification for so long, ignoring the repeated invitations from, above all, Italy and Germany, who wanted Great Britain as a valued connecting link of the European Community to the overseas world and, even more, as a mediator between France and the other members of the Community.

A deeply moving report about the gagging and isolation of an East European nation that has always been close to the West under pressure of the Soviet imperial system is given by Andrzej Ajnenkiel in his chapter "Europe from the Polish Perspective." Poland in recent history — after a short phase of independence and a remarkably advanced constitution during the French revolution — has been handed from one kind of slavery to another, interrupted only by a short interlude after the Polish nation was founded in 1918, which, in turn, fell to the aggression of the National Socialists in 1939. There can be no doubt about the European orientation of Polish culture since the eighteenth century. But it was the cultural elite especially — the Polish intelligentsia and, in particular, Polish Jews — who were either physically destroyed or driven away and scattered during the National Socialist occupation. In some respects communism enforced from the outside completed this process, turning leadership of society, business and culture over into the hands of the new bureaucracy of the so-called "real socialism" whose members were social climbers coming predominantly from the peasantry. The demonization of all relations to the West followed. Nevertheless, Polish culture maintained its orientation to the West. "Never," writes Ajnenkiel, "during the entire period of communist rule have we stopped feeling as a part of Europe."

In this manner, the new democratic Poland resolutely strives for entry into the coming European federal state politically, economically and culturally. Establishing long-lasting, good relations to Germany is crucial, as Ajnenkiel explains. There are, however, reasons for concern that the West does too little to help Poland accomplish this. Polish President Lech Walesa recently complained, as Ajnenkiel notes, that the unification of Europe unfortunately lies "in the far distance. Europe is partitioned by economic differences. . . . We citizens of poor Europe have the feeling that rich, well-to-do Europe is closing its doors to us." This appeal should give us pause.

Only a little better is the situation of the former Czechoslovak Republic, which has split up into two independent national states, not least because the serious economic problems after the liberation from communist rule have not been adequately mastered, and the poorer Slovakia hopes to do better by going it alone. This is regrettable from the European viewpoint, as Czechoslovakia was the democratic model of East Europe between the wars.

As Jiří Kořalka reports in his chapter "The Idea and the Reality of Europe Among the Czechs," the Czechs always looked largely to the West; their cosmopolitan attitudes were remarkable. To the National Socialist European ideology, which, among other things, was intended to legitimize obliteration of the Czech state, Czech politicians and intellectuals in exile countered with the idea of a future "federative Europe," in which the discarded values and ideals of European tradition were to be reinstated. During communist rule, when Czechoslovakia was compelled to join the East-Central European states in COMECON, the organization competing with the European community solidly under Soviet control, the Czechs never faltered in the feeling that they are a European nation with the need to cherish contact with the Western world. The struggle of the Czech intelligentsia against the ruling communist regime, which reached its first climax in the "Prague Spring" of 1968, was waged under the banner of a new, better Europe. The Czech dissidents of Charta 77 dreamed, as Václav Havel described it, of a new "Europe without barbed wire, high walls, artificially divided people and without gigantic munitions depots," a Europe of a "community bound in friendship, independent peoples and democratic states." The motto of a "return to Europe" was also the guideline of foreign policy of the first freely elected Czech government under the presidency of Václav Havel; and the secessionist Slovak Republic also has made it its own.

The case of Hungary is somewhat different; it was the first Eastern European state to escape the rule of Soviet imperialism, and it pursues a new democratic way in alignment with the West. Ivan T. Berend reports in his chapter, "Hungary's Place in Europe: Political Thought and Historiography in the Twentieth Century," how controversial Hungary's position between Eastern and Western Europe has been in recent historiography and how it remains so today. Hungary's location midway between East and West — Berend uses the image of a ferryboat shuttling back and forth between the Eastern and Western world — is anchored deeply in the history of Hungary, but applies in a certain sense to the history of all Eastern Europe. Since the so-called double revolution in Western Europe — what is meant are the French Revolution and the Industrial Revolution — the tendency in Hungary has always been to see itself as part of the West. But there has always been a strong opposing view holding that Hungary, as a key nation in the framework of a Central European bloc, belongs neither to the Eastern governing region nor the Western one, and that it possesses its own cultural identity. Voices also are raised to claim that, quite to the contrary, Hungary should be classified as part of the Eastern, Eurasian culture because its existing social structures correspond more to those of Eastern than of Western Europe.

Undeniably, Hungary, like other Eastern European states under Marxist-Leninist control, again moved closer to the Eastern sphere of culture right after the war, also in regard to the new social structures, which the "real socialism" planned, especially the elimination of the middle class and the native aristocracy. Yet it is also true that Janos Kadar justified the cautious communist reforms he introduced after the bloody suppression of the Hungarian uprising of 1956 with the argument that Hungary was right in the middle of Europe. This applies as well to Hungary's policies since the restoration of democracy. Berend's discussion ends on a rather cautious note; he believes that the decision for a European orientation of Hungary's policies, leading inevitably toward association and later full membership in the EEC, is not yet final. Whether the Hungarian "ferryboat" will continue on its European course or perhaps again turn toward the East some day depends essentially upon whether the country's economic and social integration into the West is successful.

Finally, the Russian historian Alexander O. Chubarian reports about "The Path to Europe from Moscow's Perspective." It is an old dispute — whether Russia is part of Europe at all, or whether it forms the core of a separate Eurasian sphere of culture. Already in the nineteenth century, Russian intellectuals were divided into two bitterly opposing factions — the Slavophiles, and among them especially the Narodniki, who insisted on the special character of Russian culture and the Russian social order as against those of the West and the Russian liberals, who pleaded passionately for Russia's union with Europe in cultural and political respects. In 1917, the Marxist-Leninists came to power in the October Revolution, which, in accordance with Lenin's maxims, strove for immediate modernization under Soviet rule based on the principles of a socialist order; not shrinking, especially under Stalin, from forceful and brutal collectivization. Fundamentally, Marxism-Leninism was an ideology completely foreign to Russia, actually a variation of Western Marxism designed in response to the Western model of advanced bourgeois industrial society. Only with the help of theoretical legerdemain did Lenin succeed in adapting the Marxist model of revolution to the uniquely Russian situation, i.e., to a country in which the industrial working class formed a small minority as against the large masses of peasants. Nevertheless, the Soviet communists attempted to extend this model of a unique Russian way of a socialist society to all of Europe. But because the revolution failed to materialize in the other European countries, nothing became of these grand plans. Instead, communist Russia saw itself thrown back to a policy of "socialism in one country" with the consequence that the old anti-intellectual messianic, nationalistic and autocratic traditions of czarist Russia returned via the back door into official ideology, diverting it from its original cosmopolitan course, turning the wheel more strongly in an "Eastern" direction.

Chubarian's chapter, which essentially discusses the official policies of Soviet Russia, shows what happened under these conditions to Russia's Western orientation which had been taken for granted since the reforms of Peter the Great. Soviet diplomacy managed as early as the twenties to gain recognition for the USSR as a European power. But in fact Soviet society was increasingly cut off from Western influences as, especially under Stalin, a growing isolation spread to the East-Central European states of the Eastern bloc after the end of World War II.

Ultimately, the experiment of "real socialism" failed because of the increasing incompetence of the "bureaucratic method of production," imposed upon the Soviet people and Eastern Europe. This is what led to Gorbachev's policy of Perestroika. It was intended in the beginning only to be a careful relaxation of the bureaucratic system by adopting Western methods of market economy, as well as Western ideals of public candor and the self-determination of the individual, but in fact it caused the collapse of the communist system of power. The policy of Perestroika essentially strove from the beginning to open Russian society to the West and to seek the economic cooperation of the European capitalist states. The democratic revolution, which since then has led to a complete reorganization of political conditions in the states of the former USSR, clearly aspires to lead these countries back to Europe again after a costly seventy-year historical detour.

Chubarian concludes his remarks with a fervent plea to "let Russia after its renewal be accepted again to the bosom of the old world," i.e., the old Europe. Failing this, the choice of a society fashioned after the Western model made by the successor states of the Soviet Union since the collapse of communist rule, could be reversed again in the turmoil of new, aggressive nationalisms. The historical arguments about whether Russia should find its intellectual bearings in the West or in the tradition of its unique Eastern past have recently erupted again; Europe cannot be indifferent about the outcome.

The chapters that follow deal with the long road to Europe, each from a different national point of view. They argue on a wavelength within a fairly narrow frequency range, although their points of departure differ greatly; they describe the historical preconditions and, at the same time, the problems confronting these countries now, and they analyze their differing views of the idea of a unified Europe. It is appropriate today to call for a realistic, rather than a merely technocratic, European policy which takes into account the historically evolved national identities of the European populations and which also finds their innermost acceptance. Then, at the end, there will be no lack of enthusiasm for Europe. This volume would like to be a modest contribution to this goal.

France and Europe—From Yesterday to Today

François Bédarida

If the statement by François Mitterand, "France is our Fatherland, Europe is our future" reflects a consensus of the majority of the French today, this comes at the end of a long historical path. Who in France shortly after World War II would have given much of a chance to a ravaged Europe that was lying in ruins and was also divided and fragmented? Even in the seventies, at a time when Raymond Aron wrote his *Plea for a Declining Europe*, who would have put his money on a future for European union? Therefore, the change that occurred in the mid-eighties appears quite spectacular, no less so than the shift of most French people toward the idea of a common future in a European setting. A poll by IPSOS in May 1992 testifies to this: a five to two majority approved the Maastricht treaty, while five to three favored a unified European currency that would replace the franc. This is a truly remarkable turnabout for a nation proud of a rich past and convinced of its own genius.

The Time of the Visionaries

In the seventeenth century, Pierre Chunu remarked, the scholarly word "Europe" had come into common use in the occident. From France, where it entered the language between 1630 and 1660, as it did in England and Holland at around the same time, the word conquered the western half of the continent. By the end of the seventeenth century it had spread over all of Europe.

But this Europe was a Europe of states—national states ruled by absolute monarchs contemptuous of any authority that might believe itself superior and where interests of state triumphed. In view of the constant state of war—wars of alliance or wars for the line of succession, continental, sea and colonial wars—some asked themselves what balances, what mechanisms, what harmonies ought to be introduced. The Abbé de Saint Pierre, for instance, saw the remedy in a "European society" guaranteeing collective security or the involvement of the government to each state by means of a perpetual alliance between sovereign rulers, who are subject to the majority decision of a "European senate" with a joint army at its command.

The ideas of these visionaries were barely noticed. But in the eighteenth century during the Enlightenment the "French Europe" was to inform a large body of writing with the same spirit. The particularism of interest groups and small countries was a thing of the past; in its place was the universalism so well expressed by Montesquieu. "If I knew something which were useful to me and of disadvantage to my family, I would ban it from my mind. If I knew something which were useful for my family and not for my fatherland, I would try to forget it. If I knew something which were useful for my native country and disadvantageous for Europe, I would view it as a crime."

In the nineteenth century, the Romantic period joined the nationalist movement to create the dream of a Europe renewed by the holy alliance of the princes. The national and liberal revolutions of 1830, and especially that of 1848, raised enormous hopes and great visions among the French public of emancipation, freedom and European unity, though none of these had much chance of success. For example, Alphonse de Lamartine, foreign minister of the French provisional government of 1848, addressed the European powers in a European Manifesto that counseled a "Marseillaise of freedom."

Victor Hugo is the great visionary who, at the opening of the 1849 peace congress, prophetically said that the day would come when we would witness the birth of a United States of Europe. Like an exorcist he repeated his conviction several times—in 1847 "France is to be admired because it is destined to die, but to die like the gods by metamorphosis; France will become Europe" or even as late as 1872 "This exceedingly grand cause, the European Republic, which we will have." Hugo even based his dream on concrete historical analyses, of which several have lost none of their meaning after more than a century: "What goes on in Serbia," he wrote in 1879, "shows the necessity of a United States of Europe (. . .), the atrocities of Serbia demonstrate beyond doubt what Europe needs: a European nationality, a government, a great fraternal court of arbitration, a democracy peaceful in itself. . . ." At the same time, although he was a follower of the principle of nationalism, Ernest Renan, supported by the will of the people, praised "a central authority, a kind of Congress of the United States of Europe which would set the laws of the nations, prevail against them and replace the principle of nationalities with the principle of federation." In 1882, in his famous polemic with Theodor Mommsen "What Is a National?" he goes so far as to maintain, "Nations are nothing eternal. They have a beginning and an end. The European confederation will probably take their place."

Between this Europe of "European agreement" and the Europe of our time, World War I created a dramatic chasm, in France, as well as the rest of Europe. Because this suicidal war set the entire continent in flames; a total war in which the issue was no longer to conquer the enemy. Instead it was to destroy him. It was a conflict which generated blood baths and deadly hatred; an absolute victory which led to a peace in which the rights of the victors and the rights of nations were all intertwined, and which led to the era of totalitarianism. In this Europe, weakened and torn by war, unable to master its own fate and ravaged by its own demon, the problem of unity was newly raised from the ground up. If union never appeared more necessary than now, it also seemed much less practical and attainable. To be sure, certain circles in France, especially the left, dreamed of a new political order founded on law and embodied in the League of Nations. But the predominant feeling was one of impotence and decline (as the books of the geographer Albert Demaneon [*The Fall of Europe*], or the political scientist André Siegfried [*The Crisis of Europe*] illustrated), even if Paul Valéry kept believing that humanity had accomplished its many and most fruitful achievements just on the small territory of this "cape of the old continent," the "western appendix of Asia." "Europe has been a privileged place, the European, the European spirit, the creator of this wonder."

The first initiative to return to the injured and fragmented continent its unity was undertaken by the pan-European movement organized in national sections and founded in 1923 in Vienna by Count Coudenhove-Kalergi to counter on one hand the Bolshevik influence and on the other American economic hegemony. This initiative in France found the support of such politicians as Edouard Herriot, Léon Blum, Aristide Briand and such authors as Claudel and Valéry. These, however, hardly represented an influential pressure group, since their appeal was to the elite and not to the masses. In addition, the European economic and monetary union did its best to propagate the idea of Europe in the business world and among the trade unionists. Similarly, pleas like *Europe, My Native Country* by Gaston Riou went unheard. In the same way, in *The Contradictions of the Modern World*, Francise Delaisi explained the irrationality of national sovereignty in a Europe that was in the process of adapting itself to world market demands with great speed.

Aristide Briand is to be mentioned here as a true pioneer, as the first Frenchman and first statesman, who in September 1929 in a speech before the League of Nations clearly suggested a formula for uniting European nations. It was, in his opinion, an ambitious undertaking which, after haunting the imagination of philosophers and authors, had now become a necessity. Briand's undertaking, the crowning of a career in the service of freedom, concerned itself with reconciling the irreconcilable, suggesting the establishment of a "federal bond" between the European nations without in this process effecting national sovereignty of the national states. However, caution dictated that his efforts be placed on the back burner with the coming of the economic crisis of 1929, when Briand himself began to vanish from the political scene. All in all, this undertaking ended in failure, leaving behind at best a memory trace in the collective subconscious. As André Gide wrote with prescience in *Incidences*, "the question of Europe occupies people very slightly, or more accurately, occupies only very few."

Gide meant a small group of intellectuals among whom were the "non-conformists of the thirties." Federalists and personalities rallied around the journals *Ordre nouveau* and *Esprit*, trying to escape the confusion of thought and systems by protesting, in the name of the European people, against the destruction, both of the individual and the Moloch state. In their view, "to be able to carry out the necessary revolution, one must start all over again at zero with a new political world view." Behind these themes as they were developed by Denis de Rougemont, Emmanuel Mounier, Robert Aron, Alexandre Marc, Georges Izard (often inspired by Maritain and Beriaev), one can detect the influence of Proudhon, a socialist thinker of the nineteenth century, who had extensively promoted the federal principle and was a decisive opponent of nationalism and apostle of the smallest entities, which were to be organized as communes at the local level or brought together regionally. But the aggressions launched after 1936 as well as the dangers emerging out of the ruins of a Europe marked by Versailles and the League of Nations put an end to the beautiful dream of a European community.

World War II and the Birth of the European Idea

From 1940 to 1944 the French felt torn between two Europes: on one side the former Europe of German hegemony and the collaboration, and on the other side the Europe of the future as envisioned by the resistance movement.

Hitler confided to Goebbels in 1943 that the "the goal of our struggle must be a unified Europe." Dominated by the victorious Reich, the "new order" had in fact become established on the continent, allowing the European idea to be revived by force under the banner of protecting civilization against the threat of "Asian and Jewish Bolshevism." In the eyes of the Parisian supporters of a collaborationist policy and the collaborators of Vichy—especially among the intellectuals—the hour of a "European France" had struck, by which they meant that the "European spirit" based on a common culture, a common ideology and a common fate was to be cultivated.

All these people believed that Hitler, instead of remaining committed to an obsolete nationalism within the framework of a national state, would play a positive and productive role for the future of the continent by halting the fragmentation of Europe and restoring unity. Drieu La Rochelle, a "long-time European," proclaimed that "only a Europe based on German hegemony is viable." For Marcel Déat, a European federation meant the only future hope for a conquered France. "The defeat in itself," he wrote in his newspaper *L'Oeuvre* in November 1940, "should bring us to the realistic standpoint of supporting Europe." As far as Pierre Laval was concerned, in his famous speech of June 1942—after he predicted the rise of a new Europe in the future—he clearly spelled out the alternative: "Either we integrate ourselves, while respecting our honor and our vital interests, into a new and peaceful Europe, or we throw up our hands and see our civilization disappear."

Despite all this, no matter how deviously Nazi propaganda advocated this Europe of race and violence, it still failed to discredit the European idea. In fact, the opposite happened. While these ideas played no part in the Allies' post-war plans (for example, no mention of them appeared in the Atlantic Charter), quite a few French, as well as Dutch and Italian resistance movements in the darkness of the underground invoked a unity-inspiring solidarity against the common enemy as a step toward a true revolution in liberated Europe; in contrast to the Vichy slogan "France Alone," the idea of a European union was mentioned more than three hundred times in the underground press. In the lead was the movement *Combat*, which called for the establishment of the United States of Europe since September 1942, a "living reality for which we fight." Its leader Henri Frenay wrote in 1943, "The men of the European resistance will be tomorrow's builders of the new Europe." *Libérer et Fédérer* (Liberate and Unify), a movement whose name denotes its agenda, declared on July 14, 1942, "To win freedom means to realize the ideal of justice and freedom, for which the people now struggle; this also means to unify the European nations and create the conditions for a permanent peace. To unify the European people to avoid new wars." Other underground groups also rallied to the United States of Europe; for example, Resistance with Christian Democratic leanings and the socialist newspaper *Le Populaire*, while Léon Blum in *A l'échelle humaine* considered the issue of how Germany will be integrated into Europe after the war.

Indeed, in Lyon a French Committee for European Federation, founded in June 1944, went so far as to envisage a European government and a European army placed above the national governments. Under the title *Our Europe*, the newspaper of the national freedom movement La Marseillaise in July 1944 supported the idea that Europe could come into being only if "all European nations accepted losing part of their political and economic as well as all their military sovereignty." Only these conditions could bring about a "European state capable of defending itself against the threat of colonization by America and Russia, whether they are allies or foes, and cause a great economic recovery on the pacified continent." Here one sees the emergence of the theory of Europe as a third force and the prescient vision of a common market.

Leading intellectuals of a free France worked on thought-provoking themes and interesting projects in London and Algiers. In London, Maurice Druon wrote a series of reports in 1943 under the title "Letter of a European," wherein he pleads for a Europe set up as an open society and a union founded on agreement instead of a perverted Europe based on racist dogma and force. Among the purely political projects is the work of Jean Monnet who handed the French Freedom Committee in Algiers a note in August 1943 explaining what in his view were the challenges of the future. "There will be no peace in Europe," he warns, "if the states again constitute themselves on the foundation of national sovereignty." Thereupon he advocates a "European federation or entity turning into a common economic union." Since 1944 Monnet envisaged the coal and steel management of the Ruhr by a European authority, while René Mayer, Commissioner for Communication, looked toward an "industrial Lorraine" in the form of a federation of Western Europe that included the Rhine-Westphalian basin.

But at that time, i.e., 1943–1944, General de Gaulle, after studying various proposals, had only a weak confederation in mind in which France would have the dominating influence. This confederation would include France and the Benelux countries and the Rhine-Westphalian basin, possibly Italy as well, and eventually Great Britain. The official French position was very candidly reviewed by de Gaulle in a speech in March 1944 in Algiers before the consultative assembly. "So that the old revived continent may find its balance in accordance with the needs of our era, it appears to us that some form of association must be brought about, without, of course, losing the sovereignty of the individual in this process. As far as France is concerned, we believe that a type of western grouping mainly based on the broadest possible economic foundations realized with us can offer great advantages." It was difficult to express oneself more cautiously about the future of Europe.

After Nazi Germany was defeated and the war was over, the French, like the other Europeans, began to raise questions about the Europe that was to be rebuilt. Between 1945 and 1949 there were a great many projects, plans and initiatives.

In a world profoundly changed by World War II, Europe was characterized by several traits: the extent of human loss and material destruction (a continent full of bleeding wounds and fields of ruins); the victory of democracy in France (where the Communist party failed to gain power by force of arms or ballots) and its restoration in Italy and West Germany; the near disappearance of the political power of fascism and authoritarianism (with the exceptions of Spain and Portugal); the quick beginning of economic rebuilding and the modernization of the West (especially thanks to the Marshall Plan). But at the same time, the history of the European people of the West became cut off from that of the Central and Eastern European people under Soviet rule and in a communist regime, who saw themselves condemned to many years as satellites under totalitarian and often bloody dictatorships. Finally the process of decolonization, begun during the war and now becoming irresistible, also accelerated. France tried in vain to oppose the freedom movements in the countries they colonized.

In this new world four main factors worked in favor of cooperation, if not European union, strongly affecting France and the vision the French had for the future of the continent. First—as noted before—resistance against the common enemy, i.e., fascism and the Nazi movement, revived the idea of a democratic and peaceful and unified Europe rich in values and culture—a true rehabilitation after the desecration of a "new order" by Hitler's Europe.

Second, Europe's disappearance from the international stage was obvious to everyone. In the era of both superpowers, Europe no longer stood in the center of the world; instead, balance and peace now depended on non-European powers. This gave birth to the idea of a "third force."

Third, it was apparent that there was no other defense except unity against the danger of communism. In view of the threat which came from Soviet imperialism and the Stalinist seizure of Eastern Europe, the time had come to form ties and work together. The rupture of 1947, "the bad year" according to General de Gaulle, is decisive here: it was "the great schism" about which Raymond Aron spoke. If, in the end, the Cold War tended to act as a brake, it was more of a stimulus for the European idea.

Last, the aggressive activity of the European movements had an influence on public opinion. Without wanting to overestimate the significance of these groups, which represented a minority though they were recruited of the elite, they nevertheless acted as pressure groups adapting European thinking to the "spirit of the times." Certain advocates exhibited a truly apostolic passion, as if they wanted to build a new Jerusalem.

As this movement for a new unified Europe grew, the French occupied an important place in it, whether by setting up international agencies, or by establishing French factions within them. But there were disputes and whenever these were resolved other differences arose, especially between union and federal advocates.

Among these active forces, one must distinguish between various movements. The first most significant and oldest is the European Union of Federalists, founded in December 1946 and strongly influenced by Proudhon. Its general secretary was Alexandre Marc, who was French (he had been fighting for the same cause back in the thirties in the pages of the journal *Cahiers du monde nouveau,* and in alliance with the former director of *Combat,* Henri Frenay). The other dominant personality was Henri Breugmans from The Netherlands. Although it began in Switzerland, the appeal of the European Union of Federalists was addressed to all of Europe, raising the hope that Eastern Europe would be included in the planned European federation. While this organization was very eclectic from a political point of view, three other movements reflected a stronger party bias. The Democratic and Socialist Movement for the United States of Europe rallied socialists and trade unionists of various countries of the continent, with the Frenchman André Philip playing a significant role. In addition, the New International Associates brought together Christian Democrats, while the European League for Economic Cooperation, a group with liberal tendencies whose spokesmen were the economist Jacques Rueff in France and Van Zeeland in Belgium, recruited members more from the right.

In Paris a purely French movement was founded in 1947, the French Council for a Unified Europe. Its president was Raoul Dautry and among its leading personalities were André Siegfried, Paul Ramadier, and Pierre-Henri Teigen. In addition there was a French branch of the European Parliamentary Union of Count Coudenhove-Kalergi (he himself returned to Europe after the war). This national French committee had Senator René Coty, who later became president of the Republic, as its chairman. If this proliferation was an indication of vitality, it also contributed to splintering the organizations, which in any event were all inclined to internal divisions. Because of this, most movements finally combined in a Coordination Committee for a Unified Europe which was founded in 1947 in Paris.

From the official French viewpoint, the underlying issue became apparent early on: The indissoluble link connecting the establishment of the European house with the question of Germany. While the French public remained fixed on the discussion of the German question, successive governments focused on the three demands formulated after the Reich's capitulation: Continuing occupation, democratic re-education, confederal fragmentation. This explains the differences between France and the Western allies, and the fear that the Anglo-Americans might back out again, as they did in 1919, from their involvement in Germany. Therefore, German-French reconciliation appeared, as it were, as a precondition and as a cornerstone for the European house. Even if France's partners in the diplomatic game more or less quietly allowed the Germans a voice in deciding their own fate, France still held the trump card as the fulcrum of the European house, having been granted veto power thanks to its key position. This put France in an advantageous position which it was to retain for over thirty years.

Thus the road to Europe was almost ignored by official France, aside from the rhetoric of official declarations. The initiatives which came from personalities and movements had a triggering effect during the initial period. General de Gaulle, for example, in September 1945 in an interview with the London *Times*, had approved economic and cultural cooperation between the Western European nations, including an internationalized Rhineland and Ruhr area, a stand quite consistent with earlier positions. After de Gaulle had resigned in 1946 he reiterated the necessity of European union in a speech held in Bar-le-Duc. In Zurich, Churchill's passionate plea for German-French reconciliation and the "United States of Europe" ("The European family must reform itself and tie its bonds anew . . . Europe arise!") had met with only a polite and unpromising reception in official French circles. It first required the treaty of Dunkirk of March 5, 1947, and also the Brussels treaty of March 17, 1948, for a Europe of five (France, Great Britain, the Benelux nations, pompously named "Western Union") members to be created. It was still an empty shell that the future proved to be unproductive.

The true starting point for a unified Europe was the Den Haag Congress, also called the Congress of Europe, which met in Den Haag from May 7–10, 1948. As a large public event it testified to the wide public support for European union. The Congress brought together 800 participants, the political, economic and intellectual elite of Europe (Eastern Europe and Spain were only represented by exiles) in an atmosphere of enthusiasm and excitement. For many, an old dream had finally become reality. Among the participants were twelve former prime ministers and sixty ministers. The French delegation, the most numerous next to the British, had in their ranks socialists (Raul Ramadier, who was chairman of one of the three commissions, the political commission), resistance activists (Henri Frenay), prewar politicians (Paul Reynaud, Edouard Daladier) as well as a young lawyer and member of parliament, who had a brilliant future before him, François Mitterand.

In addition to creating a European cultural center in Geneva, other results of the Congress included the draft plans for a European charter of human rights, a supreme court of justice and the European parliament. Even if the Congress split into two groupings, the unionists and the federalists (the first were the majority of the French, with Paul Ramadier going so far as to state, "We have seen that the reactionary idea of national sovereignty has lost practically all its supporters!") Denis de Rougemont, as a committed federalist, was not wrong when he announced at the conclusion of the passionate debate: "Maybe the most difficult battle for European unity was won in Den Haag, even if its most spectacular results will be achieved only later and somewhere else." In fact, he was to say some twenty years later: "Everything began in Den Haag in May 1948: the first European parliamentary, legal, cultural and technical institutions, the main principles of the common market, but also the rejection of institutions wanted by the people and equipped with the political decision-making powers which were thought not to be opportune then."

The European movement, which was created in October 1948 in the wake of the Den Haag Congress, gave priority to the establishment of a representative European parliament (led by Churchill, Spaak, de Gasperi and Léon Blum, who was soon to be replaced by Robert Schuman). The European Council did come to see the light of day on May 5, 1949, and held its first session in summer 1949 in Strasbourg under the presidency of Edouard Herriot (who was later replaced by Spaak). This was the first international organization based on the democratic ideals and rule of law which emerged from the common will of the Europeans.

But the excitement of 1949 quickly dissipated and the European Council was defeated by the disappointments of its members and by the indifference of the general public. It is apparent that the true power, instead of gaining strength in Strasbourg, continued solely in the hands of the national governments. In this phase the evolution of the European idea, embedded in an unclear concept, remained superficial and sentimental. In France, to a representative survey asking "Are you for or against the efforts undertaken for the unification of Europe" 61 percent answered for, 10 percent against, 27 percent had no comment. And even if the leaders of the "third force" in the middle of the political chessboard (democrats, Christians, radicals and part of the socialists) supported the idea of a European union, both extremes wrestled (Gaullists of the Assembly of the French people and the Communist party and the organizations allied to them in support of national sovereignty) with other problems, while the majority of the people, completely consumed by the problems of daily life, saw themselves trapped into political despondency by the problems of subsistence, rebuilding and troublesome social conflicts.

The French Identity and Europe

At this point, it is appropriate to place in its historical context the great debate confronting the French since the beginnings of the establishment of Europe, which debate flares up again and again at every new stage of its evolution (from the fifties until today)—the debate about national identity in a European community. France as an old nation with a long, common past, with the will for living together, and with a common culture is indeed provided with a strong national identity, which its history has strengthened for many years. One people, one territory, one law; all this has served as a foundation for this identity forged over centuries and added to this is the element which, according to Renan, marks a nation—"one soul, one intellectual principle."

Nonetheless, the vicissitudes of our time have not allowed doubts to be raised and questions to be asked. Was it completely by accident that Fernand Braudel spent the last years of his life thinking about a "French identity" and writing about it? He defines the identity issue as "taking the destiny of France into France's own hands. [There is] the living result of that, which the eternal past has discarded in successive layers, both as relics and in fusion. On the other hand, there is a dynamic at work which serves the nation as a motor for the road ahead. That is a process, a battle against oneself designed for self-perpetuation. If it stops, all else fails. A nation can only *be* for the prize of the endless search for itself, for its own change . . . , for standing up to the other without weakness, for identifying with the best, for the essential." Such an identity is recognizable in a thousand signs, in speeches, myths, beliefs, appearances. In this sense "it inevitably includes a certain national unity."

Here one must be strict with words and accurately differentiate between *nation* (the word exists in French since the twelfth century), *nationality*, (since 1808) and *nationalism* (the term that was formed in 1798 was out of use for one century until the day when Maurice Barrés again brought it back to use in 1902). If neither the concept of nation nor that of nationality is especially problematic—at least when one adheres to the French concept, which defines the one or the other by the will to live together ("homeland is, above all, the consciousness of the homeland," says Mazzini) and by the gathering in of all those, and only those, within a state who want to be a part of it—then the definition of nationalism is far from simple and clear. Starting out as a political movement claiming for a nationality the right to establish or belong to a nation, then becoming an emotion which extols the nation to which one belongs with a passion bordering on hatred of foreigners, or turning into a doctrine, which subordinates everything to the greatness and power of a country regardless of sovereignty, even now and then leading this country to dominate others—let us acknowledge that the relationship between nationalism and patriotism is far from clear. This suggests what kind of controversies and sometimes uncertainties have kept troubling the French consciousness as a European house became established.

If the problem in France is so acute, the reason for this is very simple. In France, in the revolutionary France of 1789, the nation-state had just been established. Contrary to the concept of Europe prevailing in the eighteenth century, and within the polycentric process regulating conflicts about the balance of sovereign powers, human rights merged with intellectual cosmopolitanism, becoming the greatest innovation in France of 1789. This was the metamorphosis of the national state into the nation-state. The declaration of human rights, proclaiming that the principle of sovereignty lies in the nation, shifted the source of legitimacy from the person of the king to the French people. The logic which stemmed from this carries with it not only the principle of national independence, but also a new concept of the nation and the people's right for self-determination.

The revolution, by eliminating the monarchical central state under the authority of a sovereign who serves as the instrument to integrate and unite a region in a national ensemble, had brought about a decisive change. The nation was no longer a coincidental and unanticipated assembly of populations subjugated by a dynasty, which changed its composition by force of arms (wars) or by marriages (alliances and successions to the throne). The rule of the king over his subjects was superseded by the rule of the people, now master of its own history.

Since then, revolutionary France, which accomplished the first complete model of the nation-state and propagated it to all of Europe, made from this the source and abode of a true religion founded on an equally mythic and mystic community. The citizens actually became "children of the native country." And the nation-state, due to its power, its political and military force, now disposes over the entire panoply of sainthood. As Arnold Toynbee notes, the nation acts as a religion in that it transforms its past subservience to Christianity to the person of the ruler.

Departing from this, French identity, formed by republican and democratic tradition, has assumed the aspect of a fundamentally dualistic vision, hardly protesting its appearance as a chosen people with a universal mission. This explains the historical mission of France so strikingly described by Michelet (who speaks of "The French Messiah, pilot ship of humanity") or by de Gaulle ("France is chosen for a superb and exceptional destiny"). The historical and collective memory of the French is ruled by this system of representations and fantasies; it is the mediator of its ties with the nation and at the same time experiences an undeniable anxiety at the idea of seeing this heritage destroyed in a supranational Europe ruled by the "dwarfs" from Brussels.

Moreover, this memory is structured by a double mythology—a national mythology rich in historical legacies, glory and past achievements of France, and a democratic mythology, heir of the French revolution and the universal spirit of human rights, as Clemenceau called it when he proudly proclaimed on November 11, 1918, "France, yesterday's soldier of God, today's soldier of humanity, will always be soldier of the ideal." In this way the mysticism of "eternal France" as the heir of Gallien and Rome, Jeanne d'Arc and the revolution combines two mottos: *Gesta Dei per Francos* and *Gesta Humanitatis per Francos*. Now we can understand why the rulers of France always put such great stress on teaching history. History was viewed as an essential way of making the fundamental values of the nation and the purpose of the French identity understandable to the young generation, and to hand it down. This went so far that President Mitterand in 1984 devoted a famous cabinet meeting to this problem!

It is true that this patriotic memory is in constant danger of degenerating into flagwaving nationalism, even chauvinism. Therefore there has been an attempt to introduce a subtle differentiation between two forms of nationalism. The first, that of "open nationalism," is characterized as universal, optimistic, generous and hospitable, in solidarity with other nations and the oppressed. That is the nationalism of the democratic and republican France which holds high the flag of freedom and human rights. The other, the "hidden" and aggressive nationalism, arises from fear and repression and is founded upon the concept of a closed, egoistic defensive nation mobilized for the elimination of internal and external enemies. This nationalism is characterized by a type of collective paranoia fueled by the illusion of decline and conspiracy. No one has better represented the contrast between these two views of France than Giraudoux in his novel *Bella*, where the mean, selfish, closed and unfriendly nationalism of Rebendart-Poincaré is opposed by the enlightened and generous patriotism of Dubardeau-Berthelot, the embodiment of the sunny universal genius of France.

It is also true that the lines are not always easily drawn between the different types of patriotism and nationalism, especially when they are engaging with the international community and adapting internally to the European house. This is all the more so since by nature every identity is simultaneously composed of a sharing part and a part that rejects.

In building the European edifice, a certain part of the French were beset by the feeling that their identity, already an object of doubt and fear, has become evermore fragile because of the two main problems facing their country—modernization and immigration. Here was a double threat to French identity, made all the worse by the rushed pace of European integration, while in addition to it all, the safety net provided by national sovereignty was to be abandoned in favor of a type of community superstate.

Modernization first made itself known in the demise of rural France, that ancient element of French identity. This silent revolution convulsed the rural areas when modern farming was introduced, causing a deep shock; it was the inevitable end of what was left of the old peasant memories, and with the change came the feeling that this world was lost forever. Braudel in *The French Identity* calls this "the great overthrow of peasant France," leaving its impact not only on the people, but also on the countryside and agriculture, and refashioning the country's identity with the iron hands of progress and technology. Pompidou could very well have been a child of the Auvergne, of direct rural descent, and Mitterand could very well be a great friend and protector of trees. Nothing stops the process of violation of the most durable and weakest tradition.

But modernization caught up with the cities as well as the villages. Its effect was obvious everywhere, and the sociologist Henri Mendras could give his book, which appeared in 1989, the title *The Second Revolution* to characterize the development of the last quarter century. Mass consumption created its own double—mass culture. The multiplication and wide distribution of values and objects are accompanied by a change of social characteristics and forms of social discrimination. The hierarchic tradition of social rank is abolished in favor of the standard of living. In daily life, in trade, in advertising and in leisure time one can detect a uniformity, a levelling out and deterioration (which some call Americanization), even if the feeling of uncertainty and the rise in unemployment as well as the growth of a "new poverty" challenge these earthlings to justify their egoistic and meaningless existence (like the dreams in the prophetic novel *Les choses* by Georges Perec).

The result of this is that with the loss of familiar points of reference, the personal sense of identity and social identity became very strained for many French, especially the disadvantaged, driving them to cling to a national identity, no matter how threatened, rather than disappear in an impersonal and technocratic Europe in which their identity is in even greater danger.

Moreover, the considerable influx of emigrants to France from the southern countries, especially from northern and interior Africa, has strongly increased the feeling of anxiety about the present and future of the French identity. Despite this, France is an old land of immigration. Statistics in this area are informative. While there were approximately 1 million foreigners in 1900 and 2.7 million in 1931, they are now estimated at about 4 million. There are almost 1.5 million naturalized citizens in comparison to 200,000 at the beginning of the century. In other words, 18 million French today are of foreign origin, i.e., one third of France—if one goes back to the second, third and fourth generation (parents, grandparents, great grandparents). This means the integration process in the French *melting pot* has functioned well.

Despite this historical fact, fears exist in the collective mentality; the ancient inclinations of hatred toward foreigners remain. In addition, from the legal view, the republican tradition has introduced a radical differentiation between those labelled "citizens of the nation" and the foreigner ("non-citizen") in order to shut the doors of the nation-state, because the revolution, in the surrender of the king's sovereignty to the nation, made of every citizen an owner of part and parcel of national sovereignty. The complications which arise when, for example, the other citizens of the European community are allowed to participate in certain civil rights, such as the right to vote in communal elections, are immediately evident. In this regard, the French tradition of *jus soli* (in addition to *jus sanguinis*), permitting generations of children of emigrants to be gently integrated and to receive French citizenship, was of no help. This gives rise to a variety of fantasies about foreigners, whether they are Europeans or non-Europeans.

Despite all this, hatred toward foreigners has recently been made manifest as a result of the economic crisis and under pressure of the renewed resurgence of the extreme right. Always clamoring "for the defense of the French identity" while expanding its position since the beginning of the eighties, the right has relentlessly preached "the national advantage" in all areas of social living—work, health, housing, etc.—against the "surging wave" of new immigrants from Africa and Asia. This very logically fits the political line of Front National, which combines anti-Europeanism with hatred toward foreigners. Thus the concepts "native country," "nation" and "roots," which, in the name of regaining national values, embellished speeches by Jean-Marie Le Pen. From there, too, comes the call for "the right of every one of us to be at home in France and the right of every one of us to protect our own interests first." Especially notable in this context is the frequently repeated slogan by the leader of the Front National, "I love my daughters more than my cousins, my cousins more than my neighbors, my neighbors more than strangers, and strangers more than my enemies"!

From this it is evident how disturbing the problem of national identity is in the formative stage of Europe, because this term derives its source and strength from the pure republican and democratic tradition and, simultaneously, nurtures the worst excesses of anti-foreign demagogy.

Splitting Into Six Unions

As we have seen, following the initial momentum of 1948 the European idea made only little progress. The major turning point of 1950 occurred as a result of French initiatives at a time when the European construct began concretely as a "Europe of Six." This formative phase, despite some relapses, continued within the same framework until 1969. In this development over a period of two decades one can differentiate between two stages, those characterized by the Roman treaties and those shaped by General de Gaulle's new seizure of power: the first from 1950 to 1957, the second from 1958 to 1969.

The point of departure came from French Foreign Secretary Robert Schuman, whose bold tactics bypassed the obstacles on the road to the establishment of Europe by bringing about the Coal and Steel Community. The old German-French antagonism had continued far too long for this stubborn and pious Lorraine-born minister with a strong personality hiding behind his discrete and modest appearance. He was a visionary of the future, a man whom his communist opponents called "boche" (born in 1886, he was a German citizen until the treaty of Versailles). Demilitarization and economic annexation of the Saar to France were not enough. The need was for true reconciliation.

This initiative, which Robert Schuman and Jean Monnet undertook together, found in Konrad Adenauer a committed and enthusiastic advocate of Europe. Robert Schuman, responsible for foreign policy, secured the support of his ministry, ignored parliament, and wrested approval in principle from the cabinet, which was only informed at the last minute. On May 9, 1950, his spectacular announcement followed at the Quai d'Orsay. "Europe," Schuman stated, "is not made in one stroke nor as a complete edifice; it is established by concrete achievements which first create a de facto solidarity. Bringing together the European nations requires that the French-German hostility of many decades be abolished: the act we have undertaken is one that will touch first of all France and Germany." This led to the proposal for a united coal and steel pool. "This proposal," commented Jean Monnet, "will bring about the first concrete statutes of a European federation, which is imperative for the preservation of peace."

Two new and fruitful ideas form the basis of the Schuman plan. First a political and diplomatic strategy shifting the focus of European development toward the Paris-Bonn axis. The other was part economic, part political, putting German-French coal and steel production under the control of a common agency within an organization open to participation by other European countries. The strategy was to find the chink in the armor of Europe's economic administration by a ruse designed to achieve a decisive breakthrough while preserving the partner's sovereign interests, though they would be put under the control of a political authority without effecting the property principle.

Starting from a dream, a Europe of reality took shape. The strength of the Schuman plan consisted in combining an attainable, realistic and convertible goal with a great future idea that went far beyond the immediate goal. Robert Schuman classified this ambition very clearly: "This Europe is not aimed against anyone; it knows no type of aggressive plans, has no egoistic or imperial character neither in itself nor in regard to others. It remains accessible to all who want to join. It grants international solidarity and cooperation, the right to exist (striving for) a sensible organization of the world of which it aims to become an essential part. . . . Europe must stop being a geographical conglomeration of adjoining, often antagonistic states, in order to become a community of different nations, which, however, are united in the same defensive and constructive efforts. . . . Depending on the circumstances under which it is achieved, Europe will be more or less complete. Will it ever be complete? No one is able to say. This is no reason to postpone the unification efforts until later. To undertake something is better than resignation, and waiting for perfection is a lazy excuse for inactivity."

Thus, the heart of "Europe of the Six" was created. While an additional four countries became engaged on the borders of France and Germany (Belgium, Luxembourg, Holland and Italy) and Jean Monnet, the spiritual father of this undertaking, took over the chairmanship of the high authority in Luxembourg, the CECA treaty (European Coal and Steel Community) was signed on April 18, 1951. After 1953 the coal and steel pool went into effect. Thanks to France, an essential step toward building the European house was accomplished. The Luxembourg engine became a locomotive to which the European wagon could be hitched.

Nevertheless, the first car, the European Defense Community, proved a very bad choice, because this decision was accompanied by a damaging fiasco. And that at a time when the Europe of Strasbourg appeared too big and the Luxembourg Europe too small. This affair, a direct result of the Cold War and the Atlantic alliance, occurred chiefly in France, where the "dispute about the European defense community" led to a crisis of national consciousness and unleashed passions which reached their climax in 1954. The project jeopardized French identity—a very strong identity due to the terrible trials of 1939–1945, remembrance of which was still quite recent. This even brought up talk of a new Dreyfus affair. The reference is doubtless exaggerated, but in view of the emotionally charged situation and fears of the future that this defense community created, the great national debate very quickly assumed the character of a religious war, with supporters of traditional patriotism on one side and on the other those devoted to Europe who were resolved to overcome the supremacy of national authority.

The starting point for this was simple. Ever since NATO was created, the question whether Germany was to be rearmed in the face of the Soviet threat had become inevitable. But was it permissible to rearm without danger a people who had followed Hitler ten years earlier, doing their best to conquer Europe? In the background, American pressure, intensified by the Korean War, minced no words. "I would like Germans in uniform by the fall of 1951," said Dean Acheson. Hence the October 1950 proposal by René Pleven, council president (prompted by Jean Monnet), for a European commission for defense that would include German soldiers side by side with French soldiers in a European army under supranational command. This was rearmament plain and simple, which was designed to avoid a very unpopular process, the re-establishment of the Wehrmacht. The arrangement was well planned—doubtlessly too well—to the extent that Germany would have contributed to the defense of Europe without its government having the right to dispose over its military units. The new army was, in fact, to be placed under the authority of a joint defense minister, who was to be controlled by the European assembly. But at the same time France, under this pretext of protecting itself from German danger, would lose its military independence with one stroke; it was an independence that had lasted only very briefly.

Antoine Pinay summarized this undertaking and its strong hybrid character in 1953 by saying the objective was to "bring about with one stroke Europe's security, German rearmament, and a new stage in Europe's development." But what had begun as a calculated ploy—a dictatorial and convoluted means of rearming Germany while also embellishing the drive for European unity— would in two years trigger an intense struggle within the French public.

The defense community was opposed by two homogeneous forces. First, by the Communist Party, the implacable enemy of German rearmament, who saw this, not without reason, as an anti-Soviet operation and who organized an anti-German and an anti-American left nationalism around this issue. Secondly, by the Assembly of the French People by the Gaullists, who unanimously supported General de Gaulle. For them a European army presented an unacceptable danger to national sovereignty in a key area, defense. Such a compromise would be collective suicide.

Only one party, the MRP, was a passionate defender of the project. A sign of the confusion and conflict that prevailed were the divisions within all other political forces in the country. The socialists were split; while Guy Mollet supported the entire project, the majority of the parliamentary party was against it, triggering an intense debate. Among the radicals, the Jacobins, Herriot and Daladier, were decided opponents. The classic right was also fragmented. Intense discussion took place in the army and the French garrisons and the noted military leaders General Koenig and Marshal Juin took up position against the EDC. Intellectuals, journalists (headed by *Le Monde*), left-wing Catholics, the laity of Christian-democratic Europe hostile to the "black international" all took up the fight against the European army.

An injured collective consciousness, a revived nationalism, a bloody memory—all these elements came together in a half-ideological, half-contrived dispute. The concept of Europe lost none of its standing with the public in the process. But the European army caused deeply fragmented opinions. A poll by IFOP in July 1954 shows views that are almost in balance: 19 percent are "for" and 17 percent are "more or less for"; on the other hand, 20 percent are "against" and 11 percent "more or less against," while the undecided were 33 percent. There was indeed an irreconcilable dividing line between the two, one which failed to correspond to any of the traditional divisions, like those between left-right or its opposite, Vichy-resistance.

Even though the agreement of May 27, 1952, was signed by France and its five partners, the problem of its ratification by the National Assembly still remained unresolved. Now the affair was in gridlock. Successive French governments dragged it out because of the divisions within its majority (François Fontaine, a committed European, even titled his polemic essay "The Nation on Hold"). Finally, the government of Mendés-France allowed the debate to be held anew before the National Assembly in August 1954. It did not, however, result in a real debate because a vote of 319 to 264 about procedural matters buried the proposal for a European army in an atmosphere of passion. By singing the "Marseillaise," the victors drowned out the scandalized and astonished voices of their opponents, who were soon to speak about the crime of August 30.

The EDC was dead, while the remaining Europeans pointed to France as responsible for its defeat. Despite this, the cul-de-sac, thanks to a quickly negotiated substitute solution, was avoided. The London and Paris agreement of October 1954 acknowledged the complete sovereignty of West Germany, including its possible rearmament if the West European Union should be founded simultaneously.

Even if the proposal's hybrid character was the direct cause for its failure, the advocates of supranational Europe, however, made a serious mistake. Departing from a hasty improvisation they believed they could also use the lucky formula of coal and steel for national defense. By making the EDC the second stage of the establishment of Europe they wanted to put in place a military Europe modeled on the economic Europe with the goal of a political Europe. This turned out to be a serious miscalculation because the term defense was not likely to mobilize the Europeans devoid of political will. Moreover, the public was not ready. In this sense, Europe, blown up into a bone of contention instead of an object of a community of mind and spirit, was the first victim of the EDC.

For this reason the following stages would again become the sole affairs of experts, politicians, economists and high officials. Moreover, the French were now and for many years to be occupied with the war in Algeria. While the West European Union remained an empty shell, a long way from supranational readiness (in fact, it was always to play an insignificant role), it appeared that Europe fell out of style. This was the backlash. Nevertheless, the European idea was still approved, though the lack of its acceptance by the people led to the construction of Europe under a bell jar. This is how a feeling of apathy among the general public may be explained — a feeling that was to last.

Despite all this, some of the most stubborn people among the European advocates drew a lesson from past errors. They wanted to scrap the stages, favoring "all or nothing" tactics instead of gradual steps. In the pursuit of the opposite, it became important to manifest movement by speed. Because the road to military as well as political Europe was blocked, only the path of economic Europe remained. It was imperative for it to lead to success and to prevail against the "maximalists" and the "pragmatists."

In 1955, the efforts to bring about the Roman treaties were renewed. The inexhaustible Jean Monnet, who had given up the chairmanship of the CECA (European Coal and Steel Community) in order to take over the chairmanship of the "Action Committee for the United States of Europe," made the first move. In the conference of June 1–3 in Messina, the Six, instead of going for grandiose projects, approved a simple and convertible, practical and effective idea: the Common Market (the term first appeared there). Parallel to this was the creation of Euratom, whose strongest advocate was another Frenchman, Louis Armand, a brilliant engineer, president of SNCF (French Railways), a committed advocate of the united European nuclear program. In fact, Jean Monnet in this phase thought this nuclear community was much more likely to lead to the realization of the unity of Europe than the Common Market. On the other hand, enlightened French as well as German economic circles naturally showed much more interest in setting the sights on a large market of the Six.

Two years passed before negotiations were held. From the French side, the chief negotiator, Maurice Faure, a very flexible and steadfast advocate of Europe, was instructed to fight for two points: to ensure guarantees for the adaptation of the French economy, and not to leave out the overseas regions. At the same time the foundations for a common agricultural policy were established, leading immediately to a customs union, i.e., the free flow of trade within the six European Economic Community countries.

In France, in view of established protectionist traditions, not a few reservations arose about the common European market. Of course, French economy at that time experienced very vigorous growth, but the thought of opening the borders scared many industrialists and farmers. Catastrophes were foreseen. European advocates pointed out that Europe would offer the very means to provide powerful stimulants for the modernization of the country. Eventually industry and business agreed, and so did the unions. *Force Ouvrière* and the French Confederation of Christian Workers also approved, provided employees were guaranteed social benefits. Still, the public followed the negotiations with indifference.

The Treaty of Rome, a turning point in European history, was ceremoniously signed on March 25, 1957, thanks to the determination of a "small group." The ratification debate in the French parliament took place from July 3–10. And this time there was a large majority: 342 for, 239 against. Among the opponents were the Communists, the majority of the Gaullists, the Poujadists and individual leading politicians such as Pierre Mendés-France. Supporters were the MRP, the Socialists, the Radicals, the independents (i.e., the classic right) with Valery Giscard d'Estaing, as well as leaders of the left center such as François Mitterand.

The new institutions were established at the beginning of 1958, a year in which France was stuck in the "Algerian mire," its attention monopolized by the fall of the Fourth Republic and the return of General de Gaulle to power. Two trends characterize the period between 1958 and 1969. First, the Six learned how to live together in a series of successes and crises. The French took their place in a Europe that had become an everyday environment. This period was also dominated by the personality of General de Gaulle, who himself had to overcome not a few prejudices, animosities and personal deep indignations. However, the earlier positions of Charles de Gaulle toward Europe could hardly give rise to concerns among the passionate advocates of Europe, in France as well as in other countries of the European Economic Community, although the new head of state had always expressed his hostility toward supranational institutions. The pragmatic and realistic de Gaulle (who had a completely different view toward what André Philip called a "whining nationalism") was immediately determined to carry out the treaties signed and ratified by France. He became deeply involved in the Common Market, put his stamp on it and, in addition, gave it much impetus for acceleration.

His immediate goal was to put an end to the paralysis that had gripped France since the Algerian war. Beginning with 1962, thanks to a well-formulated doctrine and an unshakable will, he developed his own policy. According to his usual philosophy the problem had to be seen globally. "To erect Europe means to unify it," he emphasized, "this is what is most essential." From this followed an unqualified European conviction. "How can we allow that this large crucible of civilization, of reason and prosperity, becomes extinguished under its own ashes?" But when it came to giving up any portion of sovereignty he was adamant. De Gaulle never wanted to tolerate a true European executive, because "it is clear that no European people will entrust its fate to an airplane crew primarily composed of foreigners." In short, the Gaullist doctrine can be summarized in this way: organize European solidarity without infringing on national sovereignty.

General de Gaulle approved close cooperation between the states, with German-French détente as the pivotal point. He constantly rejected the loss of national identity in a Europe he described in hyperbole as "thinking and writing in something like integrated Esperanto or Volapük" (international artificial language invented in 1880 by the German Joachim Martin). He defended himself in a press conference May 15, 1962, for having used the term "Europe of the fatherlands" ("As far as I am concerned, I have never, in any of my statements, spoken about a Europe of the fatherlands, although I'm always charged with having done so.") On the other hand, he used the term "Europe of the states." Because "there are only the states, only they count, are legitimate and able to develop ideas. . . . At this time there can be no other Europe than that of the states, of course outside of myths, fiction and pageantry." This is how the president of the French republic contrasted the Europe of reality with the Europe of lip service.

On the basis of this Gaullist concept of Europe, the German-French détente was created, symbolized by the personal relationship between General de Gaulle and West German Chancellor Adenauer, "this old French-man and ancient German." The world witnessed the quick disappearance of the century-old antagonism which, with the friendship agreement signed in 1963 and widely approved by the public, confirmed the stability of the German-French alliance. Half of the French saw this as a great step forward. In 1968 a SOFRES survey showed that three-fourths of the sample believed the wars between France and Germany belonged to the past. However, fear had not completely disappeared; a large majority expressed the wish that

Germany not become independent, and two-thirds were against a political Europe which excludes Germany.

As far as the candidacy of Great Britain for admission to the Common Market was concerned, the position of General de Gaulle was categorical. In two attempts, 1963 and 1967, he used the French veto. De Gaulle said no with such determination because Britain's candidacy faced two problems: the island and maritime country was not ready, and it was too closely associated with American policy. For the well-nigh fanatical goal of Gaullist diplomacy was to wrest Europe from domination by the United States. This is precisely the *indispensable* condition of European development—there could be only one unity of the continent, one removed from American hegemony.

The rejection of Britain's candidacy left behind some uneasiness among France's partners (chiefly West Germany), followed by a stalemate of common agricultural policy. The Fouchet plan of 1961–62, which intended to complement the Economic Community with political union using a very restrictive formula, proved a bitter disappointment and failure. During the subsequent crises of 1965–66 General de Gaulle did not hesitate to put his partners under pressure and pursue the policy of the empty chair himself.

Finally, de Gaulle's policy remained steadfast in all the eleven years he was in power: uncompromising rejection of the supranationalities in the name of French independence; pursuit of an independent Europe, a "European Europe," stress on the Paris-Bonn axis. Instead of relying on the stateless technicians of the Brussels Commissions, future development should build on the states as "the only unit with the right to command; and a power that commands obedience."

In other ways, the French public followed General de Gaulle fairly faithfully. He was seen as the determined advocate of Europe, the surveys indicating that there was wide agreement with his European policy. Among indications for this trust was a report by the IFOP in 1965, showing that 52 percent of the French would have put Charles de Gaulle in first place if they were to elect the first president of Europe!

The French in the Expanded Community: The Long March to European Unity

The year 1969 marked a great turning point. With General de Gaulle's death in the spring, a commanding personality had departed. A French initiative at the summit of the Six at the Haag Conference in December produced a new spurt of activity for a united Europe. The new president of the Republic, Georges Pompidou, was anxious to make a conspicuous entrance on the European stage. Wanting to create a climate of trust and to escape from the blind alley in which European development now found itself, he believed that by admitting Great Britain he could take an important step forward in the Community, which was preparing to submit the candidacy of the U.K. for the third time. The three principles suggested by France were: completion, expansion and extension. However, the cautious and realistic Pompidou was determined to pursue a cooperation that would follow the guidelines set by de Gaulle, i.e., a Community based on the states eschewing all supranationality.

The first of de Gaulle's three points provided for shoring up the two pillars of the European Economic Community (customs union and the common agricultural policy). The results of a common policy in the industrial, technological and social areas remained meager and progress slow. As for the third point, extension, its most important objective was an economic and monetary union. But as soon as these principles were defined the dollar collapsed, followed by a crisis which hit the European national economies and currencies with full force and again fanned the differences between the states. The impact of all this was such that, after several years, the record of the European economic and monetary union proved a failure.

On the other hand, the Community's expansion recommended in The Haag was completed, because on January 1, 1973, three new countries joined: Great Britain, Ireland and Denmark. The Six thus became Nine at the end of the negotiations. The Anglo-French entente was decisive, especially in the crucial encounter between the British Prime Minister Edward Heath and President Pompidou in May 1971 in Paris. At the beginning of 1972 agreement became reality and the treaty of admission of the new European Economic Community members was signed.

The expansion of Europe by including England no doubt corresponded to a wish generally favored by the French. Surveys showed that since the beginning of the common market, three of five persons in 1965 supported expansion and only one in five was against it. Among the countries mentioned in an expansion of the European economic community, England always ranked first. If its inclusion in the community met with wide agreement, it was because many assumed Britain's association with the continent would strengthen the bonds among Europeans, while the bond between Britain and America would weaken.

But when Pompidou decided to allow the French to give their blessings to the expansion, by referendum, i.e., vote on England's membership, he was only partly successful. And that was because the matter was badly arranged and because internal political fears influenced the election campaign as well as the outcome of the vote. First of all, every past negative record of voting participation (only 47 percent of the electorate!) and invalidated votes was beaten. Even if the yes votes won with 68 percent of those who voted, it was only one-third of the electorate. This poor result for President Pompidou was the fault of the Communist opposition, the absence of the Socialists and the grumbling of the Gaullists. But this result was not to carry much weight in the construction of Europe.

When in 1974 Valéry Giscard d'Estaing, a committed European, moved into the Elysée Palace, France took a new step in its engagement for Europe. In fact, the views of the new president of the Republic (who was ready to yield certain sovereign rights to the Community's institutions and to strengthen the authority of the Brussels commission) differed from those of his predecessor, who for his part was very careful not to deviate from the Gaullistic idea of a Europe of separate states. In addition, Giscard d'Estaing developed a good relationship with West German Chancellor Helmut Schmidt, so the Paris-Bonn axis was revived. He himself had some considerable time ago put his belief in Europe in these words: "One must invent Europe," he explained in 1966, "and the task of our generation will be to define an original structure and propose it step-by-step. It will be the existential Europe. . . . France must suggest a method and time table which must end in a European union in 1980."

Nevertheless, it must be said that the achievements in the second half of the seventies, as real as they were, took place only slowly. The two major accomplishments were first achieved in 1979—the European monetary system and the Ecu (common monetary unit of European currency defined by a "basket").

Even more complicated was the way which led to the general election of the European Parliament, an instrument (so one hopes) that replaces the Europe of the bureaucrats with the Europe of the citizens. Valéry Giscard d'Estaing supported it after initial hesitation and the measure received its approval in 1977 by the French National Assembly, but not without reviving the old arguments; for example, in addition to the Communists, the Gaullists were opposed as well, fearing a gradual shift to supranationality. But the French public approved of these measures by a large majority, and in June 1979 the first direct election of the Strasbourg European Parliament took place with 180 million Europeans voting. A Frenchwoman, Simone Weil, a former member of parliament and minister, became the first president. Although the European Parliament now had democratic legitimacy, it has not been able to widen its authority.

By the way, it must be admitted that at the end of the decade, the European union promised for 1980 (the term was replaced in 1972 by political union) still remained to be realized. Without a doubt, the European Council superseded the "summit" at the suggestion of Valéry Giscard d'Estaing. However, the difference was very minor. Despite the ritual memory of the intended goal and invoking the "European identity," little success was in sight because the future union lacked clear definition because of little determination to bring it about.

With the beginning of the eighties, the Community experienced new misfortunes because a long-lasting crisis began in 1981 due to Margaret Thatcher's inflexibility. This crisis blocked all negotiations in the dispute about the amounts the British should contribute to the Community's budget. Only François Mitterand's intervention in the European Council's session of Fontainebleau in June 1984 made it possible to emerge from the confusion of the agricultural payments and the crisis, thanks to a settlement arranged by the Ten for Britain's contributions in order to make its admission easier. In general, the agreement was welcomed by the French public, who were happy about settling this European disagreement with Great Britain, since in the setting of green Europe (agriculture) and blue Europe (fisheries) there was no paucity of friction between France and Britain.

At the same time the agreement favored admission of Spain and Portugal into the European Economic Community after 1986, while Greece, whose candidacy was very much supported by France, had already been admitted in 1981. The principle of expanding the community to the South, i.e., the Iberian countries and Greece, had been accepted at the end of the previous decade when these three countries became democratic states. But admission of Spain and Portugal was not without commotion in France, where, especially in view of competition of agricultural products such as wine, fruits and vegetables from the Iberian peninsula, great fears arose.

In France, there is often a discrepancy between approving the principle of unification of Europe and opposing certain of its effects and consequences judged harmful to French interests (primarily to various occupational groups). Correspondingly, there is also ambivalence about supporting a European federation which would better safeguard the future, and about France having to participate without giving up its national independence. Nevertheless, as time passes, the need for Europe becomes more evident to more and more people, especially the young. It is apparent that in a world shaken by ambivalence, uncertainty and conflicts, the European nations, too, small to meet the demands of the twenty-first century alone, must join in order to achieve and develop their own space of freedom and democracy.

Besides, France since 1981 is led by a president of the Republic who, just as his predecessors, is a determined champion of Europe. The development of Europe, in fact, is part of the fundamental convictions of François Mitterand. He has always described himself as "European from the ground up." Added to this are the historical aspirations of a man concerned about leaving his mark on history, a mark distinguished by having served longer than any other French president (and that as a leftist as well). What more gratifying success could there be for him than to accomplish the political union of Europe? Who would dare challenge François Mitterand his place in the history of France and the world?

Thus, too, the considerable progress of 1985 is in large part due to the initiative of François Mitterand working in close cooperation with West German Chancellor Helmut Kohl, i.e., the agreement of the United European Act concluded in December of that year in Luxembourg and signed by France in February 1986. This achievement deserves credit for finding a common denominator for two often antagonistic arguments, each logical in its own way, in the construction of Europe: the argument of cooperation between two states and the supranational argument. It accomplished this by failing to live up to the expectations of the radical "Europhiles" and, at the same time, upsetting the moderate "Europhiles," because it attempts to limit the autonomy of the national legislatures. An important point calls for the qualified majority vote to become the rule, while the unanimous vote is to be the exception.

There, in fact, is the realization of a large common domestic market of the Twelve after January 1, 1993, insuring the free flow of people, goods, capital and services. It may be expected to revive old hostilities between those favoring unqualified federalism and those for absolute national independence. Nevertheless, the treaty was ratified, thanks to "cohabitation" (i.e., the cooperation between a Socialist president of a non-Socialist government) in November 1986 and preparations for unifying legal, banking and education systems began.

Meanwhile, it has become evident that, in view of the radical changes of 1989 in the other half of Europe and the collapse of the Communist system, the tactics of small steps is no longer enough. Therefore, Mitterand and Kohl, in a message addressed to their partners in April 1990, summarized three points: To make real progress a united Europe needs first, a goal, to equip the European union with the necessary means; second, a procedure, to draft a new treaty; third, a deadline, to ratify the treaty before the end of 1992. On February 7, 1992, with the signing of the Maastricht treaty about the European union, the end of the road was reached at last.

The preamble to the European Economic Community treaty had recommended "an ever closer union of the European people." Now, thirty years later, the last goal of a united Europe is in the process of becoming an attainable reality with economic and monetary union and political union, thanks to the qualitative leap the Maastricht treaty represents.

What Kind of Europe?

At the conclusion of this outline the reader may ask himself what kind of future Europe the French strive for and what kind of Europe in turn is likely to await them. Three large challenges govern the future outlook: democracy, national identity and citizenship.

As for Europe and democracy, we first must be clear about the radical changes which occurred during the eighties. Within the span of a few years the unloved Europe actually became deeply beloved. No longer do the caricatures of steel barons or milk quotas dominate. What has done most to re-establish Europe's repute is a world exposed to turmoil and brutality; Europe appears in it as a harbor and symbol for democracy and human rights. The cultural revolution, which produced the primacy of justice and the rule of law is to a large extent due to this Europe.

Up to now, Europe for many has been identical with a past plagued by the sins of nationalism, colonialism and also racism. By becoming aware of the totalitarian phenomenon, by disowning the third world mythology and turning increasingly toward the values of freedom, peace and tolerance Europe has done much to redeem itself. The word "plural" which has become fashionable in French testifies to the total victory of pluralism. There is constant talk of the *pluralistic* society, *pluralistic* culture, *pluralistic* schools. . . .

The replacement of a central axiom of political philosophy—the reformist model with a revolutionary ideal, which has been in fashion for so long—has also contributed to the same development. The revolutionary ideal is discredited today and is still popular only with a few groups and sects. Now force and terror are rejected in light of the tragic non-European examples of China and Cuba or the Iranian "revolution," which displayed their fanatic and bloody face in public. In the end, European democracy has triumphed, becoming the model and object of admiration and the goal for all of Eastern European societies which escaped communist totalitarianism.

Even in France, European integration has fostered the rule of law and the promotion of a democratic ideal, receiving its legitimacy not only from the rule of the majority, but also from the articles of the European Commission for Human Rights. If there is a lack of democracy, it is very much because of indifference and apathy of the citizens as well as because of a fissure in France. As surveys have shown, there is on one side a young, dynamic, vibrant France, a France conscious of its European identity and fully supporting it; on the other side is an older France, troubled and disadvantaged and touched by unrest and therefore ready to reject the development of Europe.

Will the Europe of tomorrow be a federal Europe as its "founding fathers" had dreamed? Or will it be satisfied with becoming the Europe of nations which General de Gaulle recommended? Even if the controversy remains alive, the great political inclinations of the French public have barely changed in forty years. Europe has the approval of the majority and the approaching European union is rejected only by the left and extreme right forces, the Communists and the Front National, as well as a splinter group of the Gaullists.

We must, however, also take note of François Mitterand's many assurances that the French nation and the French fatherland would continue to exist within the framework of a future European union. Are these affirmations anything other than an attempt to reconcile a great European plan with the wish for continued national sovereignty? Incidentally, the Socialist party in "Project for France," the official program in which it attributes a federal objective to the European union, announces that the "European identity will not be created in opposition to the idea of the nation." Here is one example of the sacred value which attaches to the nation by virtue of the republican tradition; a value of belief and hope that in the innermost part of the collective soul there are latent powers; a value which can instill strength, vigor and a sense of identity.

In reality, Europe is not destined to transform itself into a state of nations. Rather, its calling is to remain an integrating organization for the nation states, which are democratic themselves and in which the right of the community will serve as motor for future European citizenship. Therefore, the nation state remains the preferred location for the practice of democracy. The crux is the division of power between the community and the member states, who, instead of being divested of their authority in the areas of education, health, social welfare and law, should retain their authority in essence, as the Maastricht treaty indeed provides in accordance with the minority principle.

But a sound domestic democracy in every country is the fundamental precondition for the success of the European edifice. For its objective is not a national superstate since the nations are remaining alive; rather, it is what Jacques Lessourne, the editor of *Le Monde*, astutely called "a community of sovereign states." This also corresponds to the avowed desire from the French side to strengthen in the union the instruments of cooperation between the states (the Council of State and, above all, the European Council, which is composed of the heads of state and government) at the expense of the supranational institutions (the European Parliament and the Brussels Commission). Therefore, we may expect the development of a federal Europe in the economic and monetary area as well as cooperation between the states in the political area.

In the final analysis, very close cooperation between democratic countries only makes sense if the citizens are part of it and if they are convinced they share a common future. Indeed, there would be no need to be content with a gigantic market within the framework of a technocratic Europe of goods. Cooperation must include all areas essential to life, such as currency and foreign policy. From this derives the need for European citizenship with all its rights and duties, because it will give legal legitimacy to a sense of belonging without forfeiting the Community's deep roots. Everyone must become accustomed to having various affiliations; nothing stops us from being French and at the same time also European.

But the sense of belonging can only develop if citizens perceive that demands for social justice are respected. For this reason, the French, in contrast to the soulless Eurocrats who try to impose the tyranny of the Brussels offices on the obedient, though unruly people with regulatory edicts emanating mostly from small quiet office cubicles, insist so much on a social Europe as a condition for participating both as citizens and people of like mind.

Moreover, what the French believe must be avoided at all costs is that the Community remains restricted to itself—a justifiable fear—and that it rejects the other half of Europe at the very moment when Central and Eastern Europe wish to join the large democratic family of the continent. But the majority of the French also believes it would be risky to give up the consolidation of the European union, and weaken or even abandon the European Economic Community in order to take the plunge into a large continental free trade zone. Even the thought of coordinating a tightly integrated community and a confederation extending as far as the Russian territory meets with wide approval. This would offer the chance of political and economic cooperation, while the strong influence which the European Economic Community represents would also be strengthened.

Thus the European union presents itself as a creation still in the process of realization by giving the obstacles definition and exploiting the areas of understanding and agreement. The product of a free and voluntary accord based on a jointly and democratically arrived at regulatory mechanism, it is where the great work of construction will take place tomorrow. In this way, after so many centuries of battles and conflicts, today's Europe, seen as history as well as consciousness, embodies increasingly more hope and determination.

The Germans
and European Unification

Wilfried Loth

German efforts to achieve the unification of Europe arose largely from the same impulses as those that impelled other European nations. Ever since the end of the imperial era, Germany has striven for larger spheres of economic influence because as productive capacities grew national borders became too stifling to organize production in a rational way. Following the end of the First World War and its hitherto unknown destructive qualities, there were attempts to establish effective institutions that could safeguard peace and which would remove the control of military forces from nation states. Finally, the idea arose that European unity could provide protection from external dangers — from the Soviet Union, whose advocacy of international revolution had made bourgeois and pre-bourgeois leaders fearful; and from the U.S., whose spectacular economic rise had become a threat to producers within the geographically smaller European markets.

Taken together, these impulses had led to a broad-based movement during the Weimar republic. Parliamentarians and other public leaders participated in the activities of the "Paneuropa-Union" of Austria's Count Richard Coudenhove-Kalergi, which promoted renewal of the old continent with a step-by-step program for unification of all the nations "from Poland to Portugal."[1] A Union for European Understanding (Verband für Europäische Verständigung), founded in 1926 under the chairmanship of the Deutsche Volkspartei (DVP) member of parliament Wilhelm Heile, followed in the tradition of liberal pacifism in advocating more power for the League of

Nations. It found support predominantly from the Deutsche Demokratische Partei (DDP) and the Sozialdemokratische Partei Deutschlands (SDP), but there were connections to the political center and the Deutsche Volkspartei (DVP) as well. The SPD included support for a United States of Europe in its 1952 Heidelberg party platform. Business leaders and economists who opposed the proliferation of customs barriers after World War I and pleaded for a return to free trade joined in the German section of the International Committee for a European Union. Alfred Weber in his book analyzed *The Crisis of Modern State Theory in Europe;* Edgar Stern-Rubarth pleaded for a European customs union.

One of the characteristics that differentiated the German movement for Europe from that of other nations was its very specific weighting of motives. The pacifist basic principle was not as strong here as it was in France, where the fear of trench warfare on French soil had made the idea of securing peace through a strong League of Nations popular. To the Germans, who had experienced war largely through reports from returned soldiers "undefeated in the field," the League appeared to be far more an element of the Versailles system; it, in turn, was perceived as a shackle, the removal of which had to be an important goal of German policy. For that reason, German voices promoting a larger economic community were more numerous. The enormous economic dynamism developed by the German Reich in its phase of intensive industrialization made national borders seem more like inhibitors of productivity here than elsewhere.

In contrast, owing to its geographical position and the size of the Reich, concepts of Europe were associated more frequently in Germany than elsewhere with hegemonic ambitions. This is particularly true of diverse Central European ideas aimed at European integration with a German central core, which would necessarily make German participation in the integration process top heavy. These ideas were especially popular as part of the policy pursuing a German-Austrian bloc before and during World War I; there were many plans for a "Central European Union of States" in internal war aims discussions. Friedrich Neumann's *Mitteleuropa*, published in 1915, was widely acclaimed.

However, these ambitious plans had little chance of getting started after the defeat of 1918. They remained latent as one possibility for German policies for Europe. In practice, the combination of integrative and hegemonic concepts of unity frequently were difficult to unravel. Thus, Gustav Stresemann founded his foreign relations strategy on an "understanding" with France, a policy in notable contrast to previous policies, in which France was seen as the arch enemy. Moreover, though flexible in method and careful in procedure, he was consistent in seeking economic integration of

Europe. But he was not interested in freezing the status quo, which was the basis of the European initiatives of his French partner, Aristide Briand; rather he sought a situation in which Germany could realize its full economic potential.

In the Third Reich, the hopes for integration were transformed completely in plans for hegemony. Hitler's policy of a "New Order" was approved until well into World War II not only because it revoked the Versailles treaty imposed after World War I, or because of enduring national frustrations; it also received support because there was an awareness of the deficiencies of an order based on national states, which gave rise to the hope for a new order under German leadership. Hitler's efforts to form a "Greater German Reich" to colonize "inferior races" as laborers, also fostered all sorts of other ideas about a Europe envisaging a more or less "voluntary" cooperation of the European neighbors with the German conquerors.

Scholars such as Alfred Six and Werner Daitz developed notions of rearranging European territory. Business leaders pleaded for European-wide economic planning; foreign ministry officials toyed with plans for a "European Confederation." As Hitler distrusted in principle voluntary cooperation of defeated nations, all these initiatives came to nothing, although they evoked significant support for a time, particularly after the German invasion of the Soviet Union. This was a period in which National Socialist propaganda was able to portray the war as an anti-Bolshevist crusade for the defense of Europe. Ribbentrop in the spring of 1943 briefly adopted the notion of a confederated Europe as his own, and Goebbels was at least concerned about the credibility of his own European propaganda.

The proponents of conservative resistance initially also followed a path parallel to liberal imperialism. Thus, in 1940–1941, Carl Goerdeler broached the idea of a "European Confederation under German leadership," to be accomplished with progressive, voluntary agreements between the participating nations. At the beginning, there were to be reductions in customs duties, economic coordination and harmonization of laws; in the medium term, "regional associations" and "customs unions" were planned; and finally, "progressive cooperation on a military level" was to lead to "joint institutions" of defense. Just as Prussia in the nineteenth century seized leadership in Germany, the German Reich was to take the initiative and thus assure for itself leadership in Europe.[2]

In addition, there were a number of resistance groups predicting creation of a European federation without envisaging a special leadership role for Germany. Some authors, such as Helmuth von Moltke in his proposals for the Kreisauer Kreis (Kreisauer circle), linked belief in a new federal-type order to an explicit disavowal of power politics and nationalism. As the turn in the war became clear, Goerdeler also gave up claims to German leadership; at the same time he urged far more energetic steps to develop a European union than he had earlier. Members of the Kreisauer Kreis advised the Allies that only the prospect for a new, federated Europe would make the dictates of the victors less onerous and prevent renewal of German revanchism.

Following the unconditional surrender, this argument was, understandably, heard more frequently. Claims for German leadership were out of the question for the foreseeable future; first the Germans had to fight to relax step-by-step the absolute control of German affairs by the occupying powers. Now the goal of European integration became all the more urgent: it was the only way to offer security for its European neighbors without accepting long-term discrimination and abjuring all self-respect. The more quickly an integrated union of European states came about, the less the price that would have to be paid for the lost war; the shorter the time in which to overcome the status of loser, the less likely the danger of renewed revisionism. This European union would control all its members and therefore avoid discrimination against the Germans. Accordingly, for many Germans this project increased in urgency; there were also many who discovered it for tactical reasons or because it would help the success of democratization.

Another factor was that German nationalism and German belief in its national power had become seriously discredited because of their excesses and their ties to the Führer; Germany's collapse threatened its traditional identity in many ways. Here the goal of a united Europe offered an ideal with which to identify and it was accepted with gratitude, especially by the younger generation, which had enormous problems finding its bearings following the collapse of the Reich. But it was welcomed, too, by people from the idealistic middle class and the survivors of the old labor movement seeking a new beginning after their catastrophic experiences. It is hard to say how much of this widespread interest in the subject of Europe was due to the need for compensation or repression. With striking frequency and equally striking unconcern, regardless of political and ideological allegiance, many Germans demanded "equality" for the German nation within a united Europe. But this interest also provided an opportunity for a productive learning process leading to the realization that security in Europe could no longer be assured by defiant self-defense, but only by bonding to a larger community.

No matter how this learning process worked in detail, the variety of impulses which, at the end of the war, provided a "European" direction made a consensus possible for the goal of a unified Europe beyond the traditional social boundaries. Ernst von Schenck, a Swiss journalist, reported after a trip to Germany in December 1946 that the German people were tired of their nationalistic traditions and had fundamentally become pacifists. Among those who thought about positive future goals for Germans beyond these generalizations, there were "not very many who very consciously postulated dependency on one of the winning powers as a way out"; rather, he "frequently encountered the idea of Europe among their number."[3] In fact, no other idea was articulated as frequently. Apart from the Communists, who perceived the future of Germany inevitably on the side of the victorious Soviet Union, there was no political formation in the occupied zones expecting a future German foreign policy except in the context of a growing together of European nations.

It should be noted that at the beginning—and this thought must be rescued from its later fate of oblivion—the idea that a unified Europe could act as a "third force" against the two world powers of the United States of America and the Soviet Union outweighed all others. Heirs to the traditional ideas of the balance of power saw in such a union an antidote to absorption either by expanding American capitalism and/or the Soviet military power that was reaching into the center of the old continent; critics of existing social conditions hoped for a "third way" between capitalist democracy and dictatorial socialism. Both groups were convinced that only such a unification of Europe could prevent a breakdown between the two major victorious powers and eliminate the danger of a third world war. Here, too, the development among Germans was part of a more general phenomenon. The right was discredited by its collaboration with fascism, leading to a shift to the left everywhere in Europe. Similarly, the danger to the autonomy of Europeans, and to peace as well, due to the rise of the new, unequal world powers, was recognized not only in occupied Germany. But the presence of the unequal victorious powers as occupying powers also provided two additional motives for Europe as a "third force." It would offer the best chance for assuring the development of political order—something all occupying powers wanted—and it seemed likely to be able to avoid dividing the nation into East and West, which seemed to be the inevitable result of a split in the anti-Hitler coalition.

Accordingly, the call for a single, mediating Europe was heard frequently among those who voiced political ideas following the Reich's collapse in the four-power zones of Germany. Walter Dirks and Eugen Kogon, writing in the *Frankfurter Hefte*, advocated a socialist-oriented European federation as a basis for the success of a "second republic." Martin Niemöller proposed a "united Europe" as a "bridge between East and West," which alone could prevent a third world war. Hans-Werner Richter pleaded in *Ruf* for a socialist Europe to avoid the formation of blocs. Richard Löwenthal's political analysis of the social order and power politics in the postwar nation-states even led him to hope that the development of a third force Europe "beyond capitalism" could no longer be stopped.

The most important basic elements of the third force concept would also be found among politicians more closely wedded to the nation-state, who consequently showed less zeal in promoting the idea of a federated Europe. Thus, Jakob Kaiser probably had little sympathy for federalism and little feeling for the security requirements of France, which urged federative integration regardless of East-West tensions. He felt all the more strongly that mediation of the East-West conflict was in the interest of Germany, and he was fundamentally convinced that only a democratic socialism would be able to provide it. Despite all the emphasis on Germany's "bridge" function, his concern, beyond maintaining the unity of the Reich, was for a peaceful order within the framework of the United Nations, for which he believed the term "United States of Europe" to be entirely appropriate. Many Union leaders, such as Ernst Lemmer or Josef Müller, and prominent Social Democrats, like Paul Löbe and Ernst Reuter, had similar ideas as Kaiser. Even a man as idealistic as the Würzburg historian Ulrich Noack, who understood little of the realities of power politics of post-war Europe, had similar views in his vision of a new "Bund" of continental European states with a mediating mission.

But Germany could not translate a Europe of the "third force" into reality by its own power, and thus the European movement in the occupied zones soon slid into a deep crisis. By the time the Soviets rejected the Marshall Plan in the summer of 1947, every chance had been lost for taking any steps toward unification without contributing at the same time to the establishment of the two blocs and thus confirm the East-West division of Germany. It says a great deal about the fascination with which Germans viewed the idea of a third force that they by no means welcomed the possibilities of recovery afforded by turning to the Western powers, who offered to include the Western zones of occupation in the Marshall Plan. Instead, perplexity and cautious waiting were the predominant characteristics until well into the period of the Berlin crisis. Initially, hardly anyone was willing to own up to the consequences of the new state that had been established with shamefaced diffidence. In the fall of 1947, Carlo Schmidt pleaded for a West European third force without German participation, which was to overcome the cleavage of Europe. Until this arrangement led to the desired end, he wanted to grant Germans only a provisional "transitional settlement." When, after the beginning of the Berlin blockade, this position became untenable, the

Germans in the West no longer had a foreign policy concept acceptable to the majority.

This was the hour of the advocates of integration with the West. Unlike the mainstream of European political discussion of the first postwar years, they accepted total Soviet control over its zone of occupation as a given and, therefore, argued for integration of the Western zones of occupation into Western Europe. Often they were also convinced that the Soviet Union intended to expand its sphere of power further west. That led them to see a European community less as an instrument for mediation between East and West than as a means for Western European survival against the dangers of Soviet expansion. They accepted the likelihood that such a community would inevitably be restricted to Western Europe at first — in the more or less certain expectation that it would, in time, radiate over Eastern Europe and thus force the Soviet Union to retreat.

Moreover, very soon they began to think of continued U.S. presence as necessary for Europe to balance the weight of the Soviets. In their view, that would make European integration an essential instrument for building a Western community. This community would overcome the latent contrast between Western Germany and its Western neighbors, ensure the prosperity of the Western European region and bind the Germans of the Western zones of occupation permanently to the West. Self-assertion against the American superpower became a secondary matter, as did concerns about the possibility that the American guarantee of security might not last.

So long as there was hope for agreement between the victorious powers, only a few people could warm to a concept that pushed the integration of the eastern half of Germany into the distant future, while also harboring the risk of continuing escalation of conflict. It was Konrad Adenauer for whom the old needs for security of the western neighbors and a new fear of Soviet expansionism combined into a clear vision that had the significant advantage of accelerating Germany's restoration in the West. A similar view was taken by the federalists around the *Rheinischer Merkur* newspaper, who focused their efforts for a federalist-Christian new order entirely on the regions forming the nucleus of the old occident. Kurt Schumacher, as well, belongs in this line; although he had a socialist Europe in view, he was so mesmerized by the danger that "Eurasia will swallow Europe"[4] that he strove for the integration of the western zones into a Western Europe allied with the U.S. earlier and more energetically than his Christian Democratic opponents. At first the influence of those favoring integration with the West could do little more than prevent the articulation of the third force concept by the Germans from becoming offensive. Schumacher's passionate dispute with the SED (Sozialistische Einheitspartei Deutschlands; the East German Communists) diverted Social Democrats from careful consideration of the German situation and thus slowly pushed defenders of the third force into isolation. Jakob Kaiser lost influence among Christian Democrats, if only because of attacks from the ranks of the SPD. Adenauer's efforts to bring together the middle class and anti-Prussian forces were at least enough to keep Kaiser from claiming leadership. Initiatives for a multi-zonal representation of Germans regularly failed because those who wanted integration with the West feared Soviet influence.

As the hostilities of the Cold War became overt, the concept of integration with the West quickly gained wide plausibility, its appeal enhanced for many by growing anxiety. Many of those who had initially favored a third force now more or less resigned themselves to the idea, convinced that joining the effort for integration with the West was better than standing aside helplessly. Responding to the perceived totalitarian threat from the East, a surprisingly large segment of the population developed a readiness for integration with the West. The establishment of the Federal Republic won a broad consensus under the double impact of the Berlin blockade and the currency reform. Thus Adenauer, having secured the support of Ludwig Erhard, was able to assume leadership of the new nation.

Though the Germans opted for the West in principle, they were not yet ready to participate actively as a majority in an integration process. Adenauer had to fight hard to gain membership in the Council of Europe and in the European Coal and Steel Community. When he offered German troops for an integrated defense community of the West in 1956, he was opposed even in his own cabinet and the executive committee of his own party. Schumacher, as leader of the opposition, sought to obscure the contradictions of his own position by making maximum demands of the Western powers. According to opinion polls, not more than 40 percent of the Germans agreed in principle to the idea of a "European army with German participation"; those who expressed general agreement with Adenauer's policies fell, in the fall of 1950, to less than a fourth of the voters.[5] Despite the obvious aggressiveness of Soviet policies, the creation of a Western bloc continued to cause great concern. The fact that Adenauer was able to prevail, eventually even gaining majorities for his policies, was probably the consequence of the unprecedented economic recovery that characterized the "long years of the 50s." The initial signs of the "economic miracle," despite some critical moments in the beginning of the decade, came just in time to pose the risk of having to give up all that had already been achieved if both German states were to be joined. Eventually, everyone began to take it for granted that this affluence was guaranteed through the Western community. Further-more, Soviet clumsiness played an important role as well; Stalin delayed far too long before playing his unification card. When he finally acted in May 1952, the West Germans had already become too settled in their new nation. Adenauer's personal efforts also were of great significance; he was aggressive in pursuit of his objectives; he accepted progress one step at a time; he was flexible about how to achieve integration; he was insistent in his demands for security; and he found ways to obstruct initiatives to negotiate whether they came from the East or the West.

To fully understand why integration with the West was achieved, we must recognize that its opponents were not—as Adenauer probably assumed and as has been believed ever since—all advocating the policies of traditional nation statehood. Surely, thoughts of power politics were virulent in their ranks, though they were not fundamentally different in this respect from the opposition, where that tradition now appeared in anti-Communist, Western guise. By no means were all opponents to integration with the West ready to pay the price of neutralization of Germany, which the Soviets demanded for giving up exclusive control of the German Democratic Republic. Those ready to accept the risk of neutralization, Gustav Heinemann or Ulrich Noack, for example, as a rule did not perceive it as separatist nationalism, but as the prelude to the formation of a European security system. The old goal of a design for European peace appeared here in a new dress: cut to fit the demands of East-West confrontation; precise in terms of the first steps toward balancing opposing interests, and necessarily vague about the later stages of such an arrangement. Adenauer profited from both: from the contradictions in the position of those who objected to integration with the West while being unwilling to make concessions to the Soviet Union, and from fundamentally European allegiance of most neutralists. A broad national resistance movement, such as that urged by Rudolf Augstein, failed to coalesce against him. Rather, over time his opponents accepted, *faut de mieux*, the bonds Adenauer forged with the West. In the same year, 1950, in which at most 40 percent of German citizens were willing to accept German participation in a European army, 55 percent favored "the idea of a West European union." At the end of 1956, 75 percent of those questioned were willing to "vote for the formation of a United States of Europe." However, 36 percent believed at the beginning of 1958 that it was "very important" for the Federal Republic to "rescind all military alliances," and 32 per-cent believed it to be a German duty to "be a bridge between East and West."[6]

Two developments implied by these surveys explain why internal accep-tance of integration with the West was so hesitant: the export-oriented West

German economy was increasingly entwined with the nations of the OECD, and the values of Western civilization came to be gradually accepted. The latter was slower because it was associated with the painful confrontation with that which had been repressed after 1945. It was more the work of the new generation of intellectuals than the established social leadership and that of the broad population, and therefore it did not come to pass without some turmoil. But the leaders active in the cultural Westernization were frequently the very same people who had been skeptical about the political orientation to the West. Thus, the final result was a more solid bonding to the West.

However, as the ties to the West became more accepted, the drive for integration diminished. This reflects the fact that important functions originally assigned to the European community had now been assumed by NATO — protection from the Soviet threat, which in the era of atomic deterrence could be organized only globally; the fence erected around Germany and, as a consequence, its rise to the status of treaty partner. In addition, Europe was becoming less necessary as a substitute for national bonds: as time passed since the catastrophe of 1945 and with the growing economic and political success of the new republic, a new European order appeared less and less necessary and unreal. A united Europe playing an independent role in world politics or at least within the Western alliance was not what one side really wanted, nor what the other really understood; the European Community, exactly in accordance with Adenauer's ideas, seemed predominantly an element in the strengthening of the Western camp, and thus hardly in need of any special attention.

Under these conditions, it was especially fatal that the integration of the Group of Six, begun in 1950–51 with the European Coal and Steel Community, could be most readily continued as an economic community following the failure of the European Defense Community (EDC) project in 1954. At the time the Dutch proposed an economic community of the Group of Six, 75 percent of German exports went to nations outside the projected Common Market, while 72 percent of the imports came from there. That raised doubts in the minds of numerous representatives of commerce and industry about whether the advantages of liberalization of the internal markets of the Group of Six would not be more than compensated for by communal external customs duties, with tariffs significantly higher than those of the exporting Federal Republic. The more clear it became in the treaty negotiations that France would insist on a series of protective measures for its less competitive industries and to protect its social programs, the more these

West Germans feared that regulations governing the Common Market would lead to competitive disadvantages for the efficient German industry. In particular, the chambers of commerce and industry and broad sectors of the chemical and manufacturing industry argued for a free trade zone with the widest possible latitude instead of closer integration.

They were supported in this by neo-liberal theorists who had won acceptance for the concept of a "social market economy." Alfred Müller-Armack and Wilhelm Röpke opposed the Common Market project as a severe setback to worldwide free trade based on free currency convertibility. Ludwig Erhard called it "economic nonsense," and instead promoted the British proposal for a European free trade zone in the framework of the OEEC.[7] He torpedoed the negotiations for the Common Market to the extent possible; even after the signing in 1957, he continued for a long time to try to convert it to a larger free trade zone without structured common institutions.

Nor did German agriculture want to have anything to do with the Group of Six. While it could count on growth for the next several decades within a domestic framework because demand for agricultural products went well beyond national production, opening of the market would bring confrontation with cheaper competition from the Netherlands and France, together with a market surplus of some products. Price softening and a decreasing market share then would be inevitable. In addition, the Common Market would put in question the very regulatory system that had placed agriculture in a privileged position as a result of the Agriculture Act passed in 1956. Accordingly, the Deutsche Bauernverband (German Farmers' Association) openly opposed integrating agriculture in the framework of the Group of Six, and the Ministry of Agriculture seconded the efforts of the Economics Industry against the project.

Once again, Adenauer's entire energy (and the authority he had won with it) were needed to guide the negotiations for the Common Market and Euratom to a successful conclusion. It was not only a matter of economic integration; his goal, as in the past, was a political one. He believed that the bonds between Germans and the West remained insufficient, the danger of an understanding between France and the Soviet Union too great, and the West as a whole still too weak. Since the beginning of discussions about reducing American troop strength in Europe, Adenauer had sought to formulate a European fallback position in case of a declining American engagement. His goal consequently was a political community with a security policy dimension; he accepted the economic community—after initial hesitation—only because no other available project could win a consensus of the Group of Six.

Obviously, Adenauer hardly spoke publicly about his real motives. Deliberately, he avoided a public debate about the treaty. Negotiations took place in the twilight of diplomacy; parties and associations were not included at all. This permitted the differences within the cabinet to be played down and the response to critical voices to be held within bound; Erhard's efforts came to naught. The revitalization of the European idea, as envisaged by Jean Monnet, Paul-Henri Spaak and other supporters of the project, also was aborted. No agreement was reached about the goals of the effort and further steps toward European integration.

The treaty, at best difficult to explain because of its complicated technical detail and still open for certain decisions to be made in the future, provided no reason for either euphoric acclaim or dramatic fears. In fact, there was little interest and it finally was accepted as a step more or less consistent with Germany's own expectations of the future without affecting them in any particular manner, after no concrete details had been heard about the negotiations. The Free Democrats (FDP) and the BHE, parties which had approved all previous decisions for integration with the West as members of the previous government, now, as members of the opposition, permitted themselves the luxury of voting "No to Spaakistan,"[8] expressing the widely held fears of a worsening of the East-West split. In contrast, the SPD used the opportunity of agreeing to the Rome treaty to rid itself of the nationalistic image it had gained when it opposed military integration with the West. This vote was not, however, unconditional acceptance of integration with the West. Heinrich Deist explained the vote in the Bundestag by saying that this agreement unhitched economic cooperation in Europe from the creation of military and power policy blocs.

The consensus on which German participation in the founding of the Common Market and Euratom rested was a consequence of a rather superficial nature. Whether the signing of the treaties was to lead to an economic and monetary union or whether the integration of the Group of Six into a European free trade zone was to be given preference remained unclear. The SPD promoted both simultaneously and thus bridged the various emphases existing within the party. Within the government itself, Walter Hallstein's program for consistent strengthening of Community agencies was in rather abrupt contrast to Ehrhard's campaign for a larger free trade zone. Just as unclear and controversial was the question whether the new integration in the economic sphere would extend into the political, as the "functionalistic" theory popular among the founding fathers of the Common Market promised. The question of what part such a political Europe would play in the Western alliance and the relations between East and West also remained unclear, nor was it fully considered and debated among the various schools of thought.

Thus the policies of the Federal Republic were far from ready when General de Gaulle confronted his Common Market partners with his proposal for a political union. Certainly there was, in the dispute triggered by de Gaulle, a minority of German "Gaullists." But their protagonists had something very different in mind, which had little to do with de Gaulle's grand design of a European Community with its own autonomous security policy. Franz Josef Strauss wanted a joint German-French atomic capability; Paul Wilhelm Wenger, a Western community of fate; Paul Sethe, the priority of nations over ideologies. The aging Adenauer obliged de Gaulle the most. Because he was convinced that an insoluble linkage between France and Germany was necessary, he was prepared to accept Fouchet's plan for political union despite certain misgivings. When the Fouchet negotiations began to fail, he proposed the Franco-German treaty of 1963. Its reason, though, was less an effort for independence from American leadership than worry about a Franco-Soviet agreement. For himself, Adenauer wanted to do nothing to loosen the ties to the United States.

The majority of West Germans saw in de Gaulle's efforts for independence only an attempt to established France as a privileged partner of the Soviet Union on the European continent, at the cost of Atlantic solidarity and the price of destroying the European Community. De Gaulle thus appeared as a man of the nineteenth century, an era Germans had just learned to overcome in favor of a postnational deeply European, usually Atlantic-oriented allegiance. The problem of European independence raised by de Gaulle was not perceived. Rather, the resentment over the general's putative reactionary nationalism helped to keep it suppressed. Not only the majority of those who supported Adenauer's policies of integration with the West held this belief; they were joined by most of the Social Democrats, who had made their peace with integration to the West in 1960, and who saw in de Gaulle only a troublemaker whom one had to wait out.

Accordingly, the German Bundestag ratified the Franco-German treaty only after adding unilaterally a preamble that affirmed everything France's president wanted to prevent: the Atlantic connections, the expansion of the Brussels institutions, and (a particular affront to the pro-American position of the British) the efforts for membership in the Common Market. That was a process without precedence in diplomatic history and a resounding slap in the face for de Gaulle. Thus began a glacial period between France and Germany that stopped all further reflection about the political finality of the European Community, instead of promoting the Franco-German dialogue about political unity as intended by the treaty. De Gaulle reacted by going his own way, which led to his "policy of the empty chair" in Brussels and to withdrawal from the Atlantic alliance. For their part, Germans reacted either by hoping for better days for a supranational development of the Brussels institutions, or by giving more serious thought to national interests.

As a result, the new orientation of German foreign policy, which had become imperative when the Americans turned to a policy of détente, largely ignored the European Community. The serious division about foreign policy in the CDU/CSU, which was also a struggle for power over who would succeed Adenauer, ended with the victory of the national realists surrounding Kurt Georg Kiesinger. They combined self-assurance vis-à-vis the American superpower with readiness for a careful opening to the East. This not only left Erhard's postnational Atlantic orientation by the wayside, but European supranationalism à la Hallstein as well. The SPD slowly began to discover what possibilities for all-German policies were hidden in de Gaulle's initiatives toward the East. But they formulated their own "new East policies" without European mediation as national policies of rapprochement with the East. The SPD remained realistically bound to the Western alliance, without making clear what special role the European Community would be meant to play in a future peace arrangement.

The entry, as of January 1, 1973, of Great Britain into the Group of Six, initiated by de Gaulle shortly before his resignation, only reinforced the tendency to depoliticize the Community in German consciousness. That the British government primarily wanted economic integration and political independence when they resubmitted their application was hardly discussed in Germany. Hoping since the beginning for Britain's entry into the Community for political and economic reasons as well, most Germans looked past the problems this development was likely to cause. Some did this knowingly, because they envisaged no more than an expanded free trade zone in Europe, in addition to the political integration into NATO. Others were led to ignore the British aversion to political unification by the anti-Gaullist sentiments aroused by the controversies with the general. The Brandt/Scheel government was most active in the negotiations for successful British entry, knowing it was supported in this by a broad consensus of the Federal Republic's public.

The tacit departure from a supranational goal for the Community went hand in hand with a creeping depoliticization of the Community. Little protest was heard against the Luxembourg compromise of January 1966, which allowed governments to disregard majority decisions in matters of vital interest. When de Gaulle demanded the introduction of rotating presidencies of the EEC Commissions in the spring of 1967, the Kiesinger/Brandt government did not argue for continuing the tenure of Walter Hallstein, making way for successors less strongly favoring integration. Nor did the Brandt/Scheel government object when British Foreign Minister Edward Heath and French President

Georges Pompidou agreed in May 1971 "that the identity of national states within the framework of the developing Community should be maintained and that, in practice, the decisions of the Community would be unanimous when the vital interests of member states are involved."[9] Instead, German governments repeatedly made use of the option to cite "vital" interests and thus to veto decisions by the EEC.

Nevertheless, Willy Brandt in particular adhered to the goal of a "political union." Continuing the tradition of the third force, he favored an independent European role in world politics, one that avoided both a U.S.-Soviet condominium resulting from détente, as well as predominance of either of the superpowers. In contrast to Kissinger's efforts to place the EEC under Atlantic alliance control, he insisted on a partnership of equal status. At the same time, he was not ready to loosen the bonds with the United States. Furthermore, Egon Bahr put a stop to moves strengthening the Franco-German axis within a West European Union, because it clashed with his hopes for a future central European security system, which would lead to restoration of German unity and inhibit the creation of blocs in Europe.

The result was a contradictory policy of mediation perceived in Washington as an expression of German Gaullism and in Paris as impeding European independence. American demands for a binding relationship, proclaimed with much aplomb in Kissinger's 1973 "Year of Europe," were opposed in a declaration of principles at the Copenhagen Common Market summit conference in December 1973. There the Common Market nations declared their firm determination to act as an "independent entity" in world affairs. But four months later, Foreign Minister Walter Scheel managed to get an agreement (the Gymnich agreement) with his EEC colleagues permitting each member state to make all political actions contingent on consultation with the United States. In addition, Bonn gave its European partners to understand that it had no interest in developing a European deterrence.

The half-hearted way in which the Community's political destiny was being pursued was best expressed by the development of EPC and in the decision to schedule regular summit meetings of the Community's state and government heads. The governments of the Social Democratic/Liberal coalition had a significant part in both. In this way they insured that the idea of a political Europe survived in vague form during a period of great changes in security policies. At the same time, they were also responsible in part for the gap that developed between European expectations and the reality of the EEC's development, which increasingly destroyed the credibility of the unification project. Subsequent generations consequently found little sense in the formation of the Community: the New Left eliminated it completely from its program.

The political shape of the emerging Community became clearer again under Brandt's successor, Helmut Schmidt. For one thing, this was related to the fact that Schmidt had no use for Bahr's vision of a Central European security system. Instead, his version of a détente strategy rested on the conviction that there was a far-reaching common identity of West European interests. Secondly, American ruthlessness in financial and monetary policies, together with the decline of détente, now made the common interests of America's West European partners particularly clear. And finally, Schmidt found a congenial partner in France's president, Giscard d'Estaing, who not only recognized these common interests, but was also committed to the same pragmatic style of politics Schmidt had developed as minister of defense and finance.

First, Schmidt turned his attention to overcoming the crisis of the Common Market caused by the turbulence of the world-wide economic crisis of 1973–74. Among his steps was financial support for member states that had balance of payment difficulties, as well as efforts to limit expenditures of the Community; a restrictive course in the matter of a European regional fund, demands for reform of the wasteful EEC farm policy (this largely in vain, because of his own farm lobby), and the attempt to make the partners agree on a course to consolidate economic and financial policies. For this purpose, he agreed in 1978 with Giscard d'Estaing on the establishment of a European monetary system that would not only reduce dependence on international currency speculation, but would also force the participants into budgetary discipline. Fears of the Deutsche Bundesbank (German Central Bank) that such a system would turn the Federal Republic into the financier of an inflationary community were put aside in favor of the objective of the EEC as a functioning unit.

Simultaneously, Schmidt and Giscard d'Estaing made considerable efforts to synchronize their foreign policies. Just after taking office, they agreed to consult regularly before bilateral contacts with Moscow and to speak regularly about their relations with the United States. Then they initiated the agreement to hold EEC summit meetings in the Council of Europe, and proposed setting up the World Economic Summit of the leading industrial nations, which met for the first time on November 1975. The regular consultations in the framework of the Franco-German treaty and the EPC were used to come to agreements about numerous detailed questions.

Efforts to unify the foreign policies of the Common Market partners soon bore fruit; in the final stage of the Conference on Security and Cooperation in Europe (Helsinki Conference, CSCE), they agreed to such an extent that from the outside they were perceived as one and also were able to reach significant success in formulating the principles of détente. They offered notable resistance to the American tendency to turn away from a dialogue of détente. They managed to create some balance to President Carter's clumsy human rights campaign and, on the question of arms control, exerted so much pressure that the SALT II agreements on the limitation of strategic weapons could be ratified in the summer of 1979.

However, as Western Europe slid into a precarious security position and the U.S. government threatened to break off negotiations with the Soviet leadership after the Soviet incursion into Afghanistan, Schmidt and d'Estaing went a decisive step further. In 1980, they considered the formation of a Franco-German military alliance, which was to be the nucleus of an independent West European defense force within the framework of the Western alliance. The German Bundeswehr was to give up tactical nuclear weapons and instead build up its conventional capacity significantly. At the same time it would become part of a joint command with French forces. In turn, France would expand the duties of its *force de frappe* (over which it would continue to retain complete control) to the protection of the Federal Republic. In this way, the German chancellor and the French president wanted to counteract the fear that the growing German unrest over the danger of American foreign policy would drive Germans to the side of the Soviets. Furthermore, they hoped that by strengthening European autonomy in matters of security they would raise the nuclear threshold and thus defuse the entire security situation. They were convinced the other Western European countries would join this initiative of the Franco-German leaders sooner or later.

The ambitious plan was never carried out (and initially hidden from the public) because both proponents soon left office. François Mitterand, who replaced Giscard d'Estaing in April 1981, was initially more concerned about shoring up his position internally and abroad as well, granting Schmidt an "earnest exchange of views" about security matters. When the SPD/FDP coalition then fell apart and Helmut Kohl became the new chancellor, the project had no leadership on the German side either. Schmidt then went public with his proposal, but he failed to arouse the requisite response in either France or the Federal Republic.

Similarly, Schmidt's European policies suffered because of their institutional frugality. The Schmidt/Genscher government, although it spoke out for giving more power to the European Parliament and for direct election of its members, focused its European policies chiefly on the work of the heads of state in the Council of Europe. That was, of course, a reflection on the reality that France had little inclination to strengthen the institutions of the EEC, and that there was even discussion in Great Britain about withdrawing from the Community. But it also moved toward a Community that functioned only in accordance with the common interests of France and Germany. It did not want to see the autonomy of the Council restricted either by

Parliament or the Brussels Commission. "Eurosclerosis" of public opinion within the Community could not be overcome in this manner; and in view of the threat of a Franco-German condominium, the problem of having to pull the other members along remained unresolved.

Foreign Minister Genscher sought to deal with both problems by proposing a "Treaty Concerning the European Union" in 1981. It was to further the political goal of European unity, better coordinate existing activities, and project ways of further development in the foreseeable future. Helmut Schmidt regarded this venture from the beginning with considerable skepticism and, in fact, the French as well as the British governments soon reacted guardedly. Only the Italian government made any effort to bring the undertaking to a successful conclusion, so that Genscher's proposal came to be known as the "Genscher-Colombo initiative." The German cabinet converted the proposal into an initiative for a political statement of principle, and this was adopted by the Stuttgart Common Market Summit conference in June 1983 in the most noncommittal form imaginable.

In view of the EEC's inability to deal with problems, it was no wonder that the vague West European consensus that characterized German discussion about Europe since the end of the fifties faded still further in Schmidt's era. Only 65.9 percent of eligible voters participated in the first direct election of members of the European Parliament, for which the established parties gave their full support; in 1981 the percentage of support for the EEC fell below the 50 percent level in public opinion polls. Criticism of the "artificiality of the Europe" concept increased in public discussion. At the same time, a wide discussion began about the national identity of the Germans.

Revival of old German hopes for reunification was hardly ever behind these discussions, although it was often thought so abroad. Rather, the vacuum left by the scant presence of the EEC drove most Germans to worry more about themselves. For the broad conservative-liberal center, this meant support for the status quo along with a drift toward an ideology leaning on the tradition of nation-statehood and the resolve to pursue German *Realpolitik*. The growing number of those who felt concern about the precarious security position discovered a special community of fate shared by the two German states because of the recent escalation of the Cold War and, in the face of *de facto* neglect by the French, came to believe in a special German peace mission. Clearly, there were some nationalist feelings involved, and at times some quite bizarre alliances were made between traditional nationalists and radical pacifists. As a rule, however, the peace movement held strongly to a belief in a united Europe; at the same time, urgent warnings against upsetting existing integration with the West came from the camp of the "realists," to which there were many cross-connections.

Increased support for the status quo corresponded in the first years of the conservative-liberal coalition to an even stronger tendency not to go beyond the integration already achieved in Europe. The Kohl/Genscher government supported even more energetically than its predecessor a limitation of the EEC budget; it fought again—with as little consistency as its predecessor—for reform of the EEC farm policy to reduce agriculture's share of the budget; and it, too, did little to increase the status and effectiveness of the Commission and Parliament. The project of a monetary union, urged especially by France and other EEC partners because they wanted to free themselves from their overwhelming *de facto* dependence on the Bundesbank, was not only rejected by important groups of German economists and financiers who deemed the idea to be premature, but also repeatedly delayed by the federal government. Only in the southern expansion of the Community (to Greece, which joined in 1981 and later Spain and Portugal) did Bonn join actively. However, this reflected not only concern over the political stability of the young democracies, but also the new export opportunities for German industry.

Only in 1986 was this restrictive course relaxed, as the Uniform Internal Market Instrument adopted two years earlier began to show effects. The German government agreed that, if nothing else, future competitiveness of European industry must not be put in jeopardy and offered its partners important concessions—additional increased expenditures with simultaneous limits on production of agriculture (removal of land from cultivation); doubling of the structural fund within five years; complete elimination of monetary restrictions within the EEC, and the reciprocal recognition of university diplomas. Kohl made strenuous efforts (largely successful) to keep the reluctant British prime minister, Margaret Thatcher, on a consistent course for the internal market project.

The Federal German government, however, remained reserved about a central European bank; only Foreign Minister Genscher was ready for rapid cooperation. Under the influence of the Bundesbank, Kohl insisted on ever more difficult conditions which, in effect, would permit a monetary union only after all structural differences in the economies of the member states had been banished. Similarly, the project for a German-French security union and, following that, a political union moved ahead only slowly. Half measures, in this case on both sides, were responsible for the fact that the Uniform Internal Market Instrument formulated its joint foreign policy objectives only in vague terms and that nothing more came of the twenty-fifth anniversary of the signing of the Franco-German treaty, as far as security was concerned, than the creation of a German-French defense council and a German-French brigade stationed in southern Germany. At least this kept the security policy dialogue going between France and Germany, ensuring that the goal of a West European defense identity was not lost entirely. Yet meaningful agreement was still remote, not least because discussion of this topic was still in its infancy in both nations.

Still, as both countries came to show greater willingness to compromise, and with the return to majority rule in the Council of Ministers, as well as simpler procedures and more Europeanization in all areas of life because of the internal market project, old problems became resolved and the Community once more returned to the forefront of German awareness. The EEC again occupied a more clearly defined place in German expectations of the future, and faith that it would be able to deal with the tasks of the future rose again, though not in all places. Part of the political Left, having tired of its neutralist or pacifist illusions, only now began to discover how the European dimensions would help West Germany's ability to maneuver on the world stage.

This modest return to consciousness of the European project was of decisive strategic importance when the German question appeared on the agenda again in the winter of 1989–90 with the collapse of the DDR, an event that gave Germany a key role in the formulation of a new order on the European continent. It was up to Germany to decide whether a German national state would come into being again and whether a confederation of Europe would come next, whether that state would discard the ties to a united Europe or make them stronger, whether it would assume hegemonic qualities once more, or whether these would be transcended in a new European order.

It seems appropriate to say that the Germans have largely passed this test. Certainly, there were many who did not want to admit any alternative to the principle of a nation-state in the debate that began on November 9, 1989, accusing those who thought otherwise of national unreliability. Chancellor Kohl used the situation to bring about national unity promptly, without bothering much to ask his EEC partners or even to inform them about individual steps beforehand (an act that earned him unreserved applause from Egon Bahr, which is interesting from the point of view of continuity). The enlargement of the Federal Republic, which became inevitable with the March 18, 1990, vote of DDR citizens, did not elicit great pleasure among the European neighbors. Perhaps (but by how much must remain forever open) it also contributed to the failure of Gorbachev's attempt to achieve an orderly democratization of the Soviet Union.

But then the perseverance of the West Germans proved so great, and the success of integration with the West so obvious, that only a minority was willing to seriously risk a new beginning with both German states. Happiness over the newly achieved unification was quickly surpassed by worry about its financing. More than a few West Germans realized for the first time their deep roots in Western civilization only after their encounters with the new citizens. Those who were prudent enough to understand the need to balance the burden among the Germans as a rule also knew that the larger Germany required an even stronger bond to the European Community. And many also understood that approval by the former victors to German unity was, if not exclusively, a result of the trust gained in the West and in the East over decades of efforts toward mutual understanding.

The self-imposed treaty limitations which Kohl negotiated first with Gorbachev, i.e., rejection of atomic, biological and chemical (ABC) weapons and deep cuts in the troop strength of the Bundeswehr, met no criticism at all. Rather, they were seen as a natural and preliminary step in anticipation of the German national state. At the same time, the stipulated payments—these, too, borne by the German public without objections—signalled to the Soviet Union the readiness of the expanded Federal Republic not only to deal with the internal problems posed by reunification, but also to assume responsibility in the reorganization of the continent. These were two fundamental differences between the unification and the foundation of the Reich in the nineteenth century.

It was also important that Helmut Kohl—in evident agreement with François Mitterand—placed monetary union, which he had opposed for so long, on the agenda along with political union. While preparatory talks, called for December 1990, were still going on, it was possible to doubt Kohl's serious intent, since he had linked both projects. At the Maastricht Summit in December 1991, he finally committed himself firmly to a monetary union within five to seven years, although discussions for a political union remained vague. The undeniable risks associated with a European Central Bank, which, though independent, would still involve banks from different financial and political cultures, now appeared to be an acceptable price for further economic union, while simultaneously demonstrating German self-moderation. In view of the uneasiness which German economic power elicits among its EEC partners, the psychological effect of this demonstration cannot be overestimated.

The creation of the Franco-German Corps, proposed by Kohl and Mitterand in October 1991, and agreed to in May 1992, also had a significant dramatic effect. It proclaimed the intent of both governments truly to work toward a European defense identity as the European security system was being revamped, while compelling both nations to initiate the necessary steps. If the Corps is to be functional, France will have to move closer to NATO, while the Federal Republic will have to give up the restriction limiting the Bundeswehr's deployment only to NATO. The future European-ization of defense policies is not as clearly defined as the transition to a common European currency, but here, too, the course is clearly set in the direction of Europe.

Of course, the decisions taken at Maastricht and La Rochelle are not the ultimate victory. There has been much protest against the monetary union project from liberal dogmatists and advocates of the national power state as well as stubborn DM-nationalists since it seems to be seriously nearing realization. A similar fate may await the Franco-German Corps when its consequences are more widely recognized. Inveterate Atlanticists and paci-fist fundamentalists are likely to form a bizarre, but nonetheless effective, alliance of resistance. In general, neo-conservative complaints of German "power forgetfulness" (Hans Peter Schwarz) have become increasingly popular since the days of unification. And as German unification coincided with the rise of nationalist feelings in the East, many Germans have been led to believe that the nation-state is once again the normal organizational form of human communal life, rather than one that needs to be transcended.

Meanwhile, German society has become so highly individualistic that it is impossible to see how a national state could become the favorite or exclusive rallying point for a political movement. If in the postwar period Germans were willing to welcome integration in part for opportunistic reasons, the favorable experiences with the integrationary process have led to a funda-mental, even if belated, understanding of the problems common to all Europeans. Reservations about a European Community resulting from the unresolved German question and the division of Europe have disappeared with the end of the East-West confict. Concerns about the presence of the American protective force have lost much of their significance. If the politicians present the forthcoming unification projects with any skill at all, they will be able to bring them to fruition without any great difficulty.

The consensus of the Federal Republic, which on the whole is rather postnational in character, has been little changed by the addition of the new population from the former DDR. To be sure, the new citizens come from a tradition in which a narrow internationalism dictated from above could not destroy the memory of a world of national states; they neither experienced, nor properly understood, the complicated paths of integration of the West. But many understand, after initial disappointment over the poor national loyalty of the West Germans, that the Federal Repubic model, which they admired so much, owed its success not least to the integration it has already achieved. Moreover, some have a special sensitivity for the problems of all-

European security, whether because of official DDR policies or experience with the CSCE process. There is also a group of former DDR citizens—and their number is not insignificant—who are susceptible to an authoritarian nationalism because of the accumulated social problems in society. If the economic recovery of the new German states is delayed too long or if sections of the populace become the permanent losers of unification, they could gain significance quickly and infect similarly situated victims of modernization in the old German states. Even then, however, it would still be a long way before a structural majority could arise for strictly nationalistic policies.

More problematic is the fact that efforts to democratize the EEC have had little success so far. As more and more decisions affecting daily life are made on the Community level, interest groups have greater trouble articulating their positions, decision-making processes become more perplexing, and decisions themselves lack grassroots participation. Inevitably, there will be attempts to bring back national autonomy and to resist more integration. That is true in principle for all member states; in the course of the process, renationalization in some national societies threatens to have a reciprocal effect on others. In the Federal Republic, this threat is all the greater because the national institutions obviously work well and the European institutions are not used to balance the weaknesses of national institutions as they are elsewhere. The problem is not yet widely recognized, although the Danish vote against the Maastricht agreements ought to serve as a warning.

Finally, the danger that the Federal Republic will be pushed into going it alone by its partners who perceive a short-sighted need to establish a balance cannot be dismissed. If France and Great Britain continue to insist on their special nuclear roles, over the long term this will raise national security questions for Germany. If the West European partners delay the expansion of the Community to the East for too long, because they want to keep Germany tied to the West, they will provoke a German position of predominance in the East. As in the past, Germany plays a central role in the process of European integration although it cannot determine its course alone. That has its worrisome side but can be productive as well if Germans and their neighbors are aware of how dependent each is on the other.

Notes

1. Richard Coudenhove-Kalergi, *Paneuropa* (Vienna, 1929), p. 25.
2. Carl Goerdeler, "Prinzipien einer Friedenswirtschaft" (Oct. 1940) in Walter Lipgens (ed.), *Europa-Föderationspläne der Widerstandsbewegungen 1940–1945* (Munich, 1988), pp. 109–111.

3. *Europa* (Monthly of the Swiss "Europa-Union") Jan. 1947, p. 3.

4. Commentary of Jan. 3/4, 1946 reprinted in Walter Scholz, Arno and Walter Oschilewski (eds.), *Turmwächter der Demokratie. Ein Lebensbild von Kurt Schumacher,* Vol. 2 (Berlin, 1954), p. 67.

5. *Jahrbuch der Öffentlichen Meinung 1947–1955* (Allensbach, 1958), pp. 172, 360.

6. *European Movement,* Survey of Public Opinion (Brussels, 1950), p. 2 ff.; *Jahrbuch der Öffentlichen Meinung 1957* (Allensbach, 1957), p. 342; ibid., *Jahrbuch der Öffentlichen Meinung 1958–1964* (Allensbach, 1965), p. 534.

7. Press conference remarks March 15, 1957, cited in Karl Kaiser, *EWG und Freiheitszone* (Leiden, 1965), p. 136.

8. Formulation on an FDP handbill for the Bundestag election in 1957.

9. Cited in Karl-Dietrich Bracher, Wolfgang Jäger, Werner Link, *Republik im Wandel 1969–1974* (Stuttgart/Mannheim, 1986), p. 243.

Bibliography

Walter Lipgens, "Ideas of the German Resistance on the Future of Europe," ibid., pp. 362, 455.

Wilfried Loth, Deutsche Europakonzeptionen in der Eskalation des Ost-West-Konflikts 1945–1949. *Geschichte in Wissenschraft und Unterricht* 1984; 35: 453–470.

Wilfried Loth, Deutsche Europakonzeptionen in der Gründungsphase der EWG. In Enrico Serra (ed). *Il rilancio del'Europa e ittrattati di Roma.* Milan, 1989, pp. 585–602.

Michael Salewski, "National Socialist Ideas in Europe" in Walter Lipgens (ed.) *Documents on the History of European Integration,* Vol. 1. (Berlin/New York, 1985), pp. 37–178.

Hans-Peter Schwarz, Adenauer and Europa. *Vierteljahreshefte für Zeitgeschichte* 1979; 27: 471–523.

Ulrich Weinstock, "Wo bleibt Europa? Anmerkungen zu einer Geschichte der Bundesrepublik Deutschland." *Europa-Archiv* 1989; 44: 291–304. *Deutschlands Einheit und Europas Zukunft.* Frankfurt/M, Redaktion Bruno Schoch, 1992.

Italian Europeanism in the Twentieth Century

Valerio Castronovo

Europeanism runs like a red thread through Italian history from the time after World War I, when some leaders of business and politics formulated the hypothesis of a federation of European states, to the discussion of the problems of European unification that developed after World War II. This red thread was not entirely broken even by fascism and twenty years of dictatorship. The federalist principles to which Luigi Einaudi and other forerunners of the European ideal were committed builds on the "Manifesto per un' Europa libera e unita" (Manifesto for a Free and United Europe). With this manifesto, in August 1941, Alberto Spinelli and some of his anti-fascist colleagues, Ernesto Rossi and Eugenio Colorni, while in exile on Ventotene island, changed what had until then been a principle into a real political action program for the rebirth of Europe from the chasm into which nationalistic egotism and totalitarian degeneration had plunged it.

Twenty years earlier, the tragic consequences of another war that had immersed Europe in blood had led Einaudi, together with Giovanni Agnelli and Attilio Cabiati to take up the cudgels for the idea of a united Europe as the fundamental goal of our epoch. And just as later in 1942, when Hitler's troops appeared on the verge of imposing a "new order" of despotism and militarism on Europe, then too, the perspective of a federalist union appeared to be the sole alternative to the danger of imperialism and establishment of a hegemony.

"European Federation or the League of Nations" was the title of an August

1918 treatise signed by Agnelli and Cabiati, written when Europe was in the throes of the Great War and it seemed that the conflict would continue for several more months.[1] A good deal of faith in the future was required at the time to formulate a project for a new multinational European order.[2] But the convictions expressed by Agnelli and Cabiati did not spring from any abstract idealism. Rather, they were based on the assumption—which later, unfortunately, proved to be true—that if the sovereignty of national states and their pursuit of power were not brought to an end, the tragedy of an even more terrible and more inhuman war was inevitable.

Agnelli and Cabiati were two entirely different personalities, both in their professional interests and in their political points of view. Agnelli was an industrialist, an outspoken man of action, an important representative of Italian capitalism, a liberal member of the Italian wealthy class; Cabiati was a graduate economist who sympathized with the workers' movement and the socialists. Nevertheless, both were attracted to the same belief: the "bold new idea" of a united Europe (as they put it in the foreword to their polemic) which was to destroy the "Prussian spirit," as the authors call it, i.e., the virus of nationalism, an authoritative, aggressive nationalism as it was expressed in Treitschke's doctrine of "the power idea."[3] Therefore, they thought it to be an "absolute necessity" to achieve a "decisive victory of the Entente over Central Europe," which they regarded as the most tangible and symbolic expression of the power state, an imperialist superstate. That victory alone would not be sufficient to eliminate the danger of another outbreak of war if, as the authors add, victory over the Central Powers was not followed by profound and total changes of thinking and behavior. "Prussianism," they wrote, exists not only in Prussia, "it is in all of us; it is the real enemy that we must finally destroy."[4] Agnelli and Cabiati understood the "Prussian spirit" to include not only a concept and political practice in international relations that rested on force and imperialism. They perceived behind the "Prussian spirit" an ideological foundation which nourished it—class spirit and a political system of oligarchy, the combination of nationalism with militarism, the subjugation of science and the economy to their own autonomous laws and the illusion of power.

Agnelli and Cabiati were absolutely convinced that political democracy was the fundamental prerequisite for assuring coming generations a future of peace and stability. Thus, ran the authors' appeal, it was a primary responsibility of the Western democracies to provide a good example by committing themselves to a "just and final solution" for the postwar problems. "It is the first time that all nations with great traditions of democracy are joined in their responsibilities. The future of the principles of democracy in the world depend on how this responsibility is understood and how it is borne."[5] For Agnelli and Cabiati, victory over the Central Powers was to be only a first step; a step necessary to "restore the states according to their nationalities," to quote their words. A new structure was to arise from this foundation: "the federation of European states under a central power that bears and rules it."

Naturally, Agnelli and Cabiati did not close their eyes to the difficulties of such a project. And they were fully aware of the extent to which hate and fanaticism had grown in the flames of war. Nor did the increasing orientation of the entente governments toward a "punitive peace" escape them. But promising possibilities remained; one could place hope in the U.S. and Wilson's promise of fulfilling the longings of the repressed nations and to bring new forms of international cooperation to life.

Both authors, however, did not support the idea of a league or a combination of nations, as advocated by the American president. They deemed that idea generous but illusory. They shared the views about of the principles of self-determination and solidarity that Wilson had expounded, but believed that a League of Nations of individual states that retained their monopoly of rule and with their systems unchanged would not provide a real guarantee against revival of differences and nationalistic conflicts. Nor would a League of Nations automatically have eliminated each nation's right to erect customs barriers and other obstacles to free trade.

The only possible way to prevent the return of imperialism as well as economic nationalism, according to Agnelli and Cabiati, was to establish a European community which, together with two other great communities, the U.S. and the British Commonwealth, would provide a further element in the balance of power. It would be a link in the still-missing chain necessary for attainment of an enduring peace based on cooperation, work-sharing and all-round social and economic progress.

The transformation of the entire continent into a single production market within the framework of a unified Europe had fundamental significance for Agnelli and Cabiati. In their view, that would have meant the pooling of the resources of all nations, eliminating trade barriers, abolishing the cumbersome regulations of customs protectionism and other obstacles, and, thus, eliminating the increasingly costly and muddled apparatus of administration to the advantage of all parties. Unified Europe thus would experience a second "industrial revolution" and undergo a modernization process in all sectors of coexistence.

But Agnelli and Cabiati presented more than a Europe of trade, and that not only because of the close relationships they proposed between European unification and development of democracy. After they had detailed the economic advantages of a European community, they also described the

foundation required for such a structure, i.e., a European central government that was to function in four basic sectors: foreign policy, defense,
finance, and customs duties. For all other functions (social policy, education,
administration, etc.), the individual states were to have complete autonomy
in accordance with their traditions, requirements and preferences. On the
other hand, Agnelli and Cabiati did not underestimate the ethical and social
traditions of the various national cultures, much less did they denigrate the
significance and the right of existence of the national states. Rather, they
raised the issue of nationalism as a source of despotic and warlike tendencies, and of serious economic cost.

The political thoughts and ideals of Luigi Einaudi led in the same
direction. He claimed, in a somewhat earlier publication than that of Agnelli
and Cabiati, that nationalism was a terrible scourge that had to be eliminated once and for all. Failing this, there would be war again, and therefore it
was useless to place hope in the formation of a League of Nations or any
other form of alliance, to the extent that the sovereign powers of the
individual nations remained untouched.[6] Rather, he judged an international
organization to be necessary to guarantee peaceful cooperation between
nations. That organization was to have "direct jurisdiction over the citizens
of the individual states, with the power to levy taxes, to form a multinational
military separate from the armed forces of the individual nations and with its
own administration, separate from that of national administrations."[7]

In other words, unless the dominance of the individual states was limited,
every attempt at cooperation would fail at the first instance of a conflict of
interests. Thus Einaudi came to the conclusion that the proposed alliance of
nations was not only doomed to fail, but would indeed "multiply and
exacerbate the reasons for disagreements and war, as mutual envy about the
allocation of joint expenditures and anger over dilatory and obstinate states
would be added to the already existing reasons for a warlike dispute."[8]
Therefore, after the victory over German imperialism, according to Einaudi,
a communal solution would have to be sought to make possible the prerequisites for a unification process on political and economic levels. At that time
he did not believe it was possible to bring a true European community into
being. It seemed more sensible to him at first to limit the process to "the
formation of Roman, Germanic and Slavic states, on a higher plane than
the small European states that are apparently destined to become stars of
the second or third rank."[9]

In any case, the main problem for Einaudi was the contradiction between
the survival of the "dogmas" of sovereignty of the individual states and the
growing mutual dependence in all sectors of economic and social relations
beyond national boundaries. These contradictions could be overcome only

by coordinating the various states with multinational policies in ever greater geographic regions in the mutual interest of all.[10] In this sense, his orientation had nothing in common with a general and vague Europeanism, nor with a "preparatory federalism" in the sense of a model and a method for realizing an autonomous regional or territorial arrangement within existing states.[11]

Just as did Agnelli and Cabiati, Einaudi owed his federalist concept to the British intellectual tradition (Acton, Sidgwick, Seeley, Curtis, Bryce), but particularly to that of Robert Seeley, the most significant proponent of this line, which came into being in the period between the second half of the nineteenth century and the end of World War I. Seeley perceived federalism as the sole institutional system that could conquer "international anarchy" and bring durable peace together with a democratic regime. Furthermore, he had explicitly pointed to the need for a European federation (if only as a step on the path to the goal of a world federation); he believed the national states had long been on the way to a "historical crisis" because precipitate economic and technological developments increasingly demanded formation of states of continental dimensions.

But Einaudi and the other Piedmontese federalists did not limit themselves to repeating Seeley's themes. They attempted to find an explanation to illuminate the deeper reasons for World War I. In particular, they perceived the structural inadequacies of a League of Nations with singular perspicacity and, in contrast, stressed with an extremely cogent analysis the political and economic advantages of a European federation. This is what explains the unanimous acclaim given to the writings of these three authors in the international literature of federalism,[12] and the influence they have had on political debate in Italy. Einaudi's teaching, in particular, was destined to leave its impact. In fact, more than two decades later, and despite generational differences and a different public mood, it became the core of the Europe policy program elaborated by a group of antifascist intellectuals during the dark years of World War II.

Einaudi's voice was not the only one raised in favor of the European idea in Italy after the First World War. Gaetano Salvemini also dealt with the problem of European reconstruction from the rubble of war, a reconstruction that would not contain the nucleus of a new catastrophe. He approached the matter in another way, however. While for Einaudi the nation-state itself was not in a position to guarantee international peace and order, for Salvemini it was possible for nation-states—to the extent that they would gain a truly democratic visage—to ensure a European order without the danger of further rivalries and hegemonic battles. With this belief, he not only allied his views to Wilson's plans, but also to the intellectual legacy of two great Italian thinkers of the nineteenth century, Giuseppe Mazzini and Carlo Cattaneo. In 1834, Mazzini, together with a small group of Italian, German and Polish exiles, founded "Giovine Europa" (Young Europe) in Berne with two goals: to oppose all claims to a "national hegemony," and to create conditions for a united Europe by fighting for the "emancipation of the brotherhood of peoples." Caetano had claimed in 1848 that true peace was possible only with the founding of a "United States of Europe."[13]

Different from the position taken by Einaudi, and from those of Agnelli and Cabiati were the views of Piero Gobetti and Claudio Treves. The former, a member of Salvemini's school and a defender of a radical renewal and a liberal tradition in his *Energie nuove* (New Energies) and *Rivoluzione liberale* (Liberal Revolution), shared the goal of a new European system. But he considered the idea that the concept of a nation-state could be overcome as too abstract, and therefore found the proposals of President Wilson to be more realistic.[14] Treves, who had been a major leader of Italian reform socialism, and who shared the gradualist approach (in the form promulgated by Karl Kautsky, Otto Bauer and Karl Renner), believed that the formation of a "United States of Europe" should not take place by a simple transposition of the U.S. or the British confederational system. Rather, it was to be a process of true reconciliation between the former antagonist states and by means of an economic "amalgamation in common agreement" without any form of discrimination. Therefore he considered Wilson's project as the first important step in the direction of a new international balance.[15] This differed from the attitude of the overwhelming majority of the socialists of the time, who, because of their radicalism, tended to adopt the classic theses of the proletarian Internationale. These theses admitted to no autonomy of the international political system with respect to the internal structure of individual states, viewing international peace and order as an automatic and necessary consequence of the realization of these values within the individual states, as they saw the struggle for the realization of socialist equality as having priority.

Rejection of the principles proposed by Wilson, the harsh conditions placed on the conquered by the victors in the Versailles treaty, and the return of protectionism led, as we know, to the end of all hope for a new European order based on overriding fundamentals of equality and international cooperation. The theory of free trade, one of the principal motives of Einaudi's federalist proposals and those of Agnelli and Cabiati as well, nonetheless did not lose its influence in Italian politics and economics. The idea of the need for a new international order continued to be discussed further in some liberal circles between 1919 and 1923. This perspective was seen in part as the only effective countermeasure to the difficulties of postwar adjustment.

It was also meant as a protective wall against the wave of nationalistic resentments in response to the so-called mutilated peace (so-called because of the stripping away of Rijeka and the Dalmatians) which was to prepare the way for fascism. It was Giolitti in particular, together with several adherents of progressive liberalism who had declared themselves for neutrality in 1914 (and who remained opposed to Italy's participation in the war to the very end) who were convinced that a return to a system based solely on power relationships between the states had to be avoided. They insisted that Germany not be excluded and damned to isolation.

After the hypothesis of a European community was wiped out by the rise of a Fascist dictatorship, it returned as a democratic alternative to the totalitarian regime in certain antifascist circles, e.g., the "Giustizia e Libertà" (Justice and Liberty) movement in the course of the 1930s. "Fascism," Silvio Trentin claimed in 1930, "is anti-Europe because it is anti-democratic." And Carlo Rosselli held the view that only a strategy of multinational politics was in a position to oppose the advance of Fascism and Nazism with success. "For the European Left," he wrote in 1935, "there is no other foreign policy. United States of Europe, European parliament. All else is *flatus vocis*. All else is catastrophe."[16] Trentin and Rosselli both believed in the ideals of democratic liberalism. The former participated with Giovanni Amendola in the final battles against seizure of power by the Fascists, then had to flee to France to join the exiles. (He gave up the chair of law at the University of Venice.) Trentin believed that Europe had to find a "third way" between the United States and the Soviet Union, and saw this path—in the footsteps of the anarchistic-federalist socialism of Proudhon—in federalism under the formula of *liberer et federer*. Only a federalistic structure, in his judgment, could make a "third way" possible, i.e., a synthesis between freedom and collective property, between unity and autonomy. Rosselli, initiator of the "Justice and Liberty" movement, on the other hand, saw in federalism a central point of what he defined as "liberal socialism."[17] It is surely no coincidence that the idea of a multinational European community matured in those years in those circles of Italian anti-fascism that combined liberal principles with a new program of economic and social democracy. Among the Left, among Communists and Socialists, Europeanism was seen as something improvised and at best a marginal goal.[18] Beyond this, Lenin's argument ruled; in a famous article of 1915 he said that the uppermost goal was revolution in every country, European unity was simply a consequence of the universal adoption of socialism.[19]

The liberal-progressive idea is common as well to the initiators of the "Manifesto of Ventotene," Ernesto Rossi, Eugenio Colorni and Altiero Spinelli. Three anti-Fascists of differing political convictions, each with a different past, all agreed in the end. Ernesto Rossi, who had been among the first members of the "Giustizia e Libertà" movement, and who spent a twenty-year sentence imposed in 1929 under house arrest, was a radical liberal of the Anglo-Saxon type, a political reformer and defender of free trade. (He had chosen both Salvemini and Einaudi as his mentors.) In contrast, Eugenio Colorni was a socialist and militant member of the party of Nenni and Partini, with an interest in philosophy and science; Altiero Spinelli was an ex-Communist who, before his arrest in 1927, had been communications secretary of the party's youth organization. One year later, he disappeared in the prisons of the Fascists after his conviction for conspiratorial activity. After his break with the party because of the incompatibility of his convictions with the dogmas of Marxism-Leninism, he most strongly felt the need to reassess the future of Europe and to find a solution that not only would impede the resurrection of national egotisms from the rubble of war, but also would guarantee full enjoyment of individual rights.[20] It was he who wrote a large part of the piece, which was not originally titled "Manifesto di Ventotene," but rather simply "progetto di manifesto" (draft of a manifesto) which was soon to become a major early source of European federalism. The manifesto, which first saw the light of day on September 7, 1941, was not intended to be understood as a simple declaration of principles, but as a true political program. "With propaganda and actions," it claimed, "in attempting by all possible means to build unity and cooperation between the various movements that are sure to come about in the various nations, the foundations must be laid now for a movement that can mobilize all possible forces for a new organism which can be the greatest and most rejuvenating discovery Europe has ever experienced."[21]

Renewed reading of Einaudi's writings was of great significance in the formulation of the manifesto.[22] Spinelli was referred to these works by Ernesto Rossi, who saw in the Piedmontese economist not only a pioneer of the federalist idea in Italy, but also a champion of an anarchistic belief that was averse to both Marxism-Stalinism and monopolistic capitalism.[23] Other fundamental reference points were the ideas of federalists of the American as well as the English school. Among the former was Alexander Hamilton, one of the fathers of American independence, and among the latter, in addition to the pioneers of British federalism, there were others who, like Lord Beveridge and Lionel Robbins, had contributed in the 1930s to the rejuvenation of the federalist perspective on a new theoretical basis in a more multinational than intranational sense.

The end of fascism on July 25, 1943, opened the way for a plan that Spinelli and the other authors of the Manifesto were firmly determined to try. ("The path that we have determined to take," they said, "is neither easy nor certain, but we must take it and we will take it.") One month later, on August 27, 1943, the first members of the anti-fascist "Giustizia e Libertà" group met in the Milanese house of Mario Alberto Rolliers. The group included, among others, Manlio Rossi-Doria, Leon Ginzburg, Franco Venturi, and Vittorio Foa, who were soon joined by Adriano Olivetti and Aldo Garosci. Spinelli's suggestion prevailed not to found a federalist party, but rather a political movement of a new type, open to all proponents of European unification. Such a movement would be in a position to find support in all circles regardless of external form, and would be able to expand its activities beyond national borders.

Thus the "Movimento Federalista Europea" (European Federalist Movement) was founded, including in the beginning various representatives of the Action Party, some Socialists, Catholics and independents of various types. This was how shortly after the truce of September 8, 1943, various partisan groups were formed to resist the German occupation and Mussolini's Social Republic. The Federalists became a component of the resistance movement, with their own program and their own newspaper *(L'Unità Europea)*, of which several issues were secretly distributed. Of this Norberto Bobbio has written: "Not the entire resistance movement was federalist. But federalism was surely a common denominator for various groups which called the battle for liberation into being. . . . No one today can write the history of the resistance without taking the federalist perspective into account."[24]

Spinelli and Rossi's search for members was not limited to Italian anti-fascists. In May 1944, they took part in a meeting of representatives of resistance movements of Czechoslovakia, Denmark, France, Holland, Norway and Yugoslavia. This meeting produced a declaration of intent which foresaw a federalist European union following the end of hostilities. This union was to be led by a "government directly responsible to the peoples who elect it." The same concepts are repeated in a document prepared in the following year by the first European Federalist conference. The conference was organized in March 1945 by the French "Mouvement de Libération Nationale" and representatives of republican Spain and intellectuals such as Albert Camus and George Orwell.

The ideas presented in the "Manifesto di Ventotene" thus had made considerable advances when Spinelli, by then an important leader in the Action Party, renewed his efforts with new zeal on behalf of Europeanism. It was his intent to reach the goal he had formulated much earlier; to call a broad movement to life on the international level. This first goal was reached in Paris in December 1945 with the formation of the Federalist Movement for Europe (FME). However, in the postwar period hopes faded for a positive attitude of the Anglo-Saxon powers toward European union and the plans for a constitutional convention for Europe. Therefore Spinelli, believing there was no real chance for an effective federalist initiative at the time, declined to take the leadership of the FME. Adoption of the Marshall Plan, which revived the problem of European union, induced him to become personally involved in the fight once more, and he became general secretary of the FME, a position in which he continued without interruption until 1962.

In this difficult position it was of special significance that Einaudi's voice was raised again in favor of European ideals. In May 1947, he advanced from the presidency of the Italian State Bank to become finance minister and vice-president of the Council of Ministers. Almost in the same way that Jean Monnet became protector of a sound federalism in France, Einaudi, strengthened by his academic prestige, took on the task of revitalizing the idea of European unity. In fact, even before the end of the war, he had lamented the "idolization" of state powers that would accompany "the unaltered restoration of the absolute and perfect dominion of the states." In a speech before the constitutional assembly in the course of the debate on ratification of the peace treaty, he had expressed critical reservations about the United Nations, which appeared to him to be a repetition of the League of Nations. "The pure state alliances, the federations of states with their own sovereignty, are unable to prevent war, i.e., they are even instigators of war among these federated states." For that very reason he believed multinational unity had become an inescapable necessity for Europe, so that once and for all one had to choose between "the sword of Satan" and the "sword of God," between "the thought of domination with raw power" and the "eternal belief in free-willed cooperation for the common good."[25]

Einaudi, the most important representative after Minister President Alcide De Gasperi in the first postwar cabinet formed entirely from the parties of the center, emphasized his views once more in an article that appeared in the *Corriera della Sera* of April 4, 1948, shortly before he was elected president of Italy: "If we want to differentiate between the friends of peace and the enemies of peace, we must not waste time with lip service, because the greater the lies, the louder they are spread. Instead, we should ask: Do you want to retain the full sovereignty of the nation in which you live? Those who answer 'yes' are the most bitter enemies of peace. Are you determined, in contrast, to give your vote, your support, to one who promises to transfer a portion of the national power to a new institution called the United States of Europe? If your answer to this is 'yes,' and deeds follow words, then and only then can you call yourselves fighters of freedom. Everything else is lies."

Although he did not give the concept of political union absolute priority, the chairman of the Council of Ministers and head of the Christian Democratic Party, Alcide De Gasperi, was deeply inspired by European ideals and indeed had a decisive role in leading Italian policy in that direction. Europe was split into two parts after the Yalta treaty; an iron curtain separated the Western nations from the Eastern bloc. At that time, there was no hope of a total unification of the old continent. Still, there remained the outlook for agreement between the various West European nations that was to be the foundation for a process of political and economic union, particularly in view of the threat of Soviet totalitarianism. The discussions during the constitutional assembly, in which charges of a nationalistic character arose among the opponents of ratification of the peace treaty, were eye opening for De Gasperi. They came at a time when, in his view, the new, democratic Italy should have provided a clear rejection of nationalism — "not only to put an end to the past, but also to avoid jeopardizing the chances for effective diplomatic efforts."[26]

Under these circumstances, with the exception of Vittorio Emanuele Orlando and Francesco Saverio Nitti, the most important personalities of Italian culture and antifascism, from Benedetto Croce to Luigi Sturzo, from Salvemi to Piero Calamandrei, had spoken out for closer European and Western cooperation. Not only the leader of the Christian Democrats, but also representatives of the Republican Party such as Ugo La Malfa and Carlo Sforza held the conviction that a democratic Europe, in solidarity with the United States, had to unite its forces to present a protective wall against communist expansion. As foreign minister from 1847 to 1951, Carlo Sforza played an important role[27] in the fundamental decision taken by the Italian government in favor of European unity. This was at a time when the left wing of the Christian Democrats and a part of the Social Democratic Party retained a neutral position. Sforza's orientation in favor of a European union had matured during his long years in opposition and his exile in the United States.[28] In the period after the war, he came to the conviction that the German problem could be solved only in the framework of a true European cooperation which ensured peaceful coexistence between Germany and the other nations of the continent, at the same time also providing the foundation for general economic development and democratization of society. In particular he was of the opinion, as described by Sergio Pistone, that "Italy, in accordance with the teachings of Mazzini, had to take a leading role similar to that which Piedmont had taken in the unification of Italy."[29]

Although Sforza shared the view that all this spoke in favor of a multinational principle, he also thought it was necessary to proceed step by step in erecting a unified house of Europe, by moving from economic through military to political matters. He voiced this belief by terming it "from the Marshall Plan to political union." The Italian government thus decided on a "functional" approach in the conviction that after the various sectors of public life (economic, social, military and foreign policy) had been unified, a multinational system could be accomplished.

On the other hand, the Marshall Plan offered an important point of departure for initiating economic cooperation immediately. And Italy, like other European nations, had an urgent need to heal the wounds left by the war, to rebuild its own economy and to intensify its foreign trade. The path of functional unification was not the same as the one desired by the FME. But for now it was the only practical path, even if the Italian representatives at the May 1948 Congress organized by the "International Committee of Movements for European Union" in Aja did not share this opinion.[30] In fact, instead of the union of European democratic nations preferred by the Federalists, the European Economic Community was founded in 1948 and, three years later, the European Coal and Steel Community. In reality, establishing these unions was no mean achievement, but they were denigrated as minor events by the strict Europeanists. It required all the strength of De Gasperi, Schuman, Adenauer and Spaak, i.e., those statesmen who had acted more for European unity than any others, to seal these initial treaties.

For Italy, entry into the EEC and the European Coal and Steel Community also signified a significant political step toward complete return to the European framework and international politics. Foreign Minister Sforza had made special efforts to reach this goal. He believed Italy would be able to act more decisively and consistently after it had gained membership again in international organizations. In fact, he took the first steps as early as August 1948, in a memorandum to the French government in which he argued for the gradual achievement of "a European federation or union"; adoption of an independent role by the EEC (even beyond the original connection to the Marshall Plan); its metamorphosis into a permanent organization for economic cooperation (with the particular goal of promoting a customs union); but also for social, cultural and, in principle, military cooperation; the perfection of that organization by establishing a committee for coordinating the foreign policies of the member states, and a European court to which "all questions not settled by direct contact of the chancelleries would be referred."[31] The Italian proposals were repeated in a memorandum sent to the member states of the EEC the following October 27, in which, among other things, the goal of limiting national sovereign powers was explicitly declared. On the other hand, Sforza believed that the formation of an Atlantic military bloc was not sufficient to solve European problems, and that it was necessary, therefore, to supplement it with a true European union. This thesis was explained officially later, in March 1949, on the occasion of the parliamentary debate over Italy's entry into NATO.

Sforza's initiative making the EEC a starting point for a European federation remained unsuccessful, particularly because Great Britain, whose participation was perceived at the time as indispensable (not least for its function as a counterweight to Germany), tended to be against any multinational development in principle. In fact, the Council of Europe, founded in 1949 almost simultaneously with NATO, had no decision-making power although it included a parliamentary assembly which could serve as the official stage for the debate of national movements for European union. The Italian federalists took advantage of this stage when, in 1950, they offered a petition for a pact for European federation. In this petition, the Strasbourg parliament was requested to draw up the project for a Union treaty (on the basis of which the process of economic unification could be expanded to include the defense and foreign affairs). Member states were to be obliged to adopt this pact as soon as it had been ratified by member states with a population total of 100 million. In Italy, this memorandum was signed by more than a half million people, among them numerous figures in public life including Premier De Gasperi.

The project aimed at supporting a European Coal and Steel Community, led by Sforza with the backing of De Gasperi, was more successful. The Italian government agreed immediately to the proposal, formulated by Schuman and inspired by Monnet, which called for the merger of the steel and mining industries of the nations of Europe and their administration by a central agency. The significance of this initiative, in the belief of the Italian government, was that it presented a first concrete step in the direction of a German-French rapprochement. For that reason Sforza believed that "Italy must strongly support the Schuman plan, even against British prejudice," i.e., the conviction, which until then had contributed strongly to stalling the Italian pro-Europe initiative, that European integration cannot be continued without full participation of the London government.[32] At the same time, he strongly advocated that the Council of Europe formally declare compatible the aims of the seven nations of "little Europe" that had decided for the Union, and Great Britain and the other Council of Europe members who were not ready to take the same decision.

The difficulties to be overcome were not exclusively international. Not everyone in Italy was convinced of the usefulness of membership in the European Coal and Steel Community, not least because the metal industry saw itself subject to most severe international competition without protection of the old customs barriers. In fact, the Italian government had to engage in several thorny disputes (led by Senator Enrico Falk) with the most important private concerns in this sector before the protectionist barriers could be dismantled.[33] Membership in the European Coal and Steel Community later would prove to be very important for the development of the Italian steel industry. But initially, resistance by the trade unions was nourished by the fear of German economic domination, or at least a joint dominance of France and Germany, which would ruin the weaker nations of Europe.

The reservations held by Einaudi, the most significant supporter of removing customs barriers and creating new freedoms for economic development, were of an opposite nature. In his view, neither the European Coal and Steel Community nor the European defense union were sufficient to put a true process of multinational union into gear. For Einaudi, the most important path was that of political unification; everything else, he believed, would only be a result thereof. "The European Coal and Steel Community, the green treaties, and especially the defense union," he noted in 1953, "are only temporary and ought to be accepted only as means toward realization of the broader concepts of a political federation. It is a big mistake to claim one begins with a simpler economic concept, so that we can reach the more difficult political result. The opposite is true. One must begin with the political if one wants the economic."[34] Together with criticism of the functional and gradual approach,[35] this point of view expressed by Einaudi also included the conviction that European unity was the strongest diplomatic card Italy could play in making its presence felt on the international stage.

The aspiration of taking an important place in international relations, to make a place for himself among those responsible for Italy's foreign policy, had already begun in the 1950s. Although this ambition led to an active part in the process of European unification, it was based on the idea that Italy had to fulfill a far greater responsibility. Because of its peninsular position, it was called to serve as an outpost against the Eastern bloc, and at the same time, it had responsibilities for the security and stability of the Mediterranean region. This tendency was to become clearer between 1954 and 1955 when, with the solution of the Trieste question and the admission of Italy to the United Nations, the last barriers to the effectiveness of Italian diplomacy were removed and Italy resumed its rightful position in the international community. Signs for this development had existed some years earlier.

But no one proposed striving for major power status, which the British and American governments (in the words of Churchill and Dulles) appeared to be ready to give Italy. Italy, despite reorganization of its public finances and some very promising indications of economic development, depended in many ways on foreign nations and, in any case, held few trump cards. Nevertheless, in full recognition of these limitations, the desire to exert its own specific role in the framework of international relations, and not be relegated to the role of a "fifth wheel," was extraordinarily strong.

The attitude of the Italian government to the formation of a European defense community was especially typical in this respect. During the course of negotiations, Foreign Minister Sforza insisted on an adequate economic quid pro quo (beginning with freedom of movement for workers) for the financial efforts that Italy would have to make for participation in a joint European defense force. He insisted as well on the Council of Ministers becoming the chief organ of the EEC, and that its decisions were unanimous. In this way, he attempted more to defend the principle of national sovereignty than to define the EEC project in a multinational sense. On the other hand, Sforza never went so far as to spell out precisely the "institutional mechanisms" that were to develop the integration process, believing that the development of European unity was like a stream of which it was "certain that it would flow into the sea, but not which path it would take."[36]

Only in 1952, when the problem was put into De Gasperi's hands after the death of Sforza, did the government recognize that the development of the EEC, because it would inevitably include controls by a multinational political agency, required an analogous economic union and a federative unification process as natural support.[37] In the event, De Gasperi finally adopted as his own Altiero Spinelli's progressive ideas in the name of the federalist movement for Europe, in order to convert the EEC project into a broader project of a European union with political, military and economic dimensions marked by progressive federalist characteristics.[38] The result of this initiative was the adoption, through De Gasperi's efforts, of Article 38 into the EEC project. Among other things, this article provided for a democratically elected EEC assembly with responsibility for developing the statutes of the EEC. The completion of this project was, in fact, to clear the path for the development of a federalist union in a relatively short time. It did not happen because ratification of the EEC treaty by each of the nations had been made a condition of the adoption of the project. Thus, rejection by the French parliament in August 1964 also doomed the hopes for a conversion from a functional to a federative union.[39]

Disappointment over the fact that the EEC could not be achieved did not diminish the Roman government's determination to continue to defend a policy oriented toward Europe. Even though Giuseppe Pella, who had replaced De Gasperi as leader of the government following the elections of June 1963, appeared more careful than his predecessor in the absence of a secure parliamentary majority, Mario Scelba (who was a man of equally strong European convictions[40]) supported the establishment of the West European Union (WEU). The WEU—if only on a combined, if no longer on a united level—could have guaranteed military planning, weapons control and the definition of a convergent policy in security and defense matters.

But at the same time, the Italian government understood that the problem of European unification was closely related to other matters, from the reintegration of the Federal Republic of Germany into the international community to relaxation of East-West tensions; from the crisis of colonialism to relations to the Third World. For that reason, the difficulties arising in the development of a "European policy" were not underestimated in Rome; Italy, it was felt, must not become isolated. There were opportunities to strengthen relations with the nations of Eastern Europe, the Mediterranean countries and those of the Middle East, although that had to be done consistently with the European ideals and with complete respect for Italy's responsibilities to NATO. The basis for this line of thought, which was termed "Neo-Atlantism," was not only an economic motive (development of trade with the Soviet Union, access to the oil sources of the Middle East, etc.). Men of different political views (such as Pella, Fanfani, Martino, Gronchi) and ranking diplomats in Washington and the more important European capitals firmly believed that, despite any differences in attitude, the West could not assume the risk of leaving the nations of the Middle East to their fate, and that in addition, the real intentions of the new Soviet leaders who followed Stalin remained to be tested. The Suez crisis revealed how much special interests and the last remaining colonial privileges still weighed in the policies of the governments of London and Paris. It helped affirm the direction taken by the Italian government in pursuit of greater freedom of action lest it be tied to the positions taken by France and England, while simultaneously producing more effective ties to the U.S.

In fact, the adventure which France and England embarked upon with their military intervention on the coast of the Red Sea in October 1956, together with the worry of the Roman government about the danger of a change in alliances by the nations of the checkerboard of the Middle East, confirmed the doubts many Italian diplomats had raised about the good faith of European protestations. The Italian ambassador to Paris, Quaroni, had written to Foreign Minister Martino in April 1955: "Unfortunately, we can only wish (for) Europe, not make it happen." The Italian representative in London, Zoppi, held the same opinion. In October 1956, in the middle of the Suez crisis, he noted that the various political circles of France were willing to sign the European treaties only and exclusively because they hoped it would help form a broad coalition of forces against Nasser, perhaps even against the United States ("One calls for Europe, to throw out America and the Americans."[41])

Nonetheless, it was precisely the failure of the English-French attempt to turn back the clock that finally facilitated the progress toward establishing the EEC and Euratom. While resistance of the French parliament to the draft of the Common Market disappeared, the meeting between the Italian President of State Gronchi and Germany's Chancellor Adenauer on October

6, 1956, in Bonn demonstrated the general agreement of Rome and Bonn on the need for reintroducing the WEU and reaching a definition of the basic EEC treaties so that the question of European solidarity could have a firm foundation.

From the Italian side, liberal Foreign Minister Gaetano Martino in particular had supported the European cause. He finally crowned his work (which had begun with the meeting of the Six in Messina in June 1956 with an action program for the development of economic union) in March 1957 by signing the Treaties of Rome, which brought the Common Market and Euratom to life. As consistent as the efforts of the Italian governments of the 1950s had been in terms of Europe, it cannot be claimed that the goal of European unification was the most important motive that stimulated Italian foreign policy or the strategies of its most important economic groups.

The concept of European integration was more a drawing card with special appeal to cultural circles and those of public opinion makers. Not only because Europeanism offered an opportunity to drive out the virus of nationalism that had infected Italy and had plunged it into the catastrophe of World War II during the time of the Fascist regimes. But also because the intellectual elite was convinced that European unity was based first on a common cultural heritage,[42] a conglomerate of ethic and religious beliefs, equivalent or similar structures and institutions, even if experienced in various and different ways. Proof thereof was to be delivered a few years later in a masterful way by Federico Chabod in his *Storia dell'idea d'Europa* (History of the European Idea), published in 1961.

The attitude of industrial circles was different. Initially, there had been numerous objections to the dismantling of customs protectionism, in the conviction that this would expose Italian industry to intolerable competition. During the 1950s they had given the impression of tolerating the European initiatives of certain statesmen rather than really agreeing with them. On the other hand, they feared not only having to compete in the international market with a handicap, but were not yet ready to risk entering European trade channels. As curious as this might appear, the fears of the industrialists were shared by the parties of the Left. The Communists and the Socialist party (which still had not freed itself of certain old ideological schemata) considered European unification a creature of NATO in the service of American policies, as a typical expression of the interests of large, monopolistic concerns. On the other hand, they almost always perceived economic and employment policy measures exclusively within a nationalist framework. For this very reason their views coincided with Italian industrial concerns which still adhered to development policies dictated by internal demand and public expenditures. The real significance of expanding Italian industrial trade (begun by Fiat, Pirelli and Olivetti) dawned on industry when economic activity—instead of declining after expansion initiated by the Korean War, as had been widely predicted—developed in ever more profitable ways for the European nations. Initial pessimistic predictions which assumed that governments would not be in a position to meet their obligations turned out to be wrong. Thus insecurity quickly became euphoria. In fact, industrial production between 1952 and 1961 increased at an average annual rate of 8.3 percent, especially because of strong increases in the first years after entry into the EEC. Investment grew an average 9.9 percent while the gross national product grew by 5.8 percent annually.[43]

If Italy, despite these impressive figures, did not meet the records attained by the most developed nations, there can be no doubt that it developed quickly, so that in 1962 it took second place behind the Federal Republic of Germany in terms of the growth rate of per capita income, investments and exports.

The factors that promoted the Italian "economic miracle" were shared, in part, by many European nations (e.g., increased demand stimulated by public sector expenditures for the elimination of war damage, effects of the American economic expansion, undervaluation of currencies in relation to the U.S. dollar, renewal of production facilities, access to modern, low-cost energy sources, demand for new mass consumption products). In addition, many of the nations had an adequate supply of cheap labor, to which was added a steady stream from the poorer southern region to the principal industrial centers of the north. But the opening of the European market was surely the most important stimulus, not only permitting the Italian economy to increase its exports to other EEC nations significantly (by 26 percent annually from 1956–62), but also making possible significant advantages in production volumes and rationalization of labor.[44] In this way, production grew more profitable without noticeable inflation and with a steadily increasing external balance of trade. That is what made Italian economic growth clearly different from the English, the French and that of other European states which were constantly convulsed by large price increases and repeated crises in the balance of trade. On the other hand, it was imperative for Italy, a nation almost without natural resources and in constant need of imports, to keep increasing its exports. And not only that. It became just as imperative to satisfy the profitable market opportunities, to direct the greater part of domestic effort at satisfying consumer product demand.

The parties of the Left blamed this developing model of competition within the European market for the absence of a growth program supported by a growing domestic market based on increased production of capital goods and modernization of agriculture. Some economists defended the view that, given a close relationship between expanding foreign demand and economic growth, only a positive balance of trade and the resulting greater liquidity could guarantee higher growth rates. That would lead to making the traditional instrument of monetary policy the sole or overwhelming dominant parameter of the entire economic policy. Correspondingly, there would be greater reduction of all programs for improving the infrastructure, public and environmental expenditures, and, in consequence, the "social aspects" of development. But these and other "reverse sides of the coin" (such as constantly increasing dependence of development of the Italian economy on foreign demand) became clear in subsequent years. The fact that exports had reached almost 25 percent in 1970 (up from 19.1 percent of total production in 1960) was a sign that Italian industry finally had taken on new and more dynamic dimensions, even though some problems remained. Conversion of production to mass market items to meet foreign demand in fact had led to a series of imbalances between various industrial sectors (depending on technology, ability to meet competition and concentration of capital) and between agriculture and industry. Similarly, a greater difference developed between North and South (the North continuously approaching the economic dimensions of North-Western Europe; the South still not free of the typical agricultural and manual labor traditions of the Mediterranean region).

In view of the undoubted successes of economic union (even if not nearly complete and not without its darker sides) the critical reservations of the federalist movement faded into the background. Even Spinelli came to accept the thought of a gradual development, especially after the failed attempt to activate federalistic forces through the "Congresso del Popolo Europaeo" (Congress of the European Peoples) — though they were sufficient to force the governments to call into being a constitutional assembly for Europe. The advantages of economic union convinced him that projects theretofore realized by the EEC — the formation of a bureaucracy independent of national administrations and the interlocking of economic interests as the Common Market developed — "were far more acceptable than some may have thought in the beginning."[45] That did not mean, however, that Spinelli shared the unlimited faith in the proponents of functionalism and believed that the "Eurocracy" alone could lead to complete unification, while the introduction of true democratic and federalist authorities into European institutions could be delayed to the end.

The results achieved in the second half of the 1960s and the first few years of the 1970s produced a more complex and more differentiated stance in public opinion and in the political forces of Italy with respect to the

European unification process. On the one hand, because of the fact that the border between the two military blocs was irreversibly fixed at least for the foreseeable future, Italians began to assign more significance to European unification. On the other hand, liberalization of trade no longer seemed enough. Rather, unification would also have to include harmonization of social policies and employment policies, and adequate measures for the support of structurally weak regions as well.

However, the first goal—political independence of Western Europe—after de Gaulle had made it the highlight of his "Americanism" discussion, was burdened too much as a motive by diverse and contradictory ambitions. The Italian government therefore preferred to distance itself from the idea of political unification halfway along the process. The concept that Europeans are to be subjects, rather than objects, of history appeared to be conceived purely as antagonism to the United States and to be tailor-made for the interests and the aspirations and the "grandeur" of Gaullist France. In any case, public opinion, democratic-progressive circles and the major political parties mistrusted France which, with the new constitution of the Fifth Republic, appeared to be a nation with a semitotalitarian regime. In addition, the opinion was widespread that de Gaulle's proposal for a European confederation ("Europe of the Fatherlands") would mean a union dominated by France or a Franco-German alliance. All of which explains why it was seen as necessary that Great Britain join the EEC to counter the danger of French dominance or a directorate between Paris and Bonn.

However, it became increasingly clear that, from the point of view of Italian interests, developments in the EEC were moving in the wrong direction. Progress in the field of social legislation appeared meager; too many constraints and too much discrimination against "guest workers," and particularly against emigration, continued to exist in the various nations of the Community. Thus dissatisfaction on the Italian side increased after the Socialists joined the new parliamentary majority of the center (so much so that it found support in numerous official documents). The leaders of the Socialist Party, which had separated from the "Unity and Action Pact" with the Communists in 1966 and had taken direct government responsibility since 1963, believed that it was not possible to achieve true European unification without convincing the masses that the EEC also would tackle the problems of work and employment.

For this reason as well, the Italian Socialists deemed it imperative that Great Britain and the Scandinavian nations participate in rebuilding Europe, because they could provide more than others the political force and experience about the principles of democratic socialism. The leader of the PSI (Socialist Party of Italy), Pietro Nenni, held the view that no future was possible for Europe if its unification was not the result of a movement from below, i.e., with an effective participation by the people. This explains why Altiero Spinelli, at the risk of putting himself in conflict with the Italian leadership of the federalist movement, moved closer to the Socialist Party and even became one of the closest colleagues of Nenni while the latter was at the head of the Foreign Ministry between December 1968 and June 1969. The Socialist forces, not only in Italy but in other European nations as well, who were ambivalent, if not opposed, to European integration during its introduction, later had put their reservations aside; Spinelli now ascribed the same advance guard function to them as the Christian Democrats had assumed in the postwar era.[46] Finally, cooperation with Nenni and other politicians permitted Spinelli to muster broad support in governmental circles for direct elections to the European parliament. Another important result was the joint Italian-British declaration, signed on April 28, 1969, by Nenni and British Foreign Secretary Stewart, supporting direct elections to the European parliament and democratization of the Community.

The significance of this declaration was in the fact that it followed the resignation of de Gaulle from the French presidency, and thus preceded a new phase of French policy, one more constructive in its view of European matters. Nevertheless, three more years were to pass before Britain's entry into the EEC in 1973.

However, just when the entry of England, Holland and Denmark gave the new "Europe of the Nine" a more comprehensive and a more balanced form — something that had always been wished by the Roman government — the danger arose of Italy removing itself from the EEC. The severe economic crisis in Italy due to the significant increase in oil prices forced Italy to leave the European Monetary Rate system (currency snake), while a broad wave of labor disputes in the factories, together with low productivity rates, damaged the balance sheets of almost all large firms.

These events caused a calamitous combination of recession and inflation. As a consequence, political parties and public opinion asked for the first time whether the price of integration of Italy into the EEC was not too high and whether its benefits would be balanced by its cost. The bottom line for Italy appeared to show that the direct advantages of the Common Market resulting from the customs union had already been exhausted, while delays and treaty violations (also owing to poor foresight and negotiation on Italy's part) had failed to activate the compensating machinery provided by the EEC. Especially in agriculture, it was claimed that Italy's interests had fallen victim to those of France and Holland. Moreover, the fact that no appropriate plans had been put forward for regional development prompted criticism. For that reason, the EEC was perceived as an organization dominated by oligopolistic groups and a bureaucratic apparatus.

All that did not mean that its membership in the Community had been reduced to a passive role, at least not for the export industries in the "industrial triangle." But the agricultural policies of the Community had provided Italy with few real advantages, as far as modernization of its agrarian structure, higher farm income and territorial equilibrium of southern Italy was concerned, while it bore the costs of the agricultural fund supporting prices in Holland and France, where farms were far more efficient. Obviously, the long-standing resistance of Germany and France to expenditures for regional aid found little sympathy, even if it was true that serious problems of adjustment existed in some areas, such as Alsace-Lorraine, the Ruhr valley and the Pyrenees region of southern France.

How much these and other motives fanned dissatisfaction with the EEC in Italy may be recognized by the fact that some political circles felt that Italy should leave the Community, even if only temporarily, to avoid further distress from the "restrictions of the Community." The Socialists and the Republicans were particularly critical. Among the latter was Ugo La Malfa, a fierce supporter of Europe, who found it intolerable that there was more obstruction from Brussels than incentives for modernization of industry and agriculture. Indeed, the various governments of those years had publicly stressed Italy's efforts on behalf of political and economic integration, even at the most difficult moments; thus, the Christian Democratic government led by Rumor, when seeking a vote of confidence in Parliament in July 1973, noted that "European unity is our foremost goal and our link with a social structure to which we are firmly anchored." That does not alter the fact that despite all protestations to the contrary, a climate of mistrust and disappointment gained ground. Europe saw itself facing the same problems; overcoming them was further complicated by the social and economic consequences of the long economic crisis, by loss of competitiveness of European industry, and by the inefficient, slow, inappropriate establishment of institutions capable of making decisions without the assurance of continuity.[47] "The case of Italy," wrote a newspaper as important as *La Stampa* in an editorial of July 7, 1974, "is the result of many wasted years, not only here, but in other member states of the Community as well. Each had its own problems, with the result that our serious structural weaknesses which would have been brought under control and altered had they been attacked with a Community plan ten years ago, today place our Community membership in question while endangering the very existence of the Community."[48]

The controversy on the Italian side was about a wide range of principles as well as problems of substance. But the nature of the complaints was almost always the same: they were aimed at the policies of the government of France. With the "compromise of Luxembourg," the French had made sure the rule requiring unanimity in decisions of the Council of Europe would continue beyond the termination date of January 1966 foreseen in the Treaties of Rome. In a 1973 publication by the Italian speaker of the EEC Commission, Bino Olivi, de Gaulle's plan to be the leader of a "Europe of the Fatherlands" was blamed for blocking the admission of Great Britain, and thus the process of political-institutional unification.[49]

Rejection of a true economic union was laid to de Gaulle's "rude egoism" that had, among other things, excluded Italian agriculture to the benefit of that of France. This the author also blamed on the incompetence of Italian bureaucracy and on the fact that Italy, with the exception of Altiero Spinelli, was not represented in Brussels by statesmen on a level with Hallstein or Mansholt.

In any case, the "magic of Europe" had been lost. There was no longer any single aspect of the EEC policies that escaped criticism. Thus, for example, the regional policies that had finally been defined at the beginning of 1973, became mired in the depths of endless negotiations and in the end shattered on the rocks of German opposition. Similarly, attempts to make the use of the European Social Fund more rational in form and content, remained no more than good intentions. Similarly, the farm policies, ceremoniously adopted in 1968 in the "Agricultural Economy" memorandum and then converted into a skeleton of guidelines that became law in January 1974, during the execution phase, never left the desks of the Council of Ministers. In the meantime, Italy, after twenty years of the Common Market, had a particularly frightening agricultural trade imbalance as the member of the EEC who had increased its exports the least and its imports the most. It was not only claimed that the EEC had treated Italy as a "poor relation,"[50] but it was deemed completely absurd that the EEC now wanted to burden Italy with an exorbitant share of the conversion costs by using the weakness of the lira against the other European currencies to shift the costs to Italy's farmers through "compensation imports."

Altiero Spinelli, appointed a member of the Executive Commission of the EEC in July 1978, made himself the spokesman of these and other Italian complaints and frictions about the EEC. During his term of office, however, he reached the conclusion that the Council was frequently blocked by the impossibility of reaching the required qualified majority for all decisions (despite the agreement, in December 1974 in Paris, to dispense with the principle of unanimity) and that the Commission in turn was limited in power and in any case was strong enough to obtain direct elections of the European Parliament. Therefore in 1976, following the not very reassuring Tindemans Report,[51] he resigned to take up the political battle again as an independent candidate on the slate of the Communist Party in the elections of June of that year. (This after Enrico Berlinguer had taken the Communist Party out of the "iron chains" that had bound it up to that time to the USSR, using the slogan of the "historical compromise" and acknowledging the defensive purpose of NATO). The new communist line was hoping for cooperation with forces from the Catholic and Socialist population. Spinelli justified his decision to renew ties with the party he had left forty years before, and which permitted him (after his election) to take up a seat in the Strasbourg Parliament as a member of the Italian delegation by saying that "the Communist Party has moved during those years from a position of strict European unification to one of cautious acceptance," a position similar to that taken by the Socialist Party at the time of the signing of the treaties of Rome.[52]

The need for a balance and more widely accepted economic policy while reviving the constitutional unification process gained increasing approval during the second half of the 1960s from various political forces in Italy, including the opposition. The result of the European Council Conference of July 1976 in Bremen, where finally the political will emerged for direct elections for the Parliament of Europe (scheduled for the following year) was very much welcomed. Thus, the goal for which not only Italian supporters of the federalist movement in Europe, but also, in different ways, all governments up to that time had been fighting, was finally realized after thirty years. Even the Communist Party had accepted the new multinational power that was based not only on treaties between states, but on a broad consensus of the people. But the Communist Party opposed the decision of the Bremen Conference about monetary policy cooperation. Introduction of a European Monetary System (EMS) with the purpose of creating in Europe a zone of exchange stability by means of coordinating the policies of the member states would, in the opinion of the communists, act more as a brake than as a stimulus to the process of economic integration, so that the gap between the strongest and the weakest partners would not be reduced, but become greater. Rejection by the Communist Party of this point was so inflexible that Italy's entry into the EMS in December 1978 put an end to the "national solidarity" (i.e., the support given by the Communist Party to the governing coalition of Centrists and Socialists to meet the emergency situation caused by terrorism and two-digit inflation).

In reality, the decision permitted the government, led at the time by Giulio Andreotti, to accept the challenge of the EEC for Italy to reintegrate fully again into the EEC and to create the conditions necessary for a successful fight against galloping inflation. The Socialist Party was finally convinced after first abstaining. Not to have joined the EMS might have meant an irreversible step away from Europe, which would have damaged our economy in any case, as the Italian representative for the EEC regional policies, Antonio Giolitti, a Socialist, noted: "Not to participate in the monetary treaty would mean bearing the entire costs of supporting the lira on our own shoulders and, furthermore, accept the principle of a two-track Europe—the nations within the snake and those outside."[53]

Italy's decision to join the EMS was influenced as well by fear that the agreement between Paris and Bonn might lead to a joint German-French dominance of the EEC, while the demands of Great Britain to protect some of its special interests could shift the Community's emphasis in favor of northern Europe. While in previous decades Italian criticism had been aroused by de Gaulle's attitudes (although an opponent of the principle of majority rule, he had crippled the institutional functions of the EEC with his "empty chair" policy), Italian public opinion now feared the agreement between President Giscard d'Estaing and Chancellor Helmut Schmidt was a first sign of a Paris-Bonn preferential axis in the leadership of the EEC. After all, resistance of French foreign policy leaders to giving up the principle of national sovereignty had become weaker. The European strategy of Giscard d'Estaing allowed the Paris government to strengthen the structures of the Community without giving up its dreams of grandeur, by making France the "constant proponent" of the EEC on the large issues of world affairs, with the support of the economically stronger, but politically and militarily weaker Germany. That was not, however, Italy's only reason for concern. Germany's extraordinary development augured a Europe "on two tracks" (regional differences between Hamburg and Calabria, expressed in per capita gross social product, were at least 5 to 1). This situation offered little hope that the Bonn government would agree to support less developed regions with its aid.

For Italy, this posed the threat of being elbowed, in one way or another, into the "second tier" of the Community. For this reason as well the admission of Spain, Greece and Portugal into the Group of Nine was held to be imperative to balance the preponderance of the northern European nations. However, if Italy's rulers believed it was essential to expand the Community from nine to twelve to avoid the danger of Franco-German dominance, the economic impact of such a move was a different matter. The sensitive point was the preferential treatment the "strong regions" of the Community had previously enjoyed and which they now were loath to give up. As the protectionism favoring farm products of the continent could not be expanded to include the products typical of Mediterranean nations because consumers were spared additional price increases, there were plans to pacify Mediterranean producers by means of special measures (absorption of overproduction while covering the real costs of production, compensation for agricultural products used, price supports for semolina and olive oil). These proposed measures, however, turned out to be incompatible with long-term needs to modernize agriculture in southern Italy.

Therefore the Italian government hesitated for a long time before it gave its full agreement to expansion of the EEC to include Spain, Greece and Portugal, even though it was in favor in principle. In reality, Italy, feeling itself to be already disadvantaged by EEC agricultural policies, was concerned about even greater competition from the products of the Mediterranean region. Therefore, one of the two Italian EEC representatives (the Socialist Giolitti) proposed a policy of regional economic planning (as part of integration of the three Mediterranean nations into the EEC). Natali, Italy's other representative and a Christian Democrat, expressed a more cautious attitude, without, however, rejecting it a priori. He wanted to negotiate terms for membership point by point while simultaneously reexamining the agricultural rules of the Community.

The importance to Italy of revising farm policy can be seen from the fact that there were no differences about this in content between the strongest party in the government and the opposition. Both were concerned about the reactions of the various farm groups which, although representing only a smaller portion of the working population, were a significant force in their parliamentary representation and in votes. For the minister of agriculture, Christian Democrat Giovanni Marcora (who fought real battles on behalf of Italy in Brussels), there was no doubt of the need to overcome the imbalance between the "defense" of agriculture of northern and central Europe and the "exclusion" of that of southern Europe. "Therefore we have attempted, without arrogance," he said in November 1972, "to restore a minimum of balance between the so-called continental products and the products of the Mediterranean nations."[54] Communist Emanuele Macaluso was of the same opinion, identifying the agricultural policies of the EEC as one of the factors that "have contributed most to the imbalances." The reasons, he said, were the Community preferences for "meat, butter and generally all dairy products, wheat and sugar and we must therefore buy them in the EEC for that price, and large amounts are being accumulated. In France and Holland, some parts of agriculture produce only for storage, because the price is guaranteed."[55]

This unequal treatment became even more intolerable because Italy, together with England, was the nation contributing much more financially to the EEC than France and Germany. The bottom line was that Italy, which was still seen as one of the "less rich" nations in the Community, had a negative balance of nearly 100 billion lira, i.e., it had spent far more than it had received in sector aid and in contributions for participation in the new European currency system.

In this climate of bitterness and disappointment, the first European elections, held in June 1979, did not bring the real changes in true unification for which the federalist movement of Europe had hoped. The elections to the European Parliament were more like a broad opinion poll on a national level of how voters changed since the election a month earlier in their support of the governing and the opposition parties. On the other hand, the decision by the Council of Ministers the following November rejecting the changes in some laws proposed by the European Parliament led to new anger and disappointment. There was even talk of a true crisis in the Community in all sectors: taxes, institutions and policy. A tax crisis, because 70 percent of the Community's budget already was being spent for support of agricultural prices (a sector accounting for hardly more than 10 percent of the Western European population) to the disadvantage of the higher priority sectors (regions, energy, industry); an institutional crisis because the Executive Commission had become a "cattle market," and the new democratic Parliament seemed destined to be powerless. And, finally, political crisis because at a moment when the Community more than ever needed a common answer to difficult problems (energy crisis, unemployment, regional imbalances), solutions that would have led from the "negative union" of the Common Market to a "positive union" of an economic and currency union, the clash of contradictory interests and votes crippled the Community's ability to function and its future growth.[56]

For Italians, the low point in relations with the EEC was reached following the Council of Ministers' conference in Athens in December 1982, when the attempt, started in Stuttgart six months earlier with the "solemn declaration" to eliminate the conflicts, failed miserably because of irreconcilable differences between the governments about agricultural policies. This initiative, corresponding in broad outlines to the "European Contract" proposed by German Foreign Minister Genscher and European Parliament President Emilio Colombo in November 1981, had been ensured Italy's full support. It dealt with the formal obligation, signed by the heads of the member states of the Community, to draft a unification treaty for the European Union no later than June 30, 1988, following a complete review of the entire question.

This explains the discomfort in Italy following the repeated, wearying battles over agriculture ("for a pail of milk," as some commentators wrote). The image that seemed to emerge was of a divided and short-sighted Europe, with each nation attempting to make a few pennies for itself at the expense of the others, while all of them together forgot about the greater issue of forming a comprehensive power potential that could hold its own against the United States and Japan in the open battle of postindustrial nations.[57] For the first time, leaders of Italian industry openly took up positions against the Community, charging it with continuing decline instead of promoting renewal. One such leader, Gianni Agnelli, the chairman of Fiat, complained there was no uniform industrial policy for research and technology that could close the steadily growing gap with the other great Western industrial powers. Another, Olivetti chief Carlo De Benedetti, deplored the alarming development of a "continuous exodus of money and top people from Europe to the United States."[58]

The Brussels summit meeting in March 1984 improved matters only in part. After the worst disagreements had been patched up to avoid complete ruin, the European governments once again were busy with the same problems of allocating each nation's share of sacrifice. It had been viewed by all as unavoidable before, but each still calculated sacrifice in his own way. This time it was primarily Margaret Thatcher, who demanded a drastic reduction in British contributions and who was ready to put the EEC's ability to function into question, who was the target of Italian criticism. But the Franco-German agreement caused considerable apprehension, as it seemed intended exclusively to form a bloc in order to defend self-interests. The suspicions and fears of the Rome government were confirmed by the fact that Italian farmers were to bear the costs of the solution found by the "agricultural compromise." Actually, those costs should have been allotted to those producing surpluses who, along with the nations of the old "green Europe" favoring unlimited guarantees, had ruined the finances of the Community.

Bettino Craxi had been president since August 1983, but it appeared that Italy and France, despite the presence of a Socialist at the head of each government, could not come to a complete agreement. In Paris, François Mitterand, following his victory in the presidential election of 1981 and the success of his party in Parliament, finally broke the coalition with the PCF and won the same decision Italy had taken in 1978: to remain in the currency snake in full knowledge of all the consequences and to turn in the direction of more free trade, taking a number of steps to cut public spending and hold down the wage-price spiral. Craxi's government had tried to bring Italy on a par with the other EEC partners in almost the same way. Nonetheless, Craxi and Mitterand were still divided by all the old controversies they had never been able to settle between Italy and France. Rome had never overcome the suspicion that Paris gave preference to its relations with the Federal Republic of Germany and Great Britain, while Paris, for its part, feared that American influence on Italy was greater than that of the European Community in Italy.

It became possible only in February 1984 at a meeting between the two heads of government in Milan, to settle these knotty problems, setting the stage for agreement at the subsequent Brussels conference. It also helped establish a common front in support of a European constitution, which was ratified by a large majority of the Strasbourg Parliament in February, thanks to the efforts of Altiero Spinelli. Taking up the tiresome work of European unification again, Spinelli had founded the "Crocodile Club" within the Parliament of Europe in July 1988 to mobilize forces that could exert the necessary pressure on the European governments.

Backed by Mitterand's commitment that May in Brussels to find a "political justification for the existence of the Community," Spinelli's stubborn determination (he was re-elected to the Strasbourg Parliament in June 1984) was finally rewarded precisely at the most critical moment for the Community—just as discussion about a European Union was resumed.[59] The conference of European governments meeting in Luxembourg in 1985 produced the "United European Accord." The Community's basic flaw—veto power in matters of "essential interest" allowing each nation to block all the others—had become insupportable. Thus it seemed absurd that a popularly elected parliament should have only an advisory function. All of Italy's significant political forces, from the Christian Democrats, to the Socialist Party and the Communist Party, were united in both of these goals: the need for action based on European unification, and giving effective decision-making authority to the European Parliament.

For its part, Italian diplomacy played an important role during Italy's EEC presidency in settling the difficult negotiations for expanding the EEC to include Spain and Portugal in March 1985. Adding to the total political power of the EEC and moving its center of influence further south outweighed, in the view of Italy's government, serious concerns that the admission of the two Iberian nations posed for Italian agriculture. What remained was to put into action the project adopted by Parliament sixteen months earlier, i.e., providing the Commission and the Parliament with broader powers and replacing the crippling practice of deciding by unanimous vote with the majority vote. Together with the decision early in 1986 to expand the Community from nine members to twelve, this was the most important point of discussion at the summit meeting in Milan in May 1986. The document prepared by the ad hoc committee (formed immediately after the Fontainebleau summit of June 1984), named for its president Irish Senator Dodge, agreed in substance with the proposals of Altiero Spinelli calling for a "qualitative improvement" of the EEC and proposed the introduction of a simple majority vote together with the introduction of the Common Market.

The Milan summit therefore had special importance. Not because it had solved all of the problems that remained, but because it demonstrated a fundamental convergence of the various governments around Mitterand's initiative for a new European unification treaty, even if some of the details and nuances were different. The fact that the Socialist group had become the strongest party in the Strasbourg Parliament after the most recent elections made things easier. The representatives of the Socialists had come to recognize the necessity of accelerating political unification if Europe was not to belong exclusively to the technocrats and boards of directors of private and public high finance. In particular, Italian Socialists insisted that the High Council of the Governments, and their political representatives (the Council of Ministers and the Commission of the EEC) no longer exercise its prerogatives. It was to be forced, while formally retaining its rights, to delegate these powers more and more to high administrative offices and to technical commissions to be formed for the purpose. They would take over initiating and executing Community functions. For that reason, the conditions needed to develop a true representative democracy had to be established within the framework of the Community, so that a strong government also was confronted by a strong parliament, and vice versa. On this point there was also agreement with representatives of the Christian Democrats, not only because they had been Europeanists for a long time, but also because they were convinced that political union was indispensable for a prosperous Europe that also had solidarity as its goals.

While Socialists and Christian Democrats agreed in essence on the necessity for a unification based on the principles of more democracy and decision sharing, all political forces shared the belief that, in response to the enormous changes in the world situation, Europe had to demonstrate a more effective presence. The new dynamics of Gorbachev's Soviet Union and the tendency of the United States to monopolize the dialogue with the Kremlin without consulting its allies overseas were additional reasons why the governments and the public opinion of nations that in the past had been skeptical about all ideas going beyond national boundaries began to look with new interest at a more decisive "Europeanization." The Italian government, as well, believed that for Europe the moment had come for major decisions. It would have to meet the challenge of history and become a point of attraction for the nations of the Eastern bloc who had taken the path to reform, and at the same time become an important factor for other nations (from the United States to Japan), one with which, for better or worse, one had to count. In the light of these considerations, Italy agreed to support the strategy of the chairman of the EEC Commission, Jacques Delors, so that political-institutional unification could be taken up quickly.

The participation of the Italian government at the European Conference in Luxembourg in December 1985 was, in fact, decisive for the adoption of the United Europe Accord, which marked the end of a long period of decline and paralysis of the Community's institutions. That accord, signed in February 1986, took up the goal of the European Union once more, even if its execution was made dependent on cooperation of the signatory states in foreign policy and on "provision of sufficient means." Initially it set December 1992 as the effective date for the Common Market and proposed that five years after the Accords come into force the parties would have the opportunity to revise the "Rules for Foreign Policy Cooperation." As to the monetary union, the governments indicated they wanted to go ahead with further action. According to what the proponents of the Accord had hoped, the European institutions of the "second generation"—more efficient and more democratic—would thus be brought to life, while making the internal market more perfect would eventually lead to an economic and monetary union. Furthermore, the new forms and decision-making processes with respect to the environment and the Community's working conditions were to give the Community an indispensable "social dimension," while a "harmonious development" would allow the EEC to enjoy the positive effects of the Common Market to the fullest.

Altiero Spinelli, whose forty-year battle for the European ideal had been his life's work, died in May 1986. He had lived to see the project to convert the EEC into a political-economic union revived; only a short time ago the idea was thought to be too risky. But it was not the realization of all his hopes. The United Europe Accord left the most important powers in the hands of the Council of Ministers and reconfirmed the principle of unanimous agreement. Had the project of a European Union treaty been accepted by the member states, this would have opened the way for the rapid completion of European unification on a federal basis. For that reason, Spinelli, in his last appearance before the Commission of the Strasbourg Parliament on February 4, proposed that the new Parliament of Europe, to be elected in 1989, be charged with a precise "mandate for writing a constitution" for the reform of the EEC with the aid of a referendum in as many nations as possible to set the proper guidelines. He was convinced that the European Parliament would have a chance only if it was able to mobilize public opinion effectively in its favor.[60]

Spinelli's death left a permanent gap in the ranks of the European movement, not only in Italy. As a man of the highest moral principles, he had been able to combine passionate personal commitment with great ability, with extreme realism (without ever losing the coherence of his ideals); he used every opportunity to further the project of European unification on a multinational and democratic basis. In Italy, the political and spiritual heritage of Spinelli, who was recognized as the intellectual father of the new Europe, was taken up not only by the federalist movement, but also by large parts of public opinion and by important representatives of the government and the opposition. A survey taken six months after the Accords had become effective indicated that the Italians were more inclined than any of the other citizens of the Community to give the Strasbourg Parliament the mandate to prepare a new constitution. This result was confirmed in June and December 1986, a few months after the election of the new European Parliament, when a second and third survey each showed that two thirds of those questioned agreed with the need for a multinational government responsible to the European Parliament.[61]

Increasing trust also spread in industrial circles. If the agricultural policies had turned out to be significantly more expensive than had been assumed, the European monetary system had turned out to be a useful instrument for a nation such as Italy (which had reached a 20 percent inflation rate) to take the right corrective actions. The need to develop industrial and scientific cooperation was much more widely recognized. There were far more official documents of the Confindustria (the organization representing Italian industrialists) proposing regulations to improve competitiveness of European firms (by mergers, intercompany agreements or business combinations) and by defining opportunities for public intervention with clearer and more enduring common standards. Italy was represented in nearly fifty scientific research projects by "Eureka," the joint program started at the international conference in Hanover in November 1985. Italy was to participate in 1988–90, by providing additional funds, particularly in robot technology, laser techniques, information on technology, telecommunications, environmental technology and transportation.[62] It was in these areas that Italian industry and finance staked out a role for itself, its representatives taking part in the various preparatory phases for the monetary union. Among them were the working group headed by Tomaso Padoa Schioppa, established by mandate of Jacques Delors in April 1987, the program of the Committee for the European Monetary Union (March 1986) and the project of the European central bank system of the "Altiero Spinelli Committee for the European Union" (May 1988).

The June 1989 elections for the Parliament of Europe provided an additional occasion to demonstrate the Europeanism of the Italians. The political parties as well as the majority of public opinion spoke out in favor of going ahead with the development of the Community as it was proposed by "Project Spinelli." The government also promised to support the petitions voted in the referendum of June 18, 1989, and the resolutions subsequently adopted by Parliament the following November, which renewed the call for the formulation of the constitution of the United States of Europe to be drafted by the European Parliament.

On the other hand, the radical changes of the world scene and the political configuration of the old continent resulting from the fall of the Berlin Wall and the dissolution of the Communist regimes in the Eastern bloc also intensified in Italy demands and initiatives to accelerate the European unification process. This was thought indispensable in order to restore equilibrium in international relations and to create conditions which would check the virus of resurging nationalism and social instability.[63]

At this point in time, all interest was focused on the problem of Germany's reunification. The Council of Europe took up the matter for the first time at its conference in Strasbourg in December 1989. On that occasion, Italian Foreign Minister Andreotti, in agreement with Mitterand, preferred the formulation "free expression of the people's will," a more political and less binding phrase than that used by Chancellor Kohl, "free self-determination." However, both sides freely agreed to the Bonn proposal after making sure that the process of German reunification was tied expressly to the development of the EEC, i.e., that it would take place together with and within the framework of the EEC.[64] On the same occasion, Italian diplomats supported Mitterand's position in the Community to give concrete aid to the East European nations to avoid deterioration of the economic crisis and to avert conflicts between the various population groups.

The Italian and the French governments also agreed on the need to harmonize the social policies of the EEC nations, something that, like the monetary union, had been rejected up to then by Margaret Thatcher's Britain. For a long time, Italians had been almost alone in proposing the idea of an expanded and more comprehensive EEC, which would not be limited exclusively to the function of a free trade zone. Now, more than ever, they believed that the problem of social and territorial inequality, with a massive part of the EEC at its southern border separated from the rest of the Community, had to be attacked decisively.[65] There was yet another question of profound significance for the Italian representatives—the matter of a "social charter" frequently posed by the trade unions. It was to establish common rules for industrial relations and labor policies on the basis of criteria that would make economic legislation compatible with greater social justice and worker participation, all taking into account the important changes taking place in the labor market because of new technologies and the planned production processes.

For all these reasons, the summit meeting of December 1990 in Rome marked an important stage in the Community's development. Following the meeting of the heads of state and of government of the EEC member states, both international governmental conferences charged with the tasks of creating the institutional basis for the political and economic union and for the monetary union of the Twelve took up their work. The significance of both conferences therefore was equal to that in Messina thirty-five years earlier, which prepared the treaties founding the EEC. A definitive program was drafted after two additional meetings to be held in Luxembourg and in Holland, to set the time schedule and consider the modalities of establishing a central bank and a single monetary unit, together with other topics, i.e., joint foreign policy, security, extent of EEC rights and powers, and modification of institutional structures.[66]

Beyond the need to help the Soviet Union, already in the throes of dissolution, and the nations of East-Central Europe, the Gulf crisis also placed pressure on the EEC governments to speed up political and military unification. Furthermore, the "changing of the guard" in Downing Street with the departure of Margaret Thatcher and the arrival of the more pragmatic John Major, offered a good opportunity for strengthening the Community. The Italian government proposed to include the British objections, which remained controversial in some points, in a joint declaration so that nothing would jeopardize the chances of a European union and Great Britain would not be isolated. The six months under Italian chairmanship closed with the opening of the governmental conference on economic and monetary union and on political union, which resulted in the Maastricht treaties of December 1991.

Unfortunately, the Maastricht compromise agreement did not lead to the birth of a federal, but rather a "communal" European Union, and, unfortunately, a "card trick" was used with respect to the hottest topics. Thus, the Council of Ministers of the Union was assigned the task of "defining in unanimity the questions that were to be agreed by majority vote." The two points, therefore, which normally measure how substantive and firm the area of agreement really is, now allowed room for evasion. In addition, there was no joint agreement about social policies (except in a special protocol that bound eleven of the twelve members), while an "opting out" clause would leave it up to Britain to decide whether it wants to join the monetary union when the moment arrives in 1997 or 1999.

In any case, the British government for the first time shared the view that the European unification process is "irreversible," even if London continues to reject a "United States of Europe," and every conceivable effort must be made to standardize the policies of the individual EEC nations without, however, permitting the Brussels administration to gain the upper hand or to centralize all decision-making. Other important results of these treaties include a precise timetable for the monetary union and the award of far-reaching rights to the West European Union (WEU), although in dependence on NATO. With respect to the latter result, the solution proposed by Italy in agreement with Great Britain, giving the WEU a "bridge function" between the European Union and NATO won out over the "armed arm" concept for the WEU (without an American presence in Europe it would not be in a position to guarantee the security of the Western nations) which France and Germany had wanted. In the meantime, these two countries decided to form a Franco-German military corps. In other important points of the treaties, the Italian government reaped what it had sown in Rome, especially in relation to the new powers of the European Parliament (it was given the veto right on some important questions, as well the right to exercise control over the Commission) and on the harmonization of the social policies of the individual nations (to the extent that the protocol of the Eleven eliminated the obstacles that held up the work of the Community in this respect).

The results of the Maastricht summit and the role taken by its representatives there were largely applauded in Italy. Although the treaties concluded in that small Dutch town are the result of unavoidable compromises, they nevertheless provided for the transfer of many important decisions from a national level to that of the Community and at the same time give greater power to the European Parliament, preparing the path for realizing the European Union. With this goal in mind, the Rome government of Minister President Andreotti and Foreign Minister De Michelis offered no objections to the "conditions clause" planned for the economic and monetary union, although it will force Italy to take especially strict measures to reduce its rate of inflation to the EEC average and to adjust the relationship between national debt and gross domestic product to the level of the other advanced EEC nations. To the contrary, the Italian representatives were among the strongest defenders of this obligation, opposing the choice of "opting out" (the right to use a special exception clause).

In fact, Italy now faces a much more difficult task than it did at the end of the 1970s, when it joined the European monetary snake, if it is to meet its obligations to the EEC. In relation to inflation and to national debt as well, the Maastricht treaties require extraordinary measures to reduce public expenditures drastically and to hold the wage-price spiral within the defined bounds. At the same time, effective steps must be taken to make the Italian economy more competitive by modernizing the infrastructure and relieving industry of certain social costs they bear unjustifiably.[67] The "question of the South" also must be considered; it cannot be reduced simply to the North-South differential, but must include the fight against organized crime.

Italy intends to work together with the other most important member states of the EEC to create a new and greater political and economic Europe. Our nation has always, since the beginning, made a significant contribution to the ideals of Europeanism. Today, since the break up of the Eastern bloc,

Italy is deeply committed to the support of East European nations on the path to democratization and economic renewal. Similarly, Italy is at the forefront in the matter of solving the problem of external debt, which threatens to destroy the developing nations and which has a serious impact on the industrial nations. Among the founders of the European Community and at the center of important currents of international policy, Italy—as a natural link between Europe, the Balkans and the Middle East—is a fundamental component for stability of the Mediterranean region and thus of the postbipolarized world. Within the European Community it represents a polity of 57 million people, almost a quarter of the EEC population.

The step toward the new Europe as it emerges from the plans for the economic and political union, forces Italy not only to restructure its public finances, but also to introduce some imperative institutional reforms in order to secure two fundamental characteristics of a modern democracy, stability and change. Just as indispensable is a radical reform to return morality to the political and administrative systems that will lead the political parties back to their original functions of representing society as a whole and safeguarding the public interest, thus ensuring just and rigorous administration of public affairs.

Italy therefore is in a complex phase of transition. The connection to Europe demands enormous efforts, a kind of "second reconstruction" of the nation; it will surely not be easy. Italian society has had to master other emergencies (notably its rebirth from the ruins of the war, mobilization against the attacks of terrorism, the battle against double-digit inflation). It is a fact that Italy has always developed extraordinary capabilities to catch up at the critical moment. It has the resources and energies necessary to overcome today's challenges and difficulties as well, so long as the nation is not without able and prudent political leadership with which its citizens can identify.

Notes

1. G. Agnelli/A. Cabiati, *Federazione europea o Lega delle Nazioni?* (Turin, 1918).

2. For a better understanding of the political context that favored the federalist orientation of the Fiat founder, see V. Castronovo, *Giovanni Agnelli.* (Turin, 1971), pp. 132–135, 159–162, 725; and by the same author, *Giovanni Agnelli e l'idea federalista.* In *Atti del Convegno* "Alle origini dell'europismo in Piemonte," Fondazione Luigi Einaudi, Turin, November 28–29, 1991.

3. The Treitschke text cited by Agnelli and Cabiati is *Politik: Vorlesungen gehalten an der Universität zu Berlin* (Berlin, 1897). For an analysis of the German doctrine of the power state, see F. Meinecke *Die Idee der Statsräson in der Geschichte* (Munich, 1924).

4. Agnelli/Cabiati, op. cit. p. 122.

5. Ibid. p. 1.

6. L. Einaudi "La Società delle Nazioni è un ideale possibile," in *Corriere della Sera*, January 5, 1918, and Ibid, "Il dogma della sovranità e l'idea della Società delle nazioni." Ibid. December 28, 1918.

7. L. Einaudi, op. cit., p. 12.

8. Ibid. pp. 16–17.

9. Ibid. p. 24. Einaudi presented his thoughts in a review of the Agnelli/Cabiati book in "La Riforma Sociale," XXIX (11–12, November–December, 1918), pp. 661–662, with the claim that it would have been more careful to limit oneself to establish immediately a kind of Roman *Commonwealth*, to be organized on a federal basis, jointly with other regional groups, to aspire to the Wilson union of states. But in his subsequent writings he modified this position and accepted the idea of a European Union that also included Germany without reservations.

10. L. Einaudi, "Federazione europea o società delle nazioni (1918)," in G. Prezzolini, ed., *Gli ideali di un economista. Quaderni della Voce.* (Florence, 1921).

11. A. Colombo "Realtà e utopia dell'idea d'Europa," in *Storia e dossier VI* (September 1991), pp. 74 ff.

12. For better placement of Einaudi's writings and those of Agnelli and Cabiati in the history of the idea of the European Union, see C.H. Pegg, "Der Gedanke der europäischen Einordnung während des Ersten Weltkrieges und zu Beginn der zwanziger Jahre," in *Europa-Archiv 1962;* 21:749–758; and W. Lipgens "Europäische Einigungsidee 1923–1930 und Briands Europaplan im Urteil der deutschen Akten," in *Historische Zeitschrift 1960;* CIII:46–89, 316–363, but especially pp. 46–63.

13. For a complete analysis of Europeanistic currents in Italy in the 1850s, see M. Albertini *Il Risorgimento e l'unità europea* (Naples, 1979), and, particularly concerning Mazzini's internationalism, A. Chitibatelli "Mazzini précurseur de l'idée de la Fédération Européenne," in *Bulletin des Centre Interdisciplinaire de Recherches sur l'Italie de l'Université de Strasbourg*, January 1974.

14. P. Gobetti, *Scritti politici* (Turin, 1960), pp. 36–42.

15. C. Malandrino, "Gobetti e Treves due approci critici al progetto degli Stati Uniti d'Europa," in Atti del Concegno "Alle origini dell'europeismo in Piemonte." Turin, Fondazione Luigi Einaudi, November 28–29, 1991.

16. L. Levi, "L'internazionalismo operaio e l'unità europea," in ibid.

17. For a review of the development of Europeanistic ideals from the 1920s to World War II in Italy, see A. Colombo, op. cit.; and F. Federici, "Dal Manifesto di Ventotene all'unione europea," in *Ragionamenti 1991;* I:82 ff.

18. R. Monteleone, "Le ragioni teoriche del rifiuto della parola d'ordine degli Stati Uniti d'Europa nel movimento comunista internazionale."

19. "Zur Parole von den Vereinigten Staaten von Europa" [The slogan of the United States of Europe]. *Sozial-Demokrat* Sept. 5, Aug. 23, 1915; and *Der Imperialismus als höchstes Stadium des Kapitalismus*, esp. chapters VII, III, IX.

20. For a biography of Spinelli, see E. Paolini, *Altiero Spinelli* (Bologna, 1988).

21. For the early history and content of the "Manifesto di Ventotene," see A. Spinelli, *Il Manifesto di Ventotene,* with a foreword by N. Bobbio (Bologna, 1991); for a comment on the commemorative address at Ventotene by the chairman of the Italian Senate, Giovanni Spandolini on September 7, 1991, see his "L'Europa di Ventotene," *La Stampa,* September 7, 1991.

22. A. Spinelli, *Come no tentato di diventare saggio,* Vol. 1. (Bologna, 1984).

23. For a biography of Ernesto Rossi, see P. Ignazi, ed. *Ernesto Rossi: Una utopia concreta* (Milan, 1991).

24. See N. Bobbio, Il federalismo nel dibattito politico e culturale della Resistenza. Op. cit. Spinelli's writings from the war period are collected in A. Spinelli, *Dagli Stati sovrani agli Stati Uniti d'Europa* (Florence, 1956).

25. L. Einaudi, *La guerra del'unità europea* (Milan, 1948) p. 141.

26. Adstans, *Alcide De Gasperi in der italienischen Außenpolitik* (Milan, 1953); see also M.R. De Gasperi, ed. *De Gasperi und Europa* (Brescia, 1979).

27. C. Sforza, *Cinque anni a Palazzo Chigi: La politica estera italiana dal 1947 al 1951* (Rome, 1952).

28. For a biography of Sforza, see L. Zeno, *Ritratto di Carlo Sforza* (Florence, 1975).

29. S. Pistone, "Carlo Sforza e l'unità europea," in *Diplomazia e storia delle relazioni internazionali. Studi in onore di Enrico Sferra* (Padua, 1991), p. 615.

30. Concerning the FBE, see L. Levi and S. Pistone, eds., *Trent'anni di vita del Movimento Federalista Europeo* (Milan, 1973).

31. See S. Pistone. op. cit. p. 616; see also A. Varsori, *Il patto di Bruxelles (1948) tra integrazione europea e alleanza atlantica* (Rome, 1988).

32. Ibid, p. 620. See also L. Levi, *L'unificazione europea. Trent'anni di storia* (Turin, 1979).

33. See B. Olivi, "L'Italia e il mercato europeo," in *Istituto Affari Internazionali. La politica estera della repubblica italiana,* Vol. II (Milan, 1967), pp. 493 ff.

34. L. Einaudi, *Lo scrittoio del Presidente* (Turin, 1956). For a better understanding of Einaudi's views about the European Union, see M. Albertini, *Il federalismo. Antologia e definizione* (Turin, 1986) and L. Levi, *Federalismo e integrazione europea* (Palermo, 1970).

35. For criticism by the federalist movement of the gradualistic approach, see L. Levi, *Verso gli Stati Uniti d'Europa. Analisi dell'integrazione europea* (Naples, 1979).

36. Cited by S. Pistone, op. cit., p. 627.

37. See G. Vedovano, *Politica estera italiana e scelta europea* (Florence, 1979); G. Prado, *Difesa europea e stato europea. La vicenda della CED nelle carte della delegazione italiana (1950–1952)* (Milan, 1990). For a general analysis, see S. Pistone, "La convergenza fra interessi nazionale italiani e integrazione europea nella politica di De Gasperi," in *L'Italia e l'europa,* VI, No. 12, 1979.

38. See E. Rogati, "L'influenza del federalisti sulla politica europea dell'Italia." In op. cit.

39. See M. Scelba, *Per l'Italia o per l'Europa* (Rome, 1990).

40. For this complex of topics, see B. Vigezzi, "L'Italia e i problemi della politica di

potenza: Dalle crisi della CED alle crisi Suez" in *Storia contemporanea 1991;* XXII:221 ff.; and *Annuario di politica internazionale ISPI for 1954, 1955 and 1956* (Milan, 1955, 1957, 1957).

41. Reproduced at Ibid., p. 252.

42. See S. Romano, "Per una politica della cultura europea: limiti e possibilità," in *Città e regione,* Florence, February, 1982, pp. 10–11; and the record of the "L'identità culturale europea" conference, Venice, Fondazione Cini 1984; 3:29–31.

43. See V. Castronovo, "La storia economica," in *Storia d'Italia,* Vol. 4, pp. 402–403, 1975.

44. See S. Vinci, "Il ruolo delle esportazioni nello sviluppo economico italiano nel periodo 1951–1962," in A. Graziani, *Lo Sviluppo di un'economia aperta* (Naples, 1969); R. Zanchetti, "Il principio dell'economia aperta e la struttura degli scambi italiani con l'estero," in P. d'Alauro, ed., *La componente estera dell'economia italiana* (Genoa, 1969).

45. See S. Pistone's introduction to A. Spinelli, *Una strategia per gli Stati Uniti d'Europa* (Bologna, 1969), p. 22.

46. Concerning this phase of Spinelli's work, see A. Spinelli, *L'avventura europea.* (Bologna, 1972).

47. See Mario Salvatorelli's interview of Spinelli in *La Stampa,* July 31, 1973.

48. "Noi e l'Europa," *La Stampa* July 7, 1974.

49. B. Olivi, *Da un Europa all'altra* (Milan, 1979).

50. G. Maspoli, Ci "hanno trattati da parenti poveri," *La Stampa* March 23, 1977.

51. Concerning this difficult period of the EEC, see R. Perissich, "La Comunità europea del compromesso di Lussemburgo al Rapporto Tindemans," in *Instituto Affari Internazionali. La politica estera italiana* (Milan, 1977).

52. On the relationship between Spinelli and the Communist Party, see A. Spinelli, *La mia battaglia per un'Europa diversa* (Manduria, 1979).

53. *L'Espresso,* December 10, 1978. Also see A. Mosconi, *Dalla fine di Bretton Woods alla rinascita del Sistema Monetario Europeo* (Milan, 1980).

54. In *La due Europe,* "Nuova Società," (Turin), November 1978, p. 33; also B. Spinelli, "I Vizi dell'Europa verde," *La Repubblica,* January 18, 1979.

55. See *La due Europe,* op. cit., p. 35.

56. Concerning the problems of the EEC during this period, see P.V. Dastoli, *1992: Europa senza frontiere?* (Milan, 1989), pp. 51 ff.

57. M.L. Salvadori, *L'alternativa dell'Europa* (Rome-Bari, 1985).

58. "La vecchia Europa è morta per sempre." *La Repubblica,* December 10, 1983.

59. Concerning Spinelli's activities as a member of the Parliament of Europe, see A. Spinelli, *Discorsi al Parlamento europeo 1976–1986* (Bologna, 1987).

60. R.A. Cangelosi, "Dal progetto di trattato di Spinelli all'Atto Unico Europeo. Cronata di una riforma mancata," in *Affari Sociali* (Milan, 1987).

61. A. Flores d'Arcais, "Una constituzione per l'Europa," *La Repubblica,* December 16, 1988.

62. V. Grementieri and A. Papisca, eds., *Europa 1992 La sfida per la ricerca e l'università* (Padua, 1989).

63. L. Guazzone, ed., "L'Europa degli anni Novanta," Vol. 1. *La geopolitica del cambiamento* (Milan, 1991).

64. A. Guatelli, "Si alla autodeterminazione per i tedeschi," *Corriere della Sera*, December 9, 1989.

65. P. Saraceno, "Mezzogiorno d'Europa," *La Repubblica*, October 4, 1988.

66. For this complex of topics, see P.V. Castaldi/G. Vieella, *La nuova Europa. Dalla Comunità all'Unione* (Bologna, 1992), pp. 15 ff.

67. The problems remaining to be solved on various levels are the subject of a comprehensive economic-political literature, which is beyond the scope of this article.

The British Approach
to Europe

William Wallace

The British Isles lie off the west coast of Europe: separate from the continent, yet closely linked. The fabric of British history has been woven out of the crossing and recrossing of British and European influences: of interactions between the different nations and regions of the British Isles, and interactions between the British Isles as a whole and the different nations of the European continent—Danes and Normans, French and Spanish, Dutch and Germans. Britain is unquestionably a European country, but its people do not feel entirely European.

In Europe, but not entirely of Europe; the history, and the historical myths, of England, Scotland, Ireland and Wales revolve around that theme. For Scotland and Ireland, from the Middle Ages on, the continent offered allies against English dominance: support from France or Spain the only way to assert independence. For England the threat of continental alliances with the other kingdoms reinforced determination to unite the British Isles into a single state. Threatened by rebellion in Ireland, with Mary Stuart (Queen of Scots) closely allied with the Catholic Party in France, the government of Elizabethan England had good cause to feel ambivalent about European entanglements as any of its twentieth-century successors. A united kingdom, under James Stuart, resolved the Scottish threat, though the problem of Ireland remained, continuing to trouble British policies even now.

The sense of separateness from Europe, of a *Story of England* (the title of Seeley's influential history of 1895) which marked the island out from less fortunate peoples across the Channel, goes back to the Reformation. Shakespeare's patriotic imagery fitted the circumstances of a protestant state threatened by the Catholic powers of Spain and France:

> This happy breed of men, this little world,
> This precious stone set in the silver sea,
> Which serves it in the office of a wall . . .
> Against the envy of less happier lands,
> This blessed plot, this earth, this realm, this England . . .[1]

This concept of English exceptionalism, as handed down to those who directed British foreign policy for a generation after 1945, was widened and deepened by more recent history. The idea of the world outside Europe as an alternative to European involvement is a legacy of nineteenth-century imperialism, grafted onto earlier themes of English identity and reinforced by the experience of two world wars—above all World War II, in which British experience differed so sharply from that of other European countries. The idea of a special relationship between Britain and America, the Anglo-Saxon powers, was grafted onto Britain's self-image only in the 1930s and 1940s: the most important counterweight to acceptance of European commitments over the past fifty years, but also the most recent branch of British identity.

Anthony Eden's declaration in 1950 that "if forced to choose between Europe and the open sea," Britain would always choose the open sea, was soaked in this sense of Britain's history and destiny. When Hugh Gaitskell in 1962 spoke of accession to the EEC as the betrayal of "1,000 years of British history," he linked the myth of ancient Saxon liberties to Britain's civilizing and democratizing mission in the Commonwealth.[2] Margaret Thatcher's frequent references to the continuity and exceptional character of Britain's seven-hundred-year-old Parliament drew upon the patriotic images of the 1940s, on Edmund Burke's defense of English liberties against the revolutionary challenge of the French revolution, and the tradition on which both rested of a medieval England more democratic and more rooted in law than other European states. Prime Minister Thatcher's generation accepted and assumed that there had always been a natural partnership between Britain and America, the strongest of the "English-speaking peoples" who shared this heritage.

Several layers of historical analysis are needed to explain the ambivalence of contemporary British governments and public opinion toward the concept of "Europe"—a united Europe, into which Britain should be integrated—espoused by their West European neighbors. The first takes us a long way back, into the history of the British peoples as interpreted and reinterpreted in the great period of creative national history toward the end of the nineteenth century. Most Scots and Welsh, united to the story of England by their shared Protestantism, their common experience of the industrial revolution and the benefits they gained from imperial expansion, were content to accept their place in this English-speaking world; most Irish, clinging to their Catholicism, benefiting much less from empire or industrialization, came to reject it. The second takes us back to the nineteenth century, when Britain progressively withdrew from Europe: partly as the outcome of the global conflict with an expansionist France, which left Britain dominant outside Europe and France dominant on the continent, but more decisively as the unification and industrialization of Germany pushed British goods and interests away from the continent. The third takes us through the two world wars, which followed from the breakdown of the old protestant partnership with northern Europe, and which led to the reformulation of the British national identity in terms of the English-speaking peoples. The fourth focuses on the postwar experience, as British governments and public opinion have struggled to adjust to a changing continent and to shrinking influence and markets outside Europe.

The myth of continuity in British history, of institutions and attitudes that have evolved in these islands over centuries, makes it much harder for London to manage the discontinuities of European integration. The integration of Western Europe, it will be argued below, has contributed to a crisis of British identity. The British nation-state which emerged out of the long eighteenth century struggle with France, integrated by nineteenth-century industrialization and the shared pride of prosperity and empire, its solidarity reinforced by resistance to Germany in two world wars, is losing its coherence. But the forces of integration have also challenged French, Dutch and German identity. The distinctiveness of the challenge each nation faces is to be found more in the national history each has inherited than in the dilemmas for future policy. Each now faces the need to reinterpret its national past in order to fit the circumstances of a transformed Europe.

This Realm of England

The English state that the Tudors built up from 1485 on, after half a century of intermittent civil war, had lost almost all of the French possessions of the Anglo-Norman and the Plantagenet kingdoms, which English kings and English armies had struggled through the "Hundred Years' War" from Crecy (in 1314) to Agincourt (in 1415) to defend against the French crown. Henry

VIII (1507–47) intermittently aspired to play the role of a European power, balancing between France and the Hapsburgs; but consolidation of his dynasty's insecure hold on power at home was necessarily the first priority. The port of Calais remained as an outpost on the continent, to be lost to France under Mary Tudor while England was tied to the Hapsburg alliance. "When I am dead," schoolchildren in twentieth-century England learned Mary had lamented, "Calais will be found written on my heart."

In retrospect the abandonment of English claims in France freed the English state to strengthen its hold over Britain. Wales was already firmly held: the Tudor dynasty, Welsh nobles marrying into both York and Lancastrian branches of the English royal line, strengthened what the Plantagenet conquest had won. Scotland was a continuing risk, playing alliance with England against alliance with France; the last such adventure of the "auld alliance" ended with the disaster of Flodden in 1513, in which James IV of Scotland, many of his nobles and over 10,000 others perished at the hands of the English army. Ireland was formally under the English crown, but largely beyond English control. Tudor attempts to pacify the country succeeded only in pacifying the "Pale" around Dublin, designated for English settlement.

The break with Rome was decisive in shaping the future politics of Britain, as well as in settling the pattern of England's European policy for 150 years. "This realm of England is an Empire," the Act of Supremacy of 1534 proclaimed: free from the authority not only of the German (and Hapsburg) emperor but also the Italian (and Hapsburg client) Pope in Rome. Henry VIII's kingdom was already well penetrated by reformist ideas before the break came. John Wycliffe and his followers, teaching at Oxford a century earlier, had influenced Jan Hus. Erasmus had visited London, while many of the clerks in Henry's court had studied in Rotterdam or beyond. Henry, more interested in the wealth of the monasteries than in the radical ideas reformers were advancing, thought it enough to replace Latin with English within an English Catholic church. Under his sickly son, Edward VI, the protestants made much more headway; only to be thrown back by five years of "Papist" repression after Edward's death, as Mary began a Counter-Reformation.

With the "Elizabethan settlement" the Church of England took shape, as a careful compromise between the demands of protestant Puritans and the loyalties of English Catholics. Massacres of protestants in France, and the brutalities of Spanish troops in the Netherlands, committed the English to the protestant cause; English volunteers fought with the Dutch in their war of independence. Outbreaks of religious civil war across Europe, however, warned the monarchy against giving the Puritan Party their head. The revolts in northern England and Ireland which had followed the English

Reformation were warning enough that religious radicalism might break popular loyalties. Throughout Elizabeth's reign Jesuits were active in England, ministering to those who held to the old faith; after the papal excommunication of Queen Elizabeth in 1570, they also became agents of a foreign power, working to advance the cause of Spain.

The images of England's history which entered the school books of modern mass education stem from this period: from the propagandists of the Tudor state and of the protestant cause, taken up again in the late nineteenth century by propagandists for English imperialism. Holinshed's "Chronicles," which in the service of the early Tudors blackened the reputation of Richard III and made of Agincourt an English miracle against a corrupt France, were transformed by Shakespeare into the heart of England's poetic history. Foxe's *Book of Martyrs* of 1563, which dramatically portrayed the persecutions of Mary Tudor's short reign, was to be found alongside the English Bible and Cranmer's Book of Common Prayer in almost every Elizabethan church. (Reprinted several times for nonconformist readers in the eighteenth century, it reinforced the sense of free protestant England embattled against autocratic Catholic France.) Above all, the images of the Armada, of "Good Queen Bess" rallying her troops at Tilbury while Drake harried the Spanish fleet on its slow passage up the Channel to ferry the army across from Flanders, have sunk into English literature and self-identity.

The idea of "English liberties," rooted in the soil and the Saxon character, combined during the seventeenth century with the image of protestant resistance to Catholic autocracy. James Stuart had suffered in Scotland from both Catholic plotters and protestant antimonarchists; the preaching of John Knox had harried his mother out of the country. Scarcely had he succeeded to the English throne when the Catholic "Gunpowder Plot" attempted to blow Parliament and the King into oblivion: an act of treason converted into a national anti-Catholic festival—though the millions who still celebrate Guy Fawke's Day with bonfires and fireworks know little of its original propagandist purpose. James resisted attempts to extend Presbyterian principles from Scotland to England, as a challenge to the necessary sense of hierarchy which supported the idea of monarchy; "no Bishop, no King," he roundly replied to the arguments of the Puritan Party. But he also found it necessary to act against the Society of Antiquaries; the claims this group of scholars, historians and English common lawyers made of ancient Saxon liberties, successfully reasserted by medieval Parliaments against the pretensions of Plantagenet kings, had evident contemporary weight against the authority of a Stuart.[3]

The English civil war and the revolution of 1688–89 complete this development of historical reference points for modern British identity.

Seventeenth-century France gradually replaced Spain as the embodiment of continental and Catholic autocracy. The appeal of the French court, with the centralizing and modernizing power of Louis XIV's state, beguiled the exiled James Duke of York during the English Commonwealth, though Charles II, his elder brother, was cautious enough to recognize that Catholicism and monarchical aggrandizement were more than post–civil war England would stand. James came to the British thrones in the same year that Louis XIV revoked the Edict of Nantes, with Huguenot refugees settling in England. The French example—positive or negative—was the common point of reference for Stuart and Orange supporters in 1688, when aristocrats and parliamentarians invited "the Protestant champion," William of Orange, to displace James II, and the last Stuart king fled to exile in Versailles.

For the English, the "Glorious Revolution" of 1689 was (like the Church of England) a successful compromise: between the egalitarian radicalism that had blossomed in Cromwell's civil war army and in the protestant sects which had flourished within it, and the aristocratic elite who needed the monarchy to legitimize their position. The "genius" of the British constitution, as nineteenth-century politicians celebrated it, stemmed from the 1689 Settlement: the Protestant Succession, imposed upon a monarchy twice tempted by the Catholic doctrine of the Divine Right of Kings; the doctrine of Parliamentary Sovereignty, not displacing the monarchy but requiring the executive power to carry the Lords and Commons with it; the supremacy of the common law, of precedent and custom as well as parliamentary statute, relying on the courts as well as the Commons to protect English liberties against an over-mighty executive.

This was an *English* settlement, which had a different resonance for the other kingdoms of the British isles. The Stuart kings raised three separate armies, financed out of the treasuries of England, Scotland and Ireland. Civil wars broke out in all three kingdoms in the early 1640s, with different dividing lines within each. Rebellion started in the Presbyterian lowlands of Scotland, spreading to England when Charles I reluctantly summoned Parliament to ask for money for the army to resist the Scots. The war in Ireland was bloodiest, culminating in Cromwell's punitive expedition of 1649. While most of England and lowland Scotland had become firmly protestant, Ireland had found in Catholicism a cause which united its people against the imposition of English rule. Counter-Reformation had taken deep root in Ireland, with young men traveling to the continent and returning as priests to maintain the faith. The revolt of the O'Neills reached its most dangerous point with the invitation of Spanish troops to Ulster in 1601, their defeat in 1603 was followed by the displacement of much of the population of Ulster by protestant settlers, mostly from Scotland, loyal to the English crown.

By 1660 Catholic Irish held only a fifth of Irish land, against the nearly two-thirds of twenty years before. Disappointed in their expectations of Charles II's restoration, they looked more hopefully to his brother on his succession in 1685. The war in Ireland in 1688–89 was a European religious and civil war in miniature, with Dutch and Protestant French troops contesting with Catholic French, and Irish and English on both sides. "Orangemen" still celebrate each year the closing of the gates of London-derry by the Protestant apprentice boys to James's Catholic army; Ulster Unionist opposition to the Treaty of Rome linked the powers of the Commission to Roman pretensions of religious supremacy.

When James's two daughters, Mary, married to William of Orange, and Anne, held the throne, Scotland and England, (and reconquered Ireland) were held together by shared protestant legitimacy. But Anne's twelve children all predeceased her; and the claims of the Catholic son of James's second marriage, it was feared, might prove more attractive to discontented Scots than the Elector of Hanover, the distant cousin whom London preferred. The Union of Scotland with England in 1707 was partly a precaution against a resurgence of the "auld alliance," to hold Britain together in accepting (in 1714) the German inheritor of the Protestant succession. It proved a wise precaution; with French assistance, the Stuart pretender landed in Scotland in 1715, attracting support from the highlands and from northern England before his rebellious army was turned back. The last Stuart rebellion, in 1745, was also mounted from France, forcing the British government to bring troops back from the anti-French coalition in Germany to meet this domestic threat. Suppression of the highland clans, the prosperity which the slave and sugar trades with England's expanding colonies brought to Glasgow, and rising migration south integrated Scotland with England in the second half of the eighteenth century; with Edinburgh intellectuals styling themselves "North Britons," and Samuel Johnson protesting that "the noblest prospect a Scotchman ever sees is the high road that leads him to England."[4]

Britain in Eighteenth-Century Europe

Every eighteenth-century British statesman from Godolphin and Walpole to Burke and the two Pitts assumed that Britain's fundamental interests lay in Europe. As British prosperity and British control of extra-European trade displaced the Dutch, so leadership of the European coalition against France passed to Britain. Marlborough commanded an Anglo-Dutch army through the long War of Spanish Succession; the crucial victory of Blenheim (1704) was fought in Bavaria, joining up with Prince Eugene of Savoy. Hanoverian Britain was unavoidably involved in the politics of the German states; the Electorate of Hanover was united with the British crown until 1837, with the accession of Queen Victoria. Musicians, administrators, philosophers from the protestant states of northern Germany followed the Hanoverian kings to Britain. British regiments fought alongside Hanoverian and Hessian against the French at Dettingen, Fontenoy and Minden; though British financial assistance to Prussia during the Seven Years' War was more valued than its military actions on the continent.

The British nation was defined during the eighteenth century in contra-distinction to France: Europe's dominant power, with a population and territories in 1700 far larger than those of Britain. Seven wars between the two countries took place between 1688 and 1815 — on land and sea, within the British Isles themselves, on the continent, and overseas in America, the West Indies and India. Beyond Europe the conflict between France and Britain took on a different aspect. The victories during the Seven Years' War of Plassey and Quebec, with which the British established supremacy over the French in India and North America, were as important to Britain as Frederick II's progress in Germany. French colonial interests suffered from British naval superiority, and the establishment of British settlements over-seas. It was therefore natural for France to support, from 1776, the rebellion of Britain's American colonists. The War of American Independence was also an extension of European politics; at Yorktown in 1781 the Hessians in the British army surrendered to the Irish regiments in the French.

The struggle with France reached its climax in the revolutionary wars and the conflicts with Napoleon which followed. The English nationalism of Samuel Johnson had contrasted Tory virtues with the dandified cosmopoli-tanism of the Whigs, following French ideas and fashions. For Edmund Burke the defects of the French revolution lay in its rejection of tradition, its insistence that reason and popular will could provide sufficient basis for government. "A perfect democracy is the most shameless thing in the world": a constitutional government limited by law and by habits of government accumulated over generations was England's glory.[5] The wars with Napoleonic France closed the continent to British trade, but left the world outside dominated by the British navy. British forces played only a minor part in the land conflicts within Europe from 1792 to 1815 — compared to their central role in closing the Mediterranean and the West Indies to Napoleon's forces. Waterloo was won with only 30,000 British troops; with Hanoverian and Brunswick regiments taking the first impact of the French attack and Dutch troops in reserve, and with the arrival of the Prussian army sealing the French defeat.

Britain in the Nineteenth-Century World

The British state thus emerged into the re-established European system after 1815 as the dominant power outside Europe, but only one power among several (with France, Prussia, Austria and Russia) in Europe itself. The long struggle against France had shaped British self-image as a protestant north European people, a Teutonic race ranged with its vigorous cousins against the degenerate Latin south. The spread of the industrial revolution from Britain through Belgium and the Ruhr, with German artisans and entrepreneurs working and settling in English cities, reinforced this assumption of common origins and attitudes. The British crown was solidly German, Saxe-Coburg-Gotha succeeding Hanover and Brunswick from royal marriage to royal marriage; Victoria herself became the focal point of European dynastic politics as her extensive family became linked to the royal houses of Denmark, Prussia and Russia.

To the political and cultural influence of northern Europe must be added the cultural attractions of the Latin south. The eighteenth-century French Enlightenment had profoundly influenced ideas in England, even more so in Scotland; the young Adam Smith, tutor to a Scottish nobleman on his European "grand tour," was lionized in Paris, and visited Voltaire on Lake Geneva. While Tories maintained their distrust of French ideas after the revolution, English Liberals found in France natural allies against the reactionary stance of the European empires of Prussia, Austria and Russia. The Romantic movement swept over Britain as it swept over the continent, carrying back with it waves of travellers to the alpine mountains and the ruins of Rome. Romantics and liberals combined to support the causes of Italian and Greek independence; Lord Byron died on an island in Greece.

British reactions to developments across the channel in 1830 and 1848, to revolution and repression from France to Russia, were those of a state which saw itself an active player in the European balance. Refugees from repressive governments congregated in London — Karl Marx among them. Continental conflicts echoed in British politics, as reformers, radicals and conservatives drew differing lessons from the experience of others. British industrialists and investors were active in European markets, while British diplomats and ministers busied themselves with European international politics.

Two factors pushed Britain away from the continent in the second half of the nineteenth century: the rise of Prussia, as an industrial and military power, and the second wave of imperial expansion, above all east of Suez. The speed and determination of Prussian industrialization both fascinated and worried Victorian Britain: a powerful and efficient state, a model of administration and of education which successive British inquiries and commissions sought to emulate. Prussian protectionism offended against Britain's policy of free trade; pushing British manufacturers first out of German markets, and then, as the efficiency and scale of German industry grew, out of other European markets as well. The clamor for "Imperial Preference," which Chamberlain and other political representatives of the industrial cities raised in the 1890s was a response to the loss of markets to Germany first, an espousal of Britain's imperial destiny second.

India and the East captured the imagination of late-Victorian Britain. A sense of mission could be exercised in schemes for moral and educational improvement, or enlightened administration, without uncomfortable comparisons with competitors across the Channel. The brightest and best of Victorian society trained for the Indian Civil Service. The Indian army, the Chinese customs, district administration of expanding protectorates in Africa, advice and tuition to sheikhs in the Persian Gulf, provided employment and status for the rising middle classes. These opportunities for advancement and public service remained until after World War II, leaving behind a large segment of the British elite for whom India and the empire were closer than France and Germany; Gaitskell, like many other middle-class reformers, came from a family of Indian civil servants. In the last decades of the nineteenth century and the first decade of the twentieth, British attention and British priorities had so far turned away from Europe that when in the summer of 1914 a general war unexpectedly broke out on the continent, the British regiments sent to Belgium and France were organized into an "Expeditionary Force," as if they were accompanying Kitchener to Khartoum or Roberts to Pretoria.

On the unification of Germany under the Prussian monarchy, in 1871, much of the British elite saw the German empire as Britain's most natural partner on the European continent. By the time that Britain stumbled into war with Germany, in 1914, trust and respect had turned into suspicion and rivalry. Fritz Stern argued to a skeptical Margaret Thatcher, in a prime ministerial seminar on the reunified Germany of 1990 "that Anglo-German alienation, a mutual mistrust that took shape in the 1890s and matured into full-scale hatred in two world wars, triggered a troubled relationship that has been one of the most important, indeed tragic developments of the twentieth century."[6] Germany's surpassing of Britain's industrial and technological capabilities was only one aspect of this crucial shift in mutual attitudes. German resentment at Britain's superior "place in the sun," built up through naval supremacy and colonial acquisition before the German empire had been created, led to competition for influence and territory in Africa, the Middle East and the Pacific. German support for the rebellious Boers in the South African War caused particular offense in Britain. The drive to build a high seas German navy which followed was a direct challenge to Britain as a power, which sparked off a naval arms race. This was the high period of social Darwinism, of races claiming their right as the fittest to dominate others. British and German national and racial pride drew on overlapping mythical sources, leaving each ambivalent about its most respected (and feared) rival.

Ireland's experience throughout the nineteenth century was sharply different from Great Britain's. The revolution in France had ended hopes of help in winning freedom with the help of the Catholic monarchy; but revolutionary France and Catholic Ireland soon rediscovered common cause in their opposition to England. The Irish rebellion of 1798 followed an unsuccessful French military expedition two years earlier; a small French force landed to support the rebellion, fighting a month-long campaign before its capture. The Act of Union between Britain and Ireland followed, passed through by a London government intent upon protecting its national security in a struggle with France.

Outside Ulster, Ireland was largely untouched by industrialization throughout the nineteenth century and (like Poland) largely forgotten by the elites of Western Europe. The potato famines of the 1840s were marked by mass emigration, Irish communities springing up in most British cities and across the Atlantic. The attempted rebellion of 1867 was planned by veterans of the American Civil War—America from now on replacing France as the hope of independent Irishmen, and Ireland as an issue coming to bedevil relations between Britain and the U.S. The Irish issue disrupted British politics throughout the 1880s and 1890s but played no part in Britain's relations with other European states, where the cause of Irish independence attracted little attention.

In the summer of 1914, the issue was moving close to civil war, with guns smuggled in to arm the protestant Ulster Volunteers to resist the restoration of an Irish Parliament, and the army doubtfully reliable if called upon to defend Catholics against protestant attack. War in Europe postponed Irish "Home Rule." Loyal Ulster protestants volunteered instead for the British army, to die in the thousands in France. Radical Catholics exploited the opportunity of another European war to launch another rebellion against England, at Easter 1916, sparking off a time of troubles which lasted well beyond the division of Ireland in 1922, an outcome hardly noticed on the turbulent continent.

The Cumulative Impact of the Two World Wars

It was World War II that was *the* defining experience for those who made British policy throughout the 1950s and 1960s, and into the 1970s and even the 1980s: directly felt, while reinforcing many elements of the British approach to Europe and redirecting others into new channels. The Great War of 1914 made the French into full allies, with Marshal Foch given command over British divisions, while wartime propaganda portrayed the Germans as barbaric "Huns." Yet the interwar period witnessed a succession of uncertain policies toward the other European powers.

Divisions within domestic politics were reflected in divergent attitudes to continental developments: Socialists attracted by socialist France and revolutionary Russia, Conservatives admiring Italy's "new order" or even Hitler's revival of German prosperity and pride. Idealists fought against Franco in Spain with the International Brigade, alongside volunteers from all over Europe. For British governments struggling to rebuild a weakened economy and to maintain a much less confident global position, imperial links appeared to offer greater advantage than continental politics. Protective policies of "Imperial Preference," introduced in 1931, increased the attractions of extra-European markets. Imperial defense, through the Mediterranean to the Indian Ocean and the Pacific, preoccupied military planners more than continental problems, until the German threat brought belated rearmament from 1936 on. None of the senior ministers involved in managing the Munich crisis had more than brief previous contacts with Germany, but four of them knew India well.

Had the spring of 1940 turned out differently, the course of British postwar history would have been very different. Alliance with France, after the hestiations of the 1920s and 1930s, had brought renewed stress on the countries' shared liberal traditions — as opposed to the centuries of rivalry. When the French government wavered in its resistance to German attack, the British even floated proposals for Franco-British union: drafted, among others, by Jean Monnet, and turned down by an increasingly demoralized French cabinet. The shock of the collapse of France was immense, leaving Britain alone with its empire to face the likelihood of German invasion. There was only one other country to which Britain could turn for support: the United States, appealing to its liberal principles and its Anglo-Saxon heritage to build an alternative alliance to the broken link with France.

The conventional wisdom of British politics since World War II has been of a natural partnership between Britain and America. In reality the history of Anglo-American relations before 1940 had been marked as much by acrimony as by good relations. American nationalism had been shaped by opposition to England, including the War of Independence and of 1812–14. Irish emigration from the 1850s onward had added a new dimension to anti-English sentiment. Wealthy Americans were marrying into the British aristocracy from the 1890s onwards, fascinated by English society while decrying the effeteness of "the old world." America's late intervention in the First World War tipped the balance in favor of the exhausted armies of Britain and France against an exhausted Germany; only to disappoint British hopes on continuing alliance by withdrawing from European involvement into self-interested isolation and opposition to British imperial policies.

"Pan-Anglo-Saxonism" had its adherents in interwar Britain, among those who looked across the Atlantic to provide the support for global order which Britain could no longer provide on its own. Donald Watt has defined its basic doctrines as: "the unquestioning identification of British and American leadership, the naive assumption that British leadership would be welcomed and acceptable, the identification of Anglo-Saxon hegemony with the achievement of universal peace, and an optimistic idealism about the influence of a united Anglo-American opinion as a deterrent against the use of force to upset the world status quo."[7] But this was only one among several contending tendencies. There were many who saw close relations with France as essential to the pursuit of stability in an unstable world; and some in the 1930s who were sympathetic to Germany and to German hints of a world order in which German dominance on the continent would complement restored British pre-eminence outside Europe. The breakdown of Anglo-German understanding in the 1890s could still be seen in retrospect as an aberration after centuries of friendly contacts, which the bitterness and war propaganda of 1914–18 had damaged but not destroyed.

The collapse of France in June 1940 was a tremendous shock to the British government and public, coming as they had been returning to the image of Franco-British alliance under which their parents had fought in World War I. Apparent demoralization in the officer corps, the emergence of a collaborationist regime in Vichy, brought flooding back all the old assumptions about "the moral disease of France" which had been the staple of English periodicals in the 1780s and 1790s. Thatcher's father, a strict Methodist Sabbatarian, declared in 1942 that France was "corrupt from top to bottom."[8] Support from the United States was the only alternative to capitulation. In the popular imagination Britain stood alone, facing the German threat, as it had stood alone against Napoleon. In reality Britain depended more and more heavily on the United States for military re-equipment, production machinery, food, and transatlantic transport, in the eighteen months before America formally entered the war in December 1941, and even more heavily as the war continued for a further three and a half years.

The crisis of 1940 also gave Britain a prime minister who combined a strong commitment to Britain's imperial role with a keen sense of Anglo-American ties: Winston Churchill, the son of an American heiress and an aristocrat Tory politician. His rhetoric, his management of the wartime partnership, redefined Britain's position in the world (as that of de Gaulle did that of France). Wartime literature and propaganda conjured up symbols from Britain's past appropriate to present needs, and underlined what Britain and America shared to justify the common struggle. The "Atlantic Charter" committed the two states to fight for democracy throughout the world—a commitment understood differently in London than in Washington, which wished to extend its coverage also to the colonies of the British empire. Churchill seized on the shared Anglo-Saxon heritage, of common law, elected assemblies and distrust of government, as a theme that would both rally German resistance against continental tyranny and bind Americans and Britons together around common values.

The surge of refugees from continental tyranny who had brought to Britain and America a new intellectual elite was as strongly attracted by this heritage as those born into it. Friedrich von Hayek lectured at the wartime London School of Economics on the dangers of corporatism and the links between free markets and free societies. Lewis Namier revelled in the practical politics and patriotic spirit of the eighteenth century House of Commons. The corporatist tradition (and, some would add, the Catholic tradition) was seen as leading to authoritarian nemesis; free markets and limited government nurtured free men. The generation they helped to educate absorbed their assumptions. In a Conservative Party seminar on British policy towards the EEC in 1989, one former cabinet minister remarked on "the natural tendency to authoritarianism among continental governments."

English literature, and written English history, had carried messages about English exceptionalism since the great period of imperial self-confidence in the late nineteenth century. The Reverend Charles Kingsley, professor of modern history at Cambridge, also wrote the classic children's story *Westward Ho!* (1855) to encourage pride in protestant England's resistance to Catholic Spain, and *Hereward the Wake* (1866) to conjure up the image of Saxon resistance to Norman oppression. Paul Gallico's *The Snow Goose* (1941) draws on the same imagery, identifying the Germans with the Normans and his heroine with the Saxons, coming from a village "which was already old when the Normans came." English history as taught in the 1940s was firmly in the grip of the "Whig interpretation": a pattern of national history which demonstrated the gradual triumph of liberal principles through the evolution of Britain's institutions and their social underpinnings, which stressed the separate course of British history from that of the continent and downplayed the links between British and continental developments.

Churchill was himself a part-time historian with a strong didactic bent. In opposition between the wars he had written a four-volume popular history of *The World Crisis 1891–1918*, and an equally massive *Life of Marl-*

borough, his famous ancestor. His *History of the English-Speaking Peoples*, which set out in detail the mental map of the Anglo-Saxon world of which Britain was the core, was not published until the 1950s; but the ideas spelled out there were already contained in his wartime speeches, and developed further during his period as leader of the opposition after 1945, setting much of the tone of the postwar British view of the world.

It was painfully evident to British policy makers by 1942, as the prospect of eventual victory began to appear on the horizon, that Britain's international position would be impossible to sustain after the war without active American assistance. British investments in North America had been sold to finance supplies from the U.S.; obligations to the U.S. were accumulating under lend-lease, and to dominions and colonies in the form of sterling balances. It was vital to retain American commitment to global order after victory was won, and to harness that commitment to British objectives. British policy makers, impressed by the sheer weight of American resources applied to the war effort in comparison with their own, were in no doubt about the unequal nature of any postwar partnership. "We must be Greeks to their Romans," as Harold Macmillan is reputed to have remarked while resident British Minister at the Anglo-American headquarters in North Africa in 1942: providing the intellectual leadership to harness and counterbalance the organizational capacity and wealth of their future masters.

The closeness of the postwar partnership left a deep impression on a whole generation of British (and American) influentials: joint boards managing the supply of war materials in Washington and London; joint staffs in military headquarters; joint intelligence operations, where bright young men and women worked together under the most intense conditions. Until the 1970s the management of British-American relations was eased by friendships forged in the 1940s, as those whose experiences were shaped by the wartime alliance moved up the ladder of politics, government, the military services, business and finance. In the nature of the case few other Europeans shared this formative experience, even those representing governments-in-exile and token national contingents in the allied forces. A few French participated in the joint boards, Monnet and Marjolin among them. But for the most part the British experienced four years of naturally exclusive partnership, two leaders of the Free World throwing back the dictators and planning the shape of the postwar world.

Postwar Redefinition: Europe and the Open Sea

For Britain the victory of 1945 was paradoxical. At Teheran, Yalta and Potsdam there had been *three* great powers; the addition of France, at British insistence against American wishes, was more symbolic than real. The postwar international institutions, political and economic, were of Anglo-American design, with British representatives entrenched in privileged positions within them. British foreign secretaries, Ernest Bevin no less than Anthony Eden, thought in terms of global power and global responsibilities; and, until the Suez intervention in 1956 exposed a vast gap between Britain's prestige and its capabilities, were treated by other countries as statesmen of a superpower.

Yet underlying economic weaknesses made the claim to global status an illusion, sustainable only so long as the Americans were prepared to accept it. British industrial productivity and innovation had been losing ground to Germany since the 1880s, the deterioration only obscured by the massive shocks to the German economy of defeat in both world wars. The American revolution in mass production and management had made little headway in Britain before or during the war. British consumption and material imports had been paid for by the British services and the dividends of accumulated overseas investments; but war had sunk British ships, weakened the position of other services, forced the realization of investments and left instead the accumulation of debt. Continental countries, painfully reconstructing after defeat and occupation, could not avoid facing the need for radical domestic and international adjustments. But for the British, it seemed that victory had vindicated the Anglo-Saxon approach. "The very ritual of the victory celebrations proclaimed the continuity of British life and institutions while tyrants came, briefly puffed themselves up into a menace, and went. . . . As a consequence, the British people never had to face the reality about themselves and their future place in the world, let alone come to terms with it and adapt accordingly."[9] The reformulation of Britain's place in the world which emerged out of planning papers within the wartime Foreign Office, discussions within the government, and a developing consensus amongst those caught up in managing the allied efforts in Europe and Asia was set out most explicitly by Winston Churchill in his speech as leader of the opposition to the Conservation Party Conference of 1948. "As I look out upon the future of our country in the changing scene of human destiny I feel the existence of three great circles among the free nations and democracies. The first for us is naturally the British Commonwealth and Empire with all that comprises. There is also the English-speaking world centering upon the United States, in which we, Canada, and the other British Dominions play so important a part. And finally there is a united Europe. . . . Now if you think of the three interlinked circles you will see that we are the only country that has a great part in every one of them. We stand in fact at the very point of junction, and here in this island at the centre of the seaways and perhaps of the airways also we have the opportunity of joining them all together."[10] Britain's position as the third global power qualified it for a special relationship with the U.S.; yet that position depended upon the support of the U.S. American interests, furthermore, did not always coincide with those of Britain. Washington pressed Britain to play a full part in its plans for West European integration, from 1947 onward; American officials and congressmen were also sympathetic to dismantling the empire, which the British wanted to maintain. The relationship was, from 1945 on, more vital to Britain than the U.S. Yet for the first ten years after the war Britain acted like a partner and a great power—and was treated as a great power, and a valued junior partner.

Looking back, the confidence of the postwar British governments was dreadfully misplaced, but understandable. The "New Elizabethan Age," which the press trumpeted on the accession of the Queen in 1953, appeared to show a country reestablishing its economy while maintaining its international responsibilities. The British economy was still the largest in Europe. British high technology, in nuclear research and aircraft production, was second only to American in quality. British welfare services and housing standards were considered among the highest in the world. British democracy and national solidarity had stood the test of war. Britain had led among America's allies in the pace of its rearmament, as fears of Soviet expansionism grew after the outbreak of the Korean War: America's most important and responsible ally, bearing the cost of its domestic economy without fully appreciating what the long-term costs were.

Across the Channel they saw societies still threatened by Communist subversion, economies struggling to rebuild, weak governments coming and going. France provided for most British publicists and policy makers the dominant image of the continent: seeing the procession of short-lived Fourth Republic governments, peasant agriculture, unimproved nineteenth-century housing, unaware of the economic and administrative modernization also underway. The British sector of Germany had been efficiently and sympathetically run in the immediate postwar years; that task completed, recognition of the importance of Germany as the frontline of Western defense coexisted with the widespread antagonism to Germany, with popular British history now suggesting that the origins of the world wars were to be found in German culture and character.

For Europe was the third of the three circles, the one from which, policy makers believed, Britain derived least benefits in terms of prestige or added resources. "The stubborn resistance of the British to the idea of committing themselves to the Continent," of which Marjolin, Monnet, Spaak and so many others complained, was a reflection that their image and their preoccupations were elsewhere.[11] The continent was a front to be defended, indefensible without full American commitment. British defense planners who had fought through World War II, comparing the continued strength of communist parties in France and Italy with the problems of "Fifth Columns" ten years before, doubted how much of the continent could be held in the face of a Soviet attack. The maintenance of Britain's military position in the Middle East, the lynchpin of its imperial defense and of the West's global resistance to communist expansion, had to be weighed against the defense of Germany; the Korean invasion in 1950 forced the painful transfer of a British division from the Middle East to guard against the more immediate European threat.

British policy makers were thus partly absent from the debate about European integration during the first postwar decade because their attention and their ambitions were elsewhere. The link with the U.S. was so self-evidently more important that Monnet's attempts to involve Britain in his plans for a European Coal and Steel Community aroused little sympathy. In 1950–51 British officials were attempting to subsume the operations of the OEEC into NATO, because of the overriding importance of the American security commitment and the switch from economic to military assistance. The British did not share the overwhelming preoccupation with Germany of the French, the Belgians and the Dutch. The Malayan emergency, the Suez Canal Zone base, the Iranian crisis preoccupied British cabinets as much as the plans of doubtfully reliable French, Belgian and Italian governments.

Under intense American pressure, Anthony Eden put forward the proposal for a revised Western European Union in 1954, to provide a looser framework for German rearmament than that which the EDC proposals had attempted to build: making in the process a formal peacetime commitment of British troops to the continent, a major shift of British strategy without a comparable shift of political priorities. But the bulk of British forces was still in the Mediterranean, the Middle East and east of the Suez; as was the bulk of Britain's markets, and the overwhelming proportion of Britain's investments. The lack of attention paid to attempts to revive West European integration among the six ECSC countries in 1955–56 reflected the British government's political and economic interests.

The Long Retreat

The fiasco of the Suez shattered many of these illusions. Cooperation with the French exposed the inadequacies of both countries' armed forces. Failure destroyed Britain's position in the Middle East, which had rested on prestige as much as power. Withdrawal of U.S. support for sterling led to an immediate run on the pound, demonstrating the underlying weakness of Britain's economy. But it was not evident that adding Britain's weakness to those of its neighbors across the Channel provided an appropriate response. Federal Germany had regained its sovereignty only in 1955, under a chancellor whose relations with the British authorities under the occupation had been frosty. The French Fourth Republic was sliding toward collapse; with war in Algeria succeeding defeat in Indo-China, it looked not impossible in the years 1957 and 1958 that conflict might spread across the Mediterranean to a divided France.

Before 1956, Britain's imperial position had seemed the most important of the three circles. After 1956, it was clear that the transatlantic relationship was the most fundamental. Together with the U.S., Britain could still play a global role, sterling remain a reserve currency, nuclear and technological collaboration still provide the instruments of military power and industrial advance. Without the U.S., Britain would be little better than the Netherlands or France: an ex-imperial country coming to terms with decline. De Gaulle on his return to power in 1958 appears to have reached a similar conclusion, proposing in a memorandum to President Eisenhower and Harold Macmillan that the Anglo-American partnership should be widened into an Atlantic triumvirate.[12] Rebuffed by the Americans and British, he had no alternative but to turn to Germany: to use Germany as the British used the U.S., to supply the weight and resources to meet national ambitions which neither Britain or France would supply alone.

But the Americans, like the Germans, were not prepared to be passive partners in such a relationship. The Eisenhower administration saw the rearmament of Germany and the completion of European economic recovery under the new Economic Community of Six as enabling the U.S. to reduce troop levels in Europe, and to share the burden of Western leadership with a more integrated Western Europe, provided that Britain would accept a place within it. Washington gave little support to "the Maudling Plan" for a wider and looser European Free Trade Area, nor to the rump EFTA of seven countries which emerged alongside the Six. Federal Germany, with an economy which overtook Britain's in 1958 and an army which by 1960 was again the largest on the European continent—as well as the main base for the American military commitment to Europe—already seemed from Washington to be as vital a partner as Britain in America's European strategy. The Kennedy administration was equally determined to construct a new Atlantic partnership around a more united Western Europe.

Reluctantly, recognizing that the British economy was growing more slowly than those of its continental neighbors, that its heavy dependence on

Commonwealth markets was not the best base for future growth, that Britain could not afford to be left entirely outside European developments and that American pressure required a response, the British cabinet in 1961 agreed that Britain should apply to join the EEC. In itself this was something of a retreat, after British resistance to France's integrationist plans from the Messina talks on. There was no sense of a new political commitment; the term "Common Market" was the only one used in the domestic debate. The extensive process of consultation with Commonwealth governments provided ample opportunity for these to criticize Britain for neglecting their interests. The breakdown in January 1963 resulted from technological dependence on the U.S. for the nuclear delivery system on which Britain's claims to global status partly rested, Gaullist suspicion, and uninspired negotiation. The negotiations themselves were dealing with market access for Australian kangaroo meat when they were suspended.

In retrospect the immense importance given to the Commonwealth in these first negotiations must seem extraordinary. Yet Britain was only fifteen years from a war in which Commonwealth forces had defended "the mother country," and Commonwealth food kept Britain alive. The early 1960s were the high point of optimism about the peaceful transfer of empire into Commonwealth. The pace of decolonization was accelerated after Suez, with all of Britain's African territories, except Rhodesia, independent by 1964. Common law and Westminster democracy, complete with bewigged speaker and mace-carrier, appeared to be extending British values across an English-speaking world far wider and more vigorous than the Roman law community across the Channel. Attachment to the Commonwealth was strong both in the Labour and Conservative Parties, closely linked to support for a continuing military role east of Suez. Harold Wilson as prime minister in 1966 went so far as to suggest that Britain might station Polaris submarines to give India nuclear protection against a threat from China.

Disillusion with the Commonwealth followed, rapidly, in the late 1960s. Over Rhodesia and Southern Africa, a Labour government found itself subjected to sharp and unhelpful criticism from an increasingly multiracial Commonwealth. Democratic governments collapsed, Anglo-Saxon institutions giving way to military juntas. A rising tide of migrants from the West Indies and South Asia was coming into Britain. East African governments expelled the Asians who had settled as traders and businessmen under British rule—and as they poured into Britain the government of India disclaimed any share in the responsibility for resettling them. Continuing economic weakness forced abandonment of two other symbols of world power status—the international role of sterling, shaken by the devaluation of 1967 and ended in the international monetary adjustments of 1968–73; and the projection of power east of Suez, announced as a postdevaluation cut in 1968 and completed by 1971.

Britain thus acceded to the European Community in 1973 after losing most of the symbols of separate and superior status which had marked it out from the continent. Its then prime minister, Edward Heath, differed from his predecessors in his skepticism about the transatlantic relationship and his conviction that Britain must be fully "in Europe" — a conviction also formed by his experiences during World War II, when he (like Lord Carrington, Dennis Healey, and other "pro-Europeans" in both parties) had fought on the continent from Normandy through to Germany. British defense policy was now concentrated around the continental commitment; Dennis Healy as defense minister had taken the initiative with Helmut Schmidt to form the Eurogroup in 1969, as a signal to the U.S. of greater West European cooperation within the alliance. British trade had already reoriented itself toward European markets in the 1960s, as Commonwealth markets ceased to attract; though British investment continued to flow predominantly to the English-speaking world.

Yet Heath carried into the EEC a divided Conservative Party, a more divided Labour opposition, and a confused and skeptical public. There was little sense of a new start, let alone of any historic turning point. For most, as the referendum result of 1974 indicated, EEC membership was unavoidable, a British role within a European system the only role left; but that was not enough to provide a positive sense of commitment. It is part of the tragedy of Britain's relations with the continent that the EEC entry coincided with international economic recession and the oil crisis, bringing the British economy inflation rather than a surge of economic growth. Recession made other EEC members more resistant to accept the justice of British claims on its unbalanced budget, as agricultural production in France, the low countries and Germany surged and as Denmark and Ireland became substantial net beneficiaries. It was also tragic in terms of the redefinition of Britain's place in the world that Heath's Conservative government was replaced in 1974 by a Labour cabinet deeply divided on the European issue, concerned more to hold their party together than to persuade the British public or other EEC governments of the significance of Britain's acceptance of membership.

For Great Britain's other island, accession had an entirely different meaning. Ireland's independence from the United Kingdom had, since 1922, meant continued economic dependence, moderated by ties with the U.S., by continuing migration to the U.S., and since 1945 by active involvement in the UN. Neutrality during World War II had been neutrality against the UK, far more than any statement of abstract principle or of sympathy toward Nazi Germany. Community membership brought Ireland *real* independence:

direct and active political relations with the European continent, participation in European consultations on trade and foreign policy, reorientation of its trade away from British markets, and net transfers from the EEC budget which by the early 1980s amounted to almost 5 percent of the Irish GNP. Ireland had been cut off from Europe by its own poverty, by the inward-looking character of its society and politics, and by its double dependence on the UK and U.S. As Irish officials flocked to Brussels, as the Irish government successfully managed the EC presidency for the first time in 1975, as Irish farmers discovered continental markets, continental companies and tourists discovered Ireland, and American (and later Japanese) companies came into Ireland as a base from which to supply the European market, Ireland at last was freed from centuries of dependence on Britain.

Brussels and Bruges, Corporatism and Free Markets

Independence for Ireland, dependence for Britain: a country at the end of the 1970s in economic and political decline, unhappily accepting a place inside a European Community whose budget and many of its policies were structurally biased against it. Resistance in Bonn and Paris, as well as in Brussels, to adjustments of policy to meet British claims reinforced old suspicions of French reliability and German hostility in Parliament and in the popular press. The closeness of the Franco-German relationship under Giscard d'Estaing and Helmut Schmidt would have made it difficult even for an actively European British government to play a central role within the Community. Rapid changes in U.S. presidencies and administrations, and even more rapid changes in U.S. policies, weakened the special relationship as an alternative support.

The revolt within the Conservative Party against Edward Heath, after the narrow defeats of the two 1974 elections, was primarily against policies which the rebels labelled corporatist, based on subsidies for industry and the inefficient public sector, and compromise with vested interests. But Heath's commitment to a European Community which seemed to embody such policies, to partnership with a French government which appeared quintessentially corporatist, seemed part of the same mistaken philosophy. Canadian and Australian free trade economists combined with followers of Friedrich von Hayek in vigorous reassertion of Anglo-Saxon principles, economic and political.

For Margaret Thatcher, determined to shake her country out of the defeatist acceptance of decline which seemed to grip it in 1978–79, pride in the past provided the best foundation for renewed optimism in the present.

She was an English nationalist, a nonparticipant in World War II who nevertheless fervently held to all of its patriotic myths and symbols. A Conservative Party political broadcast in the 1987 election showed a film of British troops landing in Normandy, with the comment: "Britain's greatest contribution to Europe."

To a defender of British national interests who preferred plain speaking to carefully crafted ambiguity, the attitudes of Britain's continental partners offered a wide target for justified attack. French and German resistance to adjustment of the Community budget, to which Britain had now overtaken Germany as the largest contributor, was a classic example of corporatist defense of vested interests shrouded in Jesuitical argument about the *Acquis Communautaire*. The subtleties of French foreign policies, toward the Atlantic alliance and toward the Middle East, seemed casuistical; German tolerance of ambiguity in its relations with France, and in its policy toward the Soviet Union, was incomprehensible. The contrast with the apparent vigor of the new administration in Washington, from 1981, was striking: the same commitment to free markets at home and abroad, the same clear resistance to Soviet communism, even the same muscular Christianity—the approach which Charles Kingsley and his contemporaries had embodied, from which (to Thatcher's disgust) the Church of England now moved away.

Britain in the 1980s experienced economic growth more rapid than the rest of Europe, while pursuing economic policies more radical than the rest of Europe. The budgetary dispute settled in 1984, an increasingly confident British government set out to pursue free market principles through European cooperation, making deregulation a *European* objective: providing much of the initial impetus which led to the 1992 program. Between 1985 and 1987 the British government edged back toward a European priority; as Gorbachev found his first Western champions in London, as Washington's wanderings from star wars to schemes for superpower disarmament (in the Reykjavik proposals), and as the French and Spanish governments began to imitate Thatcherite policies.

But in the course of 1987–88 the Community agenda slipped back, from London's perspective, toward corporatism. Agricultural reform was making agonizingly slow progress; social legislation was being promoted; union representation on the boards of European companies was under discussion. The hypocrisy of the German government, professedly committed to open markets, but supporting closed public monopolies, subsidies for industry, and protective employment practices, was most strongly resented. But the wide gap between the grand schemes for further integration which continental governments were determined to pursue and their failure to open up their markets to British services, their public utilities to British suppliers, or their capital markets to cross-border flows, portrayed an approach to politics which seemed entirely foreign to British practitioners. The difference in style of government and administration seemed acute: between a British tradition of efficient administration and continental laxness in implementing agreed rules, between a majoritarian government able to press legislation through Parliament and the delays and compromises which characterized continental coalitions.

Frustration with the complications and half-spoken assumptions of the Brussels process burst out in Thatcher's September speech in Bruges, which reasserted some of the oldest themes of England's half-European identity within a new context.

> We in Britain are proud of the way in which, since Magna Carta in 1215, we have pioneered and developed representative institutions to stand as bastions of freedom. And proud too of the way in which for centuries Britain was a home for people from the rest of Europe who sought sanctuary from tyranny.
>
> We British have in a special way contributed to Europe. For over the centuries we have fought and died for her freedom, fought to prevent Europe from falling under the dominance of a single power. . . . Had it not been for that willingness to fight and die, Europe *would* have been united long before now—but not in liberty and not in justice.

Europe was wider than merely the European Community: "one manifestation of the European identity, but . . . not the only one;" stretching to include not only excluded Eastern Europe, but also "that Atlantic Community—that Europe on both sides of the Atlantic—which is our greatest inheritance and our greatest strength." But the key themes of the speech were the emphasis on Anglo-Saxon principles of minimum government, and on the importance of sovereignty, nationhood, and tradition. "We have not successfully rolled back the frontiers of the state in Britain only to see them reimposed at a European level, with a European superstate exercising a new dominance from Brussels. Certainly we want to see Europe more united and with a greater sense of national pride in one's own country, for these have been the source of Europe's vitality across the centuries."

The Challenge to British Identity

Four years after, confidence in economic recovery has given way to deep recession. Old fears of Germany have re-emerged upon German unification, old suspicions of France recurred in negotiations over European union and European defense. Yet Thatcher's fall from office came over the style of her approach to

European cooperation. Her successor, John Major, has repeated his determination to place Britain "at the heart of Europe, where we belong," while also resisting the federalist institution-building of continental governments.

The passing of the generation whose views on Europe and on national identity were shaped by World War II has weakened the sense of separateness from the continent. Opinion polls indicate a progressive decrease in identification with the U.S. and with its position in the world over the past fifteen years, and a far sharper fall in commitment to the Commonwealth. Levels of social interaction between Britain and the continent have mushroomed. Five times as many journeys across the Channel were made in 1990 as in 1970; 330,000 Britons now own holiday homes on the continent. Generational change has transformed assumptions about national exceptionalism and Britain's place in Europe. Young Britons travel around Europe for interest, education or work as if it were their own territory—as do young French, Italians and Germans.

Yet British identity disintegrates without some sense of separation from the continent. Pride in industrial and technological superiority has long since been lost. Pride in the empire was transformed into commitment to the Commonwealth, before disillusion overtook it. The prestige which accompanied the special relationship returned under President Reagan and Margaret Thatcher, to dissipate again under a Bush administration that has gone out of its way to signal the greater importance it places on its relations with Germany. Pride in the intellectual leadership which Anglo-Saxon open market philosophy had brought to the continent is challenged by doubts about Britain's own economic strategy, by the relative success of alternative French and German approaches, and by shifts of economic thinking in the U.S. itself. In a secular society where, outside Ulster, distinctions between protestants and Catholics no longer carry political significance, there remain only the symbol of Britain's nuclear deterrent and military tradition, and the distinctiveness of Britain's political history and institutions: the sovereignty of Parliament, the different style of British law, the rallying cries of those who defend nationhood against European federation.

If national identity disintegrates, the state itself is at risk. Already in the 1987 general election the Scottish National Party campaigned on the seductive slogan, "An Independent Scotland in a United Europe": rejecting the link with England as unnecessary and constraining in a Britain no longer facing any threat from the continent. The signs that proliferate across northern England, telling the passer-by that "Europe helps Bradford (or Newcastle, or Liverpool) again" carry an unwritten message "against London and the British treasury." The unifying factors which integrated the British state were a shared sense of threat, shared prosperity, shared (protestant and liberal) values. All seem now less specific to Britain, or to the English-speaking world.

Adjustment to an alternative framework for loyalty and pride would be easier if British governments over the past half-century had attempted to rediscover and re-emphasize those elements of Britain's history that place it firmly within a European context, rather than those which place it elsewhere. The Thatcher government's return to the symbolism of Anglo-Saxon partnership, its stubborn resistance to giving any symbolic weight to the conduct of British business with other European governments (even to the point of preventing the Queen from addressing the European Parliament), left the foundations of British policy weak when Reagan and Thatcher left the scene. The unifying experience—of national solidarity, of a clear sense of purpose, of Britain's particular place in and contribution to the world—of World War II has gone, without governments supplying alternative points of reference to orient opinion toward the idea of Britain itself and its appropriate relations with other countries in Europe and beyond.

That is not a problem unique to Britain. The disorientation of French foreign policy and national identity after the Cold War, with defense policies entangled in the ideology of independence, with "défense du territoire" replaced by open borders, with national industrial strategies conflicting with European, is manifest. Comparable disorientation, stemming from the impact of integration on different national histories and self-images, are evident also in Italy, Belgium, and arguably also Germany—lesser degrees of disorientation in all other European states, as they face the same contradictions between national autonomy and international economic and social integration. But that does not make redefinition of "Britain" and its place in Europe any easier.

Notes

1. *King Richard II*, act 2 scene 1.
2. Speech to the Labour Party Annual Conference, September 1962.
3. This portrayal of the English as Saxons resisting the imposition of Scottish (Roman) law and habits of government was of course a mixture of political propaganda and romantic myth. But the reader should note that the Scots term for English, still in use, is "Sassenach"—or Saxon.
4. Boswell's *Life of Johnson*, entry for July 6, 1763.
5. *Reflections on the Revolution in France*.
6. *Frankfurter Allgemeine Zeitung*, July 26, 1990; translated in *German Tribune*, August 12, 1990.

7. D.C. Watt, *Personalities and Policies: Studies in the Formulation of British Foreign Policy in the Twentieth Century* (London: Longman, 1965), p. 45.

8. Quoted in Hugo Young, *One of Us: A Biography of Margaret Thatcher* (London: Macmillan, 1989) p. 9. On eighteenth-century parallels, see Gerald Newman, *The Rise of English Nationalism: A Cultural History, 1740–1830* (London: Weidenfeld, 1987); the quotation is from p. 238.

9. Corelli Barnett, *The Audit of War* (London: Macmillan, 1986), p. 1, p. xi.

10. W.S. Churchill, *Europe Unites: Speeches, 1947 and 1948* (London: Cassel, 1950), p. 231.

11. Robert Marjolin, *Architect of European Unity: Memoirs 1911–1986* (London: Weidenfeld, 1989), p. 213.

12. The French President's Memorandum to the U.S. President and the British Prime Minister is printed in full in Alfred Grosser, *The Western Alliance: Europe-American Relations since 1945* (London: Macmillan, 1978), p. 187.

Hungary's Place in Europe: Political Thought and Historiography in the Twentieth Century

Ivan T. Berend

When the modern world system emerged between the early sixteenth and eighteenth centuries, Hungary, as a part of the Hapsburg empire (since 1526), and like most of its neighboring East-Central European countries, became an agricultural periphery of a rapidly modernizing and industrializing West European world.

The "dual-revolution" of the West at the end of the eighteenth century represented a new challenge. It was both a danger (in fact a reality) of further relative decline and a chance to exploit the "pull effect" of rapid Western industrialization and vastly greater market opportunities, offering unlimited export potential, and thus increased income, capital accumulation and development. The ability of joining a revolutionized "Europe" was strongly dependent on domestic reforms and modernization. From the early nineteenth century on, how adequate the response was to the challenge became a watershed of the history of the nations of the European periphery. To "follow Europe," to "join Europe," Hungary's "place in Europe" became central questions and expressions of the goal toward progress. To remain on the periphery, far away from the mainstream of modern transformation, unable to respond and lagging more and more behind was paramount to becoming separated from "Europe" altogether.

The "Greatest Hungarian," Count István Széchenyi, the grand reformer and political thinker of the early mid–nineteenth century, who became the best known initiator of the "Reform Age" (the Hungarian Vormärz), passionately advocated reforms after visiting Britain. He suggested replacing obsolete feudal institutions with the most important modern Western ones, including banks, wage labor, railroads and manufacturing. Attacking Hungarian backwardness and non-European attitudes, he was one of the first to argue that Hungarians originated as a "people of the East" (Kelet népe), though they "find themselves in the West"; therefore they have to adjust to their European environment. Modernization of Hungary, however, was only partly successful in the nineteenth century.

Several generations later, in the early twentieth century, another great Hungarian, the revolutionary poet and political thinker Endre Ady, also attacked Hungarian backwardness and corresponding attitudes. "Are you again going against Europe," he cried out in a drama written in 1905, "in the holy name of Asia?" In his angry prophetic style he called Hungary "a ferry-boat country," shuttling between the "coasts from East to West. Though with greater pleasure on the way back." He railed against the "big lie" that "here Hungary was already Europe." In reality, "ten thousand people run ahead and become European in their nerves, blood and mind," but there are no masses following them. Instead a "hidden Asia washes its face . . . and the ferry-boat country departs angrily toward the East . . . under the Carpathian mountains that Ghengis Khan celebrates."

Nineteenth and early twentieth century Hungarian "westernizers" from Szényi to Ady condemned the "Asian attitudes" and inertia of their countrymen and sought to create a "European Hungary." After World War I, however, there were rather mixed reactions. The only partly successful modernization and failure to catch up with the industrialized, democratic Western nation-states generated a bitter backlash all over East-Central Europe. The ferocious fury of the war, the extreme emotional repercussions and legalized violence against the "enemies" generated new types of responses. Beside trying to follow the West and becoming an integral part of Europe, there now emerged a vehement rejection of Western values and nations, and the desire to abandon Europe entirely.

At the end of World War I a great revolt began all over East-Central Europe against peripheral backwardness, triggered by the lack of a flourishing civil society, a prosperous industrial economy, and an independent nation-state. A belated national revolution, Bolshevik-type revolutionary attempts and various kinds of right-wing, often fascist rebellions occurred throughout the whole region. Extreme nationalism, authoritarian right-wing dictatorship or anticapitalist communism, which at times converged and at other times clashed with each other, all looked at Europe with equally great suspicion, rejecting Western European values. Whether it was self-contained nationalism, a "new European order," or anticapitalist radicalism, there was a general desire to create a self-centered Hungarian world, or some kind of parallel world system. Independence was equated with self-sufficiency and industrialization was to take the place of imports. These leading strategies of modernization from the early twenties on, as well as the realization of this policy in a more vigorous way throughout the thirties and forties and in the entire post–World War II period, all led to increasing isolation from Europe. Regional agreements tried to "free" East-Central Europe from either the Western dominated world economy, the domination of Hitlerite Germany or the straitjacket of the Soviet-led Warsaw pact and COMECON. Hungary, consequently, decisively distanced itself from Europe; the "ferry-boat country" almost permanently "sailed away from the West."

This was the basic political-historical (and often quite hysterical) twentieth century environment in which a permanent debate was carried on regarding Hungary's place in Europe.

A number of different views confronted each other during the last three quarters of a century, with often rather ambiguous and even confused concepts being formulated on the attitude toward Europe. One of the most important new trends was the rejection of Europe, which was repeatedly expressed by emphasizing a self-conscious "Easternness." The peasant writer Péter Veres expressed this populist concept in the most eloquent way when he wrote in the 1930s, "We could not become burghers, and therefore we should not desire it anymore. We have nothing to do with the West." Instead, the Hungarians were to develop and cultivate their own inner "Ghengis Khan soul."

Dezsö Szabó, a nationalist writer and father of Hungarian populism, advocated the "historical cooperation of East European nations" against expansionist Germans as well as devilish Bolshevism, and dreamed of an immense alliance from Poland and Hungary to Greece and Turkey. He argued for the creation of an "East-European idea and self-consciousness." To the question of *Where Should Hungary's Place Be in Europe?*, the title of his study published in 1935, he gave the answer "In Eastern Europe." His Eastern Europe was a huge region from the eastern border of Germany and Austria toward the east, incorporating Hungary, Poland, the Balkans and Turkey.

This view was reformulated by the most influential populist thinker of the 1930s, László Németh, who announced that "our East-Europeanness obliges us to be Europeans." His most important argument was the common destiny of the nations of the region. "We are living a common fate, but do not know each other. It is high time we get acquainted with our milk brothers, with whom we sucked at the dry breasts of the same destiny."

East European self-consciousness was not a monopoly of populists. Leading democratic-minded nonpopulist scholars and artists shared this view as well. Péter Váczy, an historian with a broad European horizon, maintained that the Carpathian basin geographically and historically belongs to Eastern Europe. István Gál, a left-wing democrat, writer and political thinker, described his conversation with Béla Bartók in the daily *Magyar Nemzet* in January 1940: "I often talked with him about the region we are living in. He also asserts that it belongs to Eastern Europe and explained to me in a detailed way that his research of folk music definitively proves this view."

Others sometimes angrily denied the East European character of Hungary and emphasized its Central European status. Gyula Szekfü, a leading historian of the Horthy regime, declared that the road of Hungary for a thousand years is "to follow Central and Western Europe. A peasant state which would turn toward the East would be a step back." Zoltán Szabó, a writer and participant in a left-wing populist series of literary sociology entitled "The Discovery of Hungary" remarked, ". . . the geographical Central Europe is sociologically a peasant Europe and anthropologically a Europe of small nations." The Central European concept became rather popular and gained very different meanings in interwar Hungary. *Nemzeti Ujság* (National Daily) published an article as early as December 1919 which spoke of the Hungarians' historical mission in the "separation of Slavic peoples, and blocking the road of German expansionism." The same view was reformulated more than twenty years later, but from a rather different political approach. Béla Imrédy, who became prime minister in 1938 and initiated the first anti-Jewish legislation, underlined in 1941 that the Hungarians "are staying alone," are ethnically alien in the region and are carrying the heavy burden of a historical mission to separate Germans, Slavs and Latins who are like fire and water. Hungary's key position in the region comes from its role as a "shock absorber" between the meeting point of East and West. Ferenc Szálasi, the leader of the Hungarian Nazi "Arrowcross" movement, also spoke of this balancing role of Hungary. According to his argument, a balancing power between the East and West and North and South is only possible under Hungarian leadership, which would reshape a multinational "Ancient Land" (incorporating a great part of the neighboring countries and even Russia).

In the extensive debates of the thirties and early forties, in addition to those who saw Hungary's role as separating or integrating the East and West, there were some who wanted to confirm a sort of neutral position for a Hungary belonging neither to the East nor to the West. Lajos Barta wrote in 1939: "Let's declare at last that we are not Central Europe, nor Danubian

Europe, and neither Eastern Europe. The Hungarian and Bohemian world is not quite Central European, nor is it Eastern European either. These two countries are the Western-Eastern world between East and West." A rather similar concept was held by the talented young historian Domokos Kosáry, who suggested a new term to define the area between Germany and Russia, "Carpathian Europe," with the Carpathian basin as its center. Danubian or Carpathian Europe was not only a different name for Central Europe, but it also represented a concept of differentiation between German-Central Europe and its Eastern neighbors. Let us note, however, that this latter concept came close to the German "Zwischen Europa" formula.

It is "surprising, chaotic and highly contradictory," summarized László Németh, if, in an act of "holy confusion" we call ourselves West European, East European, Central European, Central-East European, East-Central European, Carpatho-European, Danubian or a nation between East and West. In a heated press debate in the late thirties and early forties, a right-wing journalist, Tibor Baráth, bluntly urged, "it would be high time for some of our scholarly public institutions to decide . . . in what kind of historical region we are living—in Western Europe or in Eastern Europe; Central Europe or Central Eastern Europe; Carpatho-Europe of Danubian Europe . . ."

The debate, of course, failed to arrive at consensus. It continued after World War II and generated a great deal of historical research and scholarly publications, especially in the seventies and eighties. Indeed, the debate about Europe and Hungary's place in it continues to this day. Instead of trying to trace it, I intend to summarize the main (often confronting) trends of Hungarian historiography of the last half century about the regions of Europe, and the answers to the old and constantly debated question: "Where does Hungary belong?"

The point of departure is *history*. Its development, or rather its interpretation, played the leading role in the effort to define Hungary's attitude toward Europe.

The *political* definition of Eastern Europe as the region within the Soviet bloc or the Warsaw Pact is rapidly disappearing. Most of the countries involved have angrily rejected this political interpretation since 1989. This is appropriate since political Eastern Europe made no geographical common sense; Greece and Turkey became a part of the West, while Bohemia and a part of Germany belonged to the East.

The *geographical* borders of Europe, needless to say, are absolute. They lie between the Western coast of Iceland and the Ural mountains, roughly speaking from the 20th longitude West from Greenwich to the 60th longitude to the East. The dividing line between the two ends runs down the 19th longitude in the East and is thus rather near the line which links Dubrovnik (a city recently shelled in the Yugoslav civil war), Budapest (the capital of the 1956 revolution) and Gdansk (where Solidarity was born). In a strict geographical sense, Western Europe is west of this line, and Eastern Europe is east. In other words, part of Poland, half of Czechoslovakia, half of Hungary and the western republics of former Yugoslavia belong to the West, the other parts or halves and all of the other countries of the region belong to the East. The middle zone of the continent, however, absorbs most of the region east of the river Elbe, i.e., the former East bloc. In a mere geometrical and geographical sense, Central Europe lies between the 10th (western) and 30th (eastern) longitudes; its western border links Oslo, Hamburg, Milan, and its eastern border is the line between St. Petersberg, Kiev, Odessa. The geographical description of the region has little importance, even if it is often heard that "we are living in the center of Europe," or exactly "between East and West." The seemingly exact geographic interpretation might be as subjective as all the others and can serve rather different interpretations.

One can rightly declare, based on geographic evidence, that Hungary belongs to Western Europe, but also that its place is in Eastern Europe. Most of all, it is questionable that Hungary is located in Central Europe. Thus it is correct to say that Hungary is an East-Central, or Central Eastern European country. The latter definitions are based on the fact that there is a dividing line in the middle of Central Europe (this is, of course, the line dividing Europe between the western and eastern parts) and the western half of Central Europe (west from the Dubrovnik, Budapest, Gdansk line) may be designated as West-Central Europe and the eastern half as East-Central Europe. We arrive again at the starting point: one could also argue that Hungary belongs (at least the western half) to West-Central Europe, but it also (at least the eastern half) belongs to East-Central Europe. Geographical parameters, except the evident fact that Hungary is a European country, thus do not help much in defining the relationship between Hungary and Europe.

That was one of the reasons why *history* played the primary role for self-identification among the countries east from the river Elbe; indeed, they live *in* history. The words of the queen in the strange world (described by Lewis Carroll's *Through the Looking Glass*), are probably nowhere more appropriate than in the countries of the region where "people are living backwards." A glorious (and glorified) past was a sort of historical compensation for an often desperate and gloomy present. As an element of this, there was an attempt to counterbalance the lack of an independent nation-state (which had contributed to the success of the West) with the creation of a cultural-linguistic and historical nation. Given Friedrich Meinecke's thesis that Western nations were created by strong, independent absolute states, the only way to follow the model of the West in the more unfortunate central, southern and eastern parts of Europe would be to create a nation first, based on cultural heritage, common language and a long history, and then let the nation create an independent state. This situation led to the tradition of a historical self-definition.

How did Hungarian historiography define Hungary's attitude toward Europe and the nation's European consciousness in the last half of the century? Jenö Szücs published the most influential study on the subject, *Historical Regions of Europe*, in 1983. He rightly stressed that regional similarities and differences characterized the peculiarity of the relation to Europe of certain nations and regions, which developed in the process of history. "The regions of Europe which finally crystallized were identical to certain sets or types of responses given to the challenges of the world system." The special characteristics, therefore, based on the autonomous internal development of the given countries, were formulated by historical "layers" of the great transformation periods of the world system. East-Central Europe, according to this concept, showed genuine traits as early as the "beginnings" of medieval European development in the fifth to eighth centuries. The role of these genuine differences was already pointed out by Péter Váczy in 1936, when he underlined certain differences separating the Hungarian, Polish and Russian development from the rest of the continent. He found the reason for this divergence within early feudalism. From the seventh century onward, Europe was divided in two. When the immense area between the Elbe and the Urals was populated by peoples of Slavic, Finno-Ugric and Turkish origin, it created a coherent, integrated Roman-German world in the west and a separate Byzantine-Islamic world in the east. Between these two worlds lay Eastern Europe, which "was determined by the fact that its people settled there relatively late and its ethnic mix began to emerge late as well, when this process was already completed both in the West and in the East." The vast area east of the Elbe-Saale line is both a meeting ground for and a peculiar combination of the West with Asia. Eastern Europe itself mirrored developments on the continent as a whole, breaking into two parts, one with a Latin and Western orientation and the other with a Greek orthodox and Eastern orientation. Váczy stressed that "Eastern Europe as a whole joined a Christian cultural community only later, in the second half of the tenth century, when the Poles, the Hungarians and the Russians founded Christian states." Subsequent centuries did not, however, witness the establishment in the East of feudalism in the Western sense of the term, for a social and institutional system based on private law was beyond the reach of Roman legal tradition. In the East, "regnum became patrimonium," and the entire nobility became subjects in the sense of public law. The forms of feudalism might have been established there, but the substance of feudalism was never integrated into the social fabric of East European life.

About four decades later, László Makkai spoke of "genuine East European traits" based on the differences of the birth of feudalism. His point of departure is Marc Bloch's concept of feudalism. The Western "classical" model of feudalism, as Marc Bloch pointed out, was characterized by a harmonious and proportionate amalgamation of Roman (classical) and Germanic (barbaric) elements. In the East, such an amalgamation of elements proved impossible. In the northern parts of the region Asiatic (barbaric) elements became dominant. In the south, Byzantium, with a "defensive rigidity," hindered the absorption of barbaric elements.

Jenö Szücs, who researched three regions of Europe, also went back to the early medieval period to search for their origins. According to Szücs, Western Europe emerged within the well-defined boundaries of the Carolingian empire. Its eastern frontier were the Elbe, Saale and Leitha rivers. This Roman Catholic feudal society began to monopolize the idea of Europe around the end of the reign of Charlemagne in the early ninth century. By the eleventh to thirteenth centuries, however, the eastern frontier of Western Europe had shifted considerably to the east, as far as the lower Danube, the eastern Carpathians and the forest belt that separated Polish from Russian territory. "Europe," concluded Szücs, "from a mere geographical concept became synonymous with Christianity, a cultural, moreover 'structural' identity." Szücs contrasted East-Central Europe with the region from the White Sea to the Black Sea, and from the Polish plain to the Urals, and concluded that "the Russian state fashioned (and immediately absorbed it into the concept of Russia) the homogenous structure of an 'Eastern Europe' par excellence in the dawn of modern times." Crucial to this process was nearly two hundred years of Mongol occupation, starting in the thirteenth century. An Asian nomadic world drove a wedge into the body of Europe as far as Hungary. Later, in the twilight of the Middle Ages, an Ottoman Turkish wedge, advancing from the southeast, also stopped in Hungary. Both marginalized the territories they flooded to the role of a military borderland. Direct contacts with Asia in Russian territory and in the Balkans impeded the fuller unfolding of the Western type of feudal development and helped "to stiffen more or less an East-European archetype of feudalism." On the other hand, structures of the Western type, sharply distinct from autochthonous East-European structures, developed rapidly in the intermediate region of the Central-Eastern Europe, in the Carpathian Basin, in the Czech basin and in the Polish lowland. "The change from the western edge of geographical eastern Europe into the eastern fringe of a structurally Western Europe was characterized first and foremost by an extraordinarily concentrated and short period of development."

At this point, the concept of Jenö Szücs shows certain connections with those interpretations that stressed that, despite the later start, the trends and developing structures in Hungary showed basic similarities to those in the West, and their "deviations" from the Western model began only around the turn of the fifteenth to sixteenth centuries. Gyula Szekfü, for example, argues that Hungary moved in the same direction as the West and achieved essentially the same level as the West up through the sixteenth century. István Bibó basically shared this view when he spoke of 500 years of Western style development after the foundation of the Hungarian state in 1001, but he also added that Hungary produced a more "rural" version and a lower level of the Western performance. Hungarian historiography broadly shared this view; István Hajnal before, and Pál Zsigmond Pach and Jenö Szücs after the war described a rather rapid, "condensed" catching up process with the West. However, all three stressed the shortcomings of this trend; the much shorter time span did not allow the "deepening" and "digesting" of the adopted feudal structures. Szücs formulated this in the following way: "Social structural elements that developed organically in the West in several stages over almost five hundred years [ninth to thirteenth centuries] through the dismantling of parts of previous achievements and the rearranging of the main elements at every stage, appeared in the Eastern zone, including Hungary, in concentrated form and parallel with one another in little more than one-and-a-half centuries. It is hardly surprising that the forms they took were in some places inorganically truncated or raw, in others still inarticulated, rough or mixed, and in yet others demonstrating here and there various archaic features or differing from their pattern in the proportion to one another."

He also spoke about a special Janus-faced character of "the eastern region of Western Europe"; elements of basic Western structures took root, but the root stock "remained sparse." Vassalage was not strongly institutionalized and constant in its Hungarian "edition." In its rudimentary form of "familiarity," it was not able to counterbalance the strong centralized state, and thus unable to dismantle the old structures. The genuine characteristics of the Western model were, in Szücs's interpretation, the disintegration of central executive power, and the replacement of the state in the feudal system with social relations, as it were. In Western feudalism the administrative, military and judicial functions of the state, once divorced from sovereign power, were divided step by step in a feudal society based on civil law. "The embryo of a promising *contrat social* was conceived in this milieu." The separation of ideological and political, spiritual and secular spheres, and a continued detotalization of power by urban development, all led to a Western society that could not be integrated from above. A new social integration began to develop from below. On this basis Szücs distinguishes between the West and those territories "which were annexed to Carolingian Western Europe in the eleventh to thirteenth centuries," and structurally cannot be regarded as part of the West. "It is better," he suggested, "to anticipate the term of 'Central-eastern Europe' already in the Middle Ages to describe the region which adjusted to Western norms and models, whose structure was modified in each of its elements in an 'Eastern European' environment."

At this point I should note a visible contradiction in Szücs's interpretation. His Russian Eastern Europe par excellence, his Polish-Hungarian-Bohemian Central Eastern Europe (sometimes called the eastern rim of Western Europe by him) and Western Europe, while creating *three* different regions, sometimes appear as only *two* regions. His independent East-Central Europe, which adopted Western norms and institutions, is not, as he rightly noted, an integral part of the West because the Western structures are deformed and modified in the East European environment. In other words, Szücs himself speaks about an Eastern European environment in his East-Central Europe. Furthermore, he also accepted the fact that prior to the eleventh century both areas remained outside the Christian-feudal West, just as after the turn of the fifteenth and sixteenth centuries they would lean mysteriously eastward. "The sharp demarcation line between the economic and social structures that divided Europe into two parts after approximately the year 1500, made the larger eastern part the homeland of the 'second serfdom,' reproducing in a strikingly exact way the Elbe-Leitha frontier of about the year 800 A.D." Moreover, his Russian Eastern Europe par excellence was also not entirely different, since the Kiev Rus, having absorbed Norman and Byzantine influences and converted to Christianity (even if it became not Roman Catholic but Greek Orthodox), was somewhat analogous to Hungary in its social structure. From the thirteenth century onward, however, Asian influences interrupted the unfolding of a late antic-barbaric symbiosis, and put new obstacles in the way of catching up.

There is an old debate about this issue. Péter Váczy already in the early 1940s described an Eastern Europe between the river Elbe and the Ural mountains, including Russia. During the same period István Hajnal, while underlining the differing character of the Greek-Orthodox world, still maintained that Russia also became a part of Christian culture, and later did not automatically become a marginal area of Europe. The excellent medievalist László Makkai stated in the mid-1970s that "The Russian development followed the East-European version of feudalism. . . . Feudal rent was appropriated there indirectly (that is not directly by right of the feudal lord), a situation essentially identical with the Central-Eastern Europe (Bohemian, Hungarian, Polish) system of services . . ." He also mentioned the similarity of land tenure.

The Russian state, however, gradually became an isolated independent world outside of the emerging modern world system. This fact was certainly connected with the long centuries of the rule of the Golden Horde. The agrarian "price revolution" as well as the "religious revolution" of the Reformation did not appear in the country until the sixteenth century.

István Hajnal, however, did not attribute the differences between Russia and the other East-Central European territories entirely to external influences. "The difference from the West is so big that it may not be explained entirely by geographical factors or foreign occupation. There was a genuine structural defect inherent in the Byzantine heritage of the Russian society and culture." Russia's isolation, however, gradually lessened and disappeared from the eighteenth to nineteenth centuries on, and it also became a periphery of the European world system. Since it was separated earlier from and reintegrated later to Europe than its neighbors in East-Central Europe, Russia showed more pronounced differences. But the differences, compared to the Western economic, social and political model, seem generally more apparent as one travels eastward from the West. On this very basis a great part of Hungarian historiography heightens the major significance of the dividing line of the Elbe and Saale rivers. East from that line one can distinguish different variants or subregions of a general East-Central (or Central-Eastern) European model, profoundly different from its Western counterpart.

Regarding the nineteenth century, in our book, I.T. Berend—Gy. Ránki, *The Economic Development of East-Central Europe in the 19th and 20th Centuries*, published in the early seventies, we differentiated between subregions of East-Central Europe and spoke about a western subregion (Bohemia, Austria), a central subregion of the Polish-Hungarian type, and the Balkan subtype, since we excluded Russia from our analysis. According to our concept, it is as important to distinguish between the essential differences *within* the vast region from the Elbe to the Urals as it is to recognize developmental similarities there. Russian East Europe and the Balkans differ from East-Central Europe substantially; at the same time these subregions display similarities in economic, social and political development, compared *as a whole* to the "par excellence" West. The decisive internal regional similarities and the basic differences with the West, however, consolidated or "stiffened" mostly in the early modern and modern times.

Practically all Hungarian historians see an incontestable change at about the turn of the fifteenth to the sixteenth century, a serious decline in the development of East-Central Europe. Mihály Horváth in the mid-nineteenth century attributed this phenomenon to the collapse of centralized power in 1490 with the death of King Mátyás. Ignác Acsády in the early twentieth century underlined the importance of the bloody suppression of the great Hungarian peasant uprising in 1514. Gyula Szekfü in the interwar period put the emphasis on the Ottoman Turkish invasion in 1526–41. Several historians recognized a natural connection among the above-mentioned series of historical tragedies.

The tragedy (or tragedies), according to these interpretations, put a brake on the natural process of catching up, and hence decline became very noticeable. "The people," as Sándor Domanovszky wrote in the thirties, "who by the opening years of the sixteenth century had advanced to the early stages of capitalism, fell back within a single decade to the level of their nomadic ancestors." "Conditions in Hungary *for the first time*," declared Gyula Szekfü, "took a course different from that in the West." Hungary's similarity to the East European and Russian trends, however, are not organic and genuine but only secondary. To discover a major similarity between the Hungarian and Russian "peasant development," as he stressed in his *The Turan-Slavic Peasant-State*, is a mere misunderstanding.

These interruptions are self-evident in the case of Hungary, and no one could question the importance and impact of these historical tragedies. A thorough international comparison, however, makes it obvious that changes and decline cannot be attributed solely to local events, military defeats, the collapse of centralized states or foreign occupation. While Western Europe was evolving capitalist conditions, as shown by the detailed research and analysis of Pál Zsigmond Pach presented from the sixties on, the region east of the Elbe sharply deviated from that experience. Self-managing latifundia, relying on socage, were established; serfs were again bound to the soil as they had been at the time of early feudalism, and feudal dues were paid in kind and labor. The second serfdom gradually replaced the customary money rent and hindered its transformation to wage labor. This change began at the end of the fifteenth century simultaneously in the territories of Prussia, Brandenburg, Mecklenburg, Poland, Hungary and Russia. The two halves of Europe, East and West, clearly split. Though evidently influenced by local circumstances, and partly by attacks from the outside, the phenomenon had a universality in the region east of the Elbe, which indicates more general interconnections. In Pach's interpretation, it was connected with world economic changes. Medieval world trade, traditionally concentrating on luxury articles, was replaced by modern world trade of goods of mass consumption exactly at this time. This went hand in hand with a substantial change in trade routes. The traditional medieval Levantine trade route, leading from the Near East across the eastern Mediterranean Basin and Eastern Europe, was superseded by the trade routes of the Atlantic littoral — from the Baltic ports via Øresund Strait to Gibraltar and through to the western Mediterranean — as well as by overland trade routes between Western and Eastern Europe. The transport of bulk foodstuffs also began from Eastern Europe to the Baltic.

This interpretation of Pál Zsigmond Pach (which was later applied by Immanuel Wallerstein in a broader approach of his Modern World System) puts the "deviation" of Eastern European agrarian development from the Western model in the context of the modern world system. Its proponents, therefore, avoid the earlier "disaster explanations." The division of labor that took place in the modern world economy forming at the time reduced the countries of East-Central Europe to the role of suppliers of grain and livestock. This regulation was obviously related to geographical discoveries. New transatlantic shipping lanes and the overseas colonies not only put the countries of the Atlantic coast at the center of the new international commerce, but also offered them special opportunities for the primitive accumulation of capital. The inflow of precious metals and the related agrarian price revolution underlay internal structural changes and also linked the third factor of the modern world economy, the creation of the modern colonial system, to these economic and social processes.

The countries of the Atlantic littoral reacted to these changes, however, in radically different ways. (It is enough to note the remarkably different Spanish and British responses.) Hence, outside challenges created only conditions and possibilities, and what was of decisive significance in the seizing or missing of these opportunities was what we might call the domestic responsive readiness of particular countries and regions. Here we find a significant and decisive importance of genuine differences, which characterized the birth of East-Central European feudalism and had survived into the Middle Ages despite adjustment to the West. A backward, stagnant urban development, and the existence of the so-called noble society, with its strong aristocracy and gentry (even in number it represented from four to ten percent of the population of the Eastern countries) hindered the embourgeoisement of the peasantry and a general modernization of the society. Using the term of István Hajnal in 1942, "the general, common features of social structure" and the "historical-sociological problems" of the "outermost fringes of Europe" which already existed, now came into play for a decisive role in the new "position taking" made possible by world economic transformation. The stiffening of the social structure and a new (or renewed) system of bondage (Leibeigenschaft) set back the peasants, who had earlier been granted their freedom, and it made impossible the emergence of modern middle classes from the mass of society. It was not counterbalanced by certain contradictory trends which were also present in the East-Central European development. The peasantry, for example, as was proved by Imre Wellman, could rather vigorously defend their institutional freedoms. But their ambitions and wishes, given expression in law, could not become realities of life. "Liquidated economic, social and political phenomena," as István Hajnal pointed out, survived legal abolition and suppression with an often extraordinary persistence. "The organization of society may have inspired the belief that . . . the whole world was transformable by laws and orders . . . and there were no fundamental laws other than the ruler's will. But ukases often got stuck in what was now an autotelic apparatus. However frequently edicts were issued, the scribe still coolly marked them 'execution impossible,' and the provincial clerk on receiving aggressive and unrealistic instructions from above was accustomed to ignoring them." Such conditions opened peculiar historical "side doors." Natural processes became deformed by the need to take detours in order to forge ahead. The blocking of the peasantry's rise to the bourgeoisie under stiffening feudal conditions, for example, led to an overgrown nobility. It was still possible to rise in society, but the specific environment usually required the purchase of noble rank. Noble privileges thus became a strange sort of security for the embourgeoisement of peasant and urban layers.

As a result, East-Central European development not only became more contradictory, but also more receptive to other influences, even though primary historical trends prevailed. The noble layers massed behind the shield of noble privileges and blocked the road of bourgeois development. The Hungarian landlord who was still conducting trade in the sixteenth century gradually abandoned it in the seventeenth; by the eighteenth century he despised such activities as incompatible with his gentlemanly status. In the middle spheres of society, isolated from below and excluded from above, the nonindigenous immigrant strata gained ground and established for themselves a bourgeois existence in the "Lücken-Positionen" (Marx).

In sum, the countries of East-Central Europe had only a subordinate, peripheral position in the new world system. Having deviated from the ascent to capitalism, they underwent the bitterness of refeudalization and were stranded in the quagmire of a centuries-long, stagnant, and painfully slow "late feudalism."

All these processes were interlinked with the specific development of state and nation building. "The unfavorable changes in social-economic development," wrote Pál Zsigmond Pach, "made their natural impact in politics. What followed from the structure of the second serfdom resembles what in the early medieval period had followed from the first: economic exploitation and extra-economic (political-legal) compulsion again combined at the level of the village and of the landlord's domain." The consolidation of decentralized rule by the nobility, the stiffening of feudal institutions, the survival of the seigneurial and regional organs of coercion—in these and other ways the state structure suited the formation of the second serfdom as against the centralization of political power. "True, only in the Polish-Lithuanian state of the sixteenth to seventeenth centuries did this happen consistently, and the Polish *Rzeczpospolita*, the republic of the feudal nobility (or democracy of nobility) was the sole and pure example of this political process. But similar tendencies also appeared in the Hapsburg empire. The feudal *Ständestaat* gained a strong foothold in the Electorate of Brandenburg and in the Eastern German provinces, too. The triumph of the system of estates was destined to be accomplished in this part of Europe at the beginning of the seventeenth century."

To this rejuvenated feudalism, however, the growing military power of absolute states in the West and North was not only a potential threat but an immediate danger. The invading Swedish army at the height of its glory advanced in successive waves, launching attacks on Brandenburg and the Hapsburg, Polish and Russian states. By the 1640s they had already occupied a large portion of Moravia and encamped near Prague. In the next decade they took possession of Warsaw and Krakow as well. The Swedish deluge swept away the *Rzeczpospolita*, showing that the democracy of the nobility was not a viable formation, and in the course of the seventeenth century the superior might and outward pressure of the northern and western absolute monarchies gave force to aspirations in the East for a similar absolutism that would suppress internal autonomies. This tendency was to be seen in Brandenburg-Prussia, the Hapsburg monarchy and Russia. It is indicative that 1653, the year when Friedrich Wilhelm concluded his social contract with the junkers, was also the year in which the last Zemski Sobor assembled in Russia; the change from the feudal representative state to the absolute monarchy was rapid. If a country could not properly respond to the challenge and, like Poland, stubbornly retained its loose, feudal state structure, it not only declined as a nation but actually lost its independent statehood.

But newly established absolutisms were embedded in differing economic and social environments, thereby differing widely in structural terms from Western models. In societal terms they were linked to the system of the second serfdom. Historically, they were built on the precedent that, contrary to Western feudal practice, "étatized" society rather than having "socialized" state functions. This combination of circumstances ultimately created a firm basis for the establishment of an outwardly defensive, strong and rigidly autotelic central power. In contrast to the absolute monarchies of the West, these state formations did not pave the road to capitalist development. Rather, they became bases for a rigid form of feudalism, virtually incapable of adapting to new circumstances, and often pursuing aggressive expansion as a counterpoint to their internal uncertainties.

Even more significant, however, was that a central state power established in the face of an external threat was not identical with the nation in East-Central Europe. In the West the boundaries of the modern state and the nation coincide, and rising nationalism and emerging democracy took roots together during the long centuries of capitalistic transformation. In East-Central Europe, however, as analyzed by István Bibó in his *The Misery of the Small States of Eastern Europe* in 1946, "nation building was painful and troubled": Germany broke into pieces; the Hapsburg, the Ottoman and the Russian empires emerged; and the boundaries of nations and states separated from each other. Moreover, national existence and the territorial status of the nations were left permanently undecided. The collapse of the independent Bohemian, Hungarian and Polish states, the repeated partition of Poland and the long-lasting Ottoman domination over the Balkans clearly demonstrated this uncertainty, which, pointed out Bibó, "became the origin of a political hysterics of the East-Central European nations." The mostly multinational absolute states, on the other hand, could never be really successful, since central power and the nation were separated from each other. In this situation, the feudal nobility became the representative of the national cause and strengthened this separation.

In spite of the dead-ends in its development, however, East-Central Europe became a part of the emerging modern world system and made progress in producing agricultural commodities. As Immanuel Wallerstein noted, the refeudalized East-Central Europe became part of a multisectoral, capitalizing world system. Challenged by the world economy, the feudal absolute monarchy, which was not Janus-faced as its Western counterparts, still had to become a force of structural reforms, initiated and implemented from above. This pressure called into being a system of enlightened absolutisms as early as the mid-eighteenth century. This characteristically East-Central European type of state subsequently tried to overcome the weaknesses inherent in its socio-economic development and statehood. In the absence of genuine bourgeois development, the enlightened absolute state initiated and helped bring about the emergence, even if in a limited way, of an entrepreneurial stratum, mostly from nonindigenous social groups that had embarked upon the road of assimilation. Even still existing peasant village communities and noble self-governments, which represented traditional backwardness and aristocratic-feudal values, gained a new reform inspiration from their national aspirations.

In the "long nineteenth century," as we called it with Gyögy Ránki in our *The European Periphery and Industrialization* in 1982, the pressure and need for "reforms from above" became much more evident and strong. The "dual revolution" of the West, as Eric Hobsbawm named the combined effects of the British industrial revolution and the French political-social revolution, created a new and tremendous challenge. The gap between the extremely rapidly developing industrialized Western democracies and the stagnating and relatively sharply declining Eastern Europe broadened. In the first six decades of the nineteenth century, according to the calculations of Paul Bairoch, the ratio of the per capita gross national product widened from 1:2 to 1:3 between the East and the West. A new wave of lagging behind endangered the peripheries. It represented not only a further relative decline, but also political and even military dangers as well. At the same time, however, the industrializing West opened its markets to a growing amount of food and raw materials. World trade, which remained mostly inter-European trade, increased by nine times between 1820 and 1860. This "pull effect" stimulated the modernization of East-Central European agriculture, including a change from inefficient serf labor to modern wage labor and the introduction of a modern credit system which required the abolition of medieval noble privileges. A modernized and stimulated agricultural production became a self-interest of the former noble elite, which at least partly became a promoter of transformation. The Western institutions that supported the capitalistic economy also needed to be captured. The reply to this Western challenge, therefore, was a series of reforms introduced from above. This began with the Stein and Hardenberg reforms in Prussia, followed by Russian reforms starting in 1861 to the Stolypin reforms of the early twentieth century. In addition, the partial reforms introduced by the Hungarian parliament in the 1830–40s, the Hungarian revolution of 1848 and the reforms introduced by the Austro-Hungarian Compromise in 1867 all well illustrated the attempt to adjust to a transforming world. The reform measures met with an increasing internationalization of world economy: a European railroad network was built with Western investments, an international monetary system conquered and linked most of the European countries after 1860, and massive capital export and migration created a new dynamism in the old continent.

With the success or failure of the response to the global challenge, regional boundaries once again began to shift. The western zone of East-Central Europe again became the "Eastern rim of Western Europe." The western half of the Austro-Hungarian empire approached the Western economic level and Hungary carried out a semi-successful modernization. It realized a belated agricultural revolution and increased its agricultural production by three times between 1860 and 1913. This was connected with an impressive railroad construction boom, which led to a railroad density like the Western level and placed the country sixth in Europe regarding railroads in comparative parameters. Developing agriculture and transportation, moreover, generated spin-off effects and served as a basis for structural changes. Though Hungary could not become industrialized, and more than 60 percent of its gainfully occupied population and a similar share of its national product remained in agriculture, industrialization already started there before World War I. A powerful food processing industry, first of all the famous Budapest flour mill industry, became world renowned. Hungary represented one quarter of the world wheat flour exports and two-thirds of its wheat production was exported in processed form. The first railroads were built by imported rails and locomotives, but by the end of the nineteenth century the country became self-sufficient in producing rails, locomotives and rolling stock for its advanced network. (Unlike most of the unsuccessful peripheral countries; Spain, for example, imported almost all the equipment for its railroads until the war, and Rumania exported 98 percent of its grain to Europe in unprocessed form.) Increased capital imports, which financed 40 percent of Hungary's investments between 1867 and 1900, did not create isolated enclaves (such as Rumanian oil, Serbian copper or Spanish iron ore extraction, without introducing domestic processing industries and reinvested profits) but generated domestic capital accumulation. In the early twentieth century, 75 percent of Hungarian investments were covered by domestic accumulation, and the relative role of foreign capital declined.

A more or less modernizing economy, however, generated new problems; the gap widened between a more modern economy and rather rigid socio-political structures. The traditional noble ruling elite outlived its usefulness, but retained political power and decisive social influence. Both the elite, the autocratic political system, and the rule of militaristic absolutism generally came to seem like ever more flagrant anachronisms. At the head of the capitalist transformation marched the landowning aristocracy and the bureaucratic-military elite, so strongly characteristic in the area from Germany to the Balkans. A peculiar *Ersatzklasse* (substitute class) had risen because of the weakness of burghers and a middle class. The role of this *Ersatzklasse* was strengthened because the reforms were introduced from above and the modernization process was strictly guided by the state. The traditional ruling elite and the big estate preserved its dominance. As Péter Hanák relates, the former lower nobility, the gentry, having lost their privileges and most of their estates, captured state and public offices and flooded the officer corps of the army. The strong official-military "gentleman class" represented a survival of the old noble societies and hindered the peasantry from rising in the social scale. The majority of the peasants (60 percent in Hungary) were emancipated without land; moreover, even the narrow segment of richer peasants, those who owned a larger plot and already employed wage laborers, still remained outside society. In preponderantly peasant countries there were no peasant parties. Secondary schools and offices remained closed to the peasantry. This was true for the Balkans as well, where the landowning elite disappeared with the passing Ottoman rule and all the land became the property of the peasantry. In these "mutilated societies," as Zoltán I. Tóth called them, a new corrupt bureaucratic-military elite emerged and rushed to establish fortunes as they had seen under Turkish domination.

As Hungarian historiography and sociology portrayed it, a special dualism emerged in Hungary and in some other neighboring countries. Ferenc Erdei described this dualism as a special dual vertical structure of the society from the top to the bottom; within the ruling elite, a modern, mostly German and Jewish bourgeois entrepreneurial stratum developed in banks, industry and services beside the traditional landed aristocracy, which dominated the political power and state apparatus. In the middle strata this dualism was reproduced by a parallel existence of a traditional noble, gentry middle class in public offices or in professional fields linked to the state, and a rising modern petit-bourgeois, white-collar worker middle class in the modern business and freelance professional life of the society. (Judges, prosecutors, and even teachers in public schools were gentry-professionals, while lawyers, private prosecutors, journalists, medical doctors and actors all originated from burgher families.) Characteristically enough, the non-gentry middle class was also strongly recruited from formerly nonindigenous, assimilating German and Jewish families. Half of the shopkeepers, lawyers, journalists, medical doctors and clerks in private firms were of Jewish origin in prewar Hungary.

The dualism penetrated the lower social layers as well. The traditional peasantry (liberated serfs) was accompanied by a newly formed and partly also nonindigenous working class. More than one-quarter of the skilled labor force of the Budapest engineering industry was recruited from Bohemia, Austria or Germany in 1880, and the language of the first Hungarian labor movement and its journal was not Hungarian but German. Additionally, about one-third of the Jewish population was composed of industrial workers as well.

The dualism thus went hand in hand with a strange social separation based on ethnic-national differences. The traditional strata from the aristocracy to the landless peasantry were "native Hungarian" (or partly assimilated in earlier centuries), while the modern strata, from the high bourgeoisie to the skilled industrial workers, were often recent immigrants, counted as nonindigenous. Additionally, in multinational Hungary large numbers of peasants and unskilled workers belonged to certain minorities. Slovak and Rumanian peasants in northern Hungary and Transylvania worked on estates of Hungarian landlords and spent or even borrowed their money in shops and pubs owned by Jewish-Hungarian shopkeepers; if they found an industrial job, the boss was often German or Jewish.

Social questions and conflicts, consequently, were intertwined with ethnic, religious differences. Typical nineteenth-century class conflicts of early capitalism often appeared as a "national question." The society was faced with serious, unsolved problems: the "gentry question," the "peasant question," the "Jewish question." In this respect, the road toward modernization, regardless of its success or failure, led to a social and political crisis. This inevitability of crisis resulted in no small measure from the discouraging existence of an unsolved national question, i.e., from "unfinished" nation building.

As described by Endre Arató, the belated national awakening first and foremost manifested itself in the form of cultural and linguistic aspirations. The contradictory, bumpy road of catching up, however, did not lead to a satisfactory solution of social and national issues. Moreover, the earlier disturbances of national development, to cite again István Bibó's excellent analysis, " . . . caused a spurious relation of the elite of these nations to realities; they were accustomed to building upon birthright instead of reality, upon privilege instead of performance and to ignoring simple cause and effect." "Intense and intensely deceptive experiences" influenced many generations who survived the shocks of national grievance and generated mass emotions and passions. This also rendered large layers of the population susceptible to the half-truths and lies that gave vent to their emotions. Moreover, this happened in an age when advanced capitalist countries and mature parliamentary democracies seemed self-confident and "evident and accepted" values of liberalism were questioned. Is the West the real model to follow?

All these questions assumed particular importance in the aftermath of World War I. As I tried to describe and analyze in my *Decades of Crisis* in 1982, disappointed and humiliated East-Central Europe developed new patterns of revolts, prompted by belated starts and backwardness, by severe obstacles of economic and social modernization, let alone the unsolved national problems, as well as the lack of social, ethnic integration and an unfinished nation building.

In the Hungarian case, which was similar to Russia, a bitter revolt challenged capitalism as such. A socialist revolution searched for a new road to create an advanced economy and a welfare society. Wholesale nationalism destroyed private ownership and built a state-run economic system. Social justice was attempted by the expropriation of wealth and equalization of incomes. The Hungarian experiment, however, was suppressed by military intervention after 133 days in existence. Its red terror and dictatorship of the proletariat was suppressed and punished by a white terror of the dictatorial, authoritarian Horthy regime.

The attempts of socialist revolution, except in Russia, were bloodily suppressed wherever they appeared throughout East-Central Europe. But another type of revolt, the national revolution, became more successful. In the view of the East-Central European political, intellectual elite, the failure or semisuccess of modernization was in most cases a direct consequence of the lack of a strong nation-state that could promote industrialization and successful modernization. A belated national revolution engulfed the region, and the dreams of early nineteenth-century national movements were suddenly realized with the help of the victorious great powers, who wanted to build a new Europe with guarantees against a dangerous German rival. The newly formed independent East-Central European countries, some of them small multinational formations which had never existed before, sought to follow the example of Western national integration of previous centuries. They were ready to homogenize their "nations" by centralized power and thereby create a "Yugoslav" or "Czechoslovak" nation. (Tomas Masaryk, a genuine democrat, did not accept the notion of the existence of a Slovak nation.) Hungarian "national defense" became territorial revisionism; a permanent effort to regain the territories cut off by the Trianon treaty and given to neighboring countries, which actually comprised two thirds of the former "historical" Hungary and contained about three million Hungarians, whose majority lived next to the Hungarian borders. National policy in every country in the region was also linked with "economic nationalism," which equated national independence with economic self-sufficiency. Export-led economic growth which had characterized the prewar decades was urgently replaced by protectionist import-substituting industrialization (as Gyögy Ránki and I described in our *The Economic Development of East-Central Europe in the 19th and 20th Centuries*, in 1974). Whether from a "Kondratiev down" cycle or a great depression as part of a "Kuznets cycle," or more evidently a "structural crisis" generated by "a whole set" of technological changes, as Joseph Schumpeter described it, the new economic policy orientation in East-Central Europe during the troubled interwar decades could not lead to the catching up and an attainment of the modernization that was lacking, but to a tragic economic collapse of the early 1930s. A dramatic decline of agricultural prices and the terms of trade as well as an insoluble indebtedness crisis led to insolvency and the one-sided dependence on aggressively rising Hitlerite Germany. The gap between the advanced West and East-Central Europe widened. The countries of the region could not follow a technological-structural adjustment to the new, modern trend of the international economy. Hungary (with Poland, Austria and Spain) belonged to the economically less successful countries of interwar Europe.

The default of the Christian-national course that triumphed in Hungary after the failed Bolshevik-type revolution, the potential danger of new, bitter revolutionary attempts and a deep disappointment in market capitalism all over Europe, all led to a new type of right-wing revolt. The Fascist-Nazi type of revolt began to arise immediately after the war, but it could not gain wide support in the 1920s. During the Great Depression, however, it overwhelmed East-Central Europe. Most of the countries of the region proclaimed war against the Western values of the French enlightenment and British liberalism. Mystic racial-national ideologies took root. Moreover, as these countries' attempts to catch up failed, they were driven further to the periphery, and their leading national trends became more and more interlinked with the irrational ideas of fascism. Ruthless dictatorships, Nazi-type regimes, royal autocracies, and frenzied nationalist pseudofascisms consumed the entire region from Germany to the Balkans. The only surviving bridgehead of postwar left-wing revolution, the Soviet Union, which aimed for a new, just, egalitarian, well-to-do and genuinely democratic society, was deformed and merged with a ruthlessly dictatorial, national-imperial modernization model.

East-Central Europe rapidly departed from Europe again. A small intellectual community still angrily debated how to most adequately define Hungary's place in Europe in 1940. As István Gál wrote, all the small nations share the same concept about their mission as safeguards of Europe: *propugnaculum Christianitatis, antemurale Christianitatis.* As Gyula Künszery remarked in the course of the debate, meanwhile ". . . a new public view is emerging in Europe, which is giving up the concept of Central Europe and enlists Hungary to the Balkan countries, thus, to a *Balkan-Europe.*" Hungarian historiography in the 1960–70s agreed: "ferry-boat Hungary" (as Endre Ady called it at the beginning of the century) sailed eastward and rapidly departed Europe.

World War II shattered the old continent. There were no similar massacres, no comparable destruction in history. East-Central Europe, the most troubled part of Europe, clearly suffered the most. It survived the murder of 20 to 25 million people, saw the disappearance of huge communities of ethnic, religious minorities (about 10 to 13 million Germans escaped or were expelled, about 4 million Jews were killed and nearly 1 million of the survivors emigrated), and suffered a migration and a war destruction of national wealth of unprecedented proportions. (About half of the railroads of Poland, Yugoslavia and Hungary were destroyed, 50 to 80 percent of Warsaw and 27 percent of Budapest was damaged or destroyed, and about one quarter of the capacity of their nondeveloped industries annihilated.)

East-Central Europe experienced a new cessation of historical continuity. Previous political regimes collapsed and almost the whole ruling elite physically disappeared. Along with Governor Horthy, a great part of the former Hungarian politicians, landlords, officers and entrepreneurs left the country. Along with Ferenc Szálasi, the Hungarian Nazi head of state in the dramatic last few months of the war, quite a few former prime ministers of the country between 1938 and 1944 were tried and executed as war criminals. Another few thousand were imprisoned and about 60,000–70,000 people were purged from public positions as Nazi collaborators.

Hungary, like every other country in the region, and unlike Western Europe, could not return to its old ways after a period of reconstruction and revitalization. From one (right-wing) extreme, East-Central Europe dropped into another. In part of the Balkans, a genuine communist takeover followed years of heroic communist-led antifascist partisan war which coincided with a bitter, ruthless civil war. In other countries East from the river Elbe, a liberating and later occupying Red Army of Stalin's Soviet Union imposed a Sovietization between 1945–48. As Jenö Szücs said, the dividing line between the two different Europes, Eastern and Western, was mysteriously re-created along the Carolingian boundary of the year 815 A.D. Socioeconomic development after the turn of the fifteenth to the sixteenth centuries reinforced this division of the continent along the Elbe-Leitha line, and this is, with astonishing precision, where American and Russian armies met and where Germany was divided again after World War II. In the area of *historical* East-Central Europe, a *political* East-Central Europe was formed—the Soviet bloc, or (from 1955) the Warsaw Pact countries united for the first time in their history into one single political-military organization. They also tried to establish, again for the first time in history, a separate and independent world market, (beginning in 1949) the Council of Mutual Economic Assistance, (or, using its more often used name, COMECON). This *economic* East-Central Europe abolished the market economy and introduced central, compulsory planning with fixed prices, expropriated private ownership and established a state-owned and state-run economic system of forced capital accumulation and industrialization, reoriented its trade and canceled its economic ties with the West.

Stalin and his chief ideologue Zhdanov declared, in 1947, the existence of two camps or two world systems inside an "enlarged" Europe. Whether it deliberately chose to or was forced to do so, East-Central Europe began to follow a new model of catching up, different from the Western one. Instead of imitating the West, instead of being linked with it as its periphery of food and raw material supplier, it adopted an all-out program for regional self-sufficiency, an outrageous policy of import substitution. Paradoxically enough, the overall rejection and neglect of the West aimed to catch up with it: Stalin himself declared he would achieve the Western level of industrialization in ten years in 1931. Khrushchev, who posthumously dethroned Stalin and announced a new course of Soviet socialism, declared, however, the same goal. From 1960 he sought to catch up with Western industrialization, productivity and living standards in twenty years, and no longer alone, but together with East-Central Europe as a whole.

The post–World War II history of Hungary is an ambiguous mixture of departure from and an approach toward Europe. The departure was pronounced by Hungary's political separation from the West, by its monolithic state-socialist political structures, by its nonmarket economy with a one-sided (two thirds of its exports and imports) trade orientation to East-Central Europe. It was physically expressed for long by the closed borders with barbed wire fences, minefields and watch towers, and by the jamming of Western radio broadcasts. Official ideology and politics stressed Hungary's place in the "Socialist camp." At the height of the Cold War, in the late forties and early fifties, Hungary and every other country of the Soviet bloc urgently and excessively prepared themselves for World War III, which was seen as unavoidable. By the turn of the fifties and sixties, with the warning example of international relations and in the aftermath of the dramatic people's uprising of 1956, the official Hungarian view of Europe changed. When János Kádár participated at the closing session of the Helsinki meeting on European security and cooperation in August 1975, he stressed in his address, "We are representing the Hungarian people . . . which founded its state 1100 years ago . . . in the middle of Europe, thus both our past and our future are linked with the destiny of the peoples who are living on this continent." Kádár also stated that "The Hungarian People's Republic is a firm advocate of the peaceful coexistence of countries of different social systems." In this changed concept the two camps, the competing socialist and capitalist worlds, did not have to face an unavoidable war. To belong to the socialist bloc no longer implied being antagonistic to the idea of increasing cooperation and coexistence. The first secretary of the Hungarian Socialist Workers Party, János Kadár, spoke in 1975 about a "mutually advantageous economic connection" with the West and expressed his readiness for broadened cultural cooperation and information. He spoke of a "universal scientific world," a "universal culture of mankind" and an "open door" of international tourism. "In spite of existing ideological and political differences," he summarized his view, "we have to understand and cooperate with each other and agree on common tasks and actions . . ." In these decades there was no longer a huge gap between declarations and practice in Hungary. The attitude toward Europe changed radically, and the Helsinki agreement definitely strengthened this trend. The Communist Party and state, however, did not change its concept and policy regarding Hungary's place in Europe. As an important party document on "The actual problems of socialist patriotism and proletarian internationalism" said in 1974: "The most important antagonism of our age is the irreconcilable conflict between socialism and imperialism. In the condition of a world-wide confrontation, each socialist nation is responsible for the defense and strengthening of its social order and the international positions of socialism." Later in the document it was written: "There are two radically different socio-economic systems in Europe. Their competition is an element of the world-wide struggle between them."

Hence Hungary, according to the official party and governmental attitude, counted itself as a firm, integral part of a Soviet-led, socialist East-Central Europe, but on that basis it sought to participate only in peaceful cooperation with the other European countries and to become part of Europe as a whole. In this interpretation, both cooperation and competition was only a part of the irreconcilable confrontation and struggle between the two systems.

Separation from Europe thus accompanied the existence of state-socialism in Hungary. On the other hand, there was a process of social-economic transformation which, against the dominant ideological attitude, paved the way toward approaching Europe. A dramatic social transformation and integration ruthlessly destroyed the traditional rigid social hierarchy, the strong remnant of "noble society," land tenure of feudal origin and the precapitalistic value system. Drastic state intervention transformed the villages and caused tremendous pain and injustice, while at the same time increasing social mobility. Rapid industrialization led to radical structural changes in terms of the occupations of the population, and decreased the share of the agricultural population from 56 to 13 percent. Urbanization accelerated and modernized the lifestyle, changed the pattern of family, and modified eating habits and leisure. A more egalitarian and significantly enlarged school system, which offered education free of charge at each level, including university, improved the cultural-educational level of the population. The country's economic structure changed, and the per capita gross national product rose from 70 percent of the level of the European average to equality in the mid-1970s. The pattern of industrialization, though based on early twentieth century technological and structural standards, and unable to adjust to the dramatic structural crisis of the 1970–80s, still crept closer to Europe. Hungarian scholarship became an integral part of the international scientific community and nearly a tenth of its scholars periodically visited Western countries and universities, and indeed worked there from the late sixties on, though most of all in the 1980s. Mass tourism made a great part of the population more Europe-oriented, informed and "European" than ever before.

The primitive anticapitalism and one-sided critical attitude of the West in official propaganda and ideology was not sustainable, because the strict isolation of the country was abandoned in the mid-1960s and the borders became increasingly open long before the actual collapse of the iron curtain. The lies of a declining and "rotten" capitalism and of the superiority of the "socialist" Soviet Union became evident for the masses, who themselves had rather different personal experiences. In this environment, anti-Western propaganda became even counterproductive, leading to an idealization of the West. It was strengthened by the impact of the new waves of emigrants. The first wave of emigration (about 1.3 million people) left Hungary around the turn of the nineteenth and twentieth centuries. About 200,000 followed in the interwar decades. As a part of post–World War II emigration, including the Germans who were expelled from the country, about 400,000 people left between 1944 and 1948. After the suppressed revolution, another 150,000 emigrated at the end of 1956. From the early sixties on, there was no further mass emigration from Hungary, but a sort of rather limited, but almost permanent emigration of intellectuals and young people created a special connection and even familiar relations with different Western countries. Since almost three million Hungarians lived in neighboring countries of no more than one day's travel away, a rather personified and diversified sociological and political experience was assured for a great many families. Moreover, a gradually increasing economic and trade connection with the West strengthened the Western ideal. From the mid-1970s to the late 1980s, COMECON trade steadily declined from 66 percent to about 40 percent of Hungarian foreign trade, and Western products flooded the country. "Shopping tourism" became a regular practice and culminated in a Hungarian mass exodus of shoppers to Vienna in the late 1980s before the collapse of state socialism. In the personal experience of the masses, "western" became a synonym of better quality and superiority in a rather idealized way.

From the 1980s on, parallel with the erosion of the system, (the extended reform process followed by the peaceful collapse of state socialism), a strong and gradually strengthened political-intellectual-spiritual trend aimed at expressing the need of differentiation between Hungary and the Soviet Union, as well as Hungary and most of the other parts of the Soviet bloc. One of the expressions of distancing from Eastern Europe and attempting to draw nearer to the West was reflected by the renewal of the historian's debate regarding Hungary's place in Europe. The concept of *historical* East-Central Europe was challenged and an effort was made to emphasize the organic link with Western or Central Europe.

The poet laureate Gyula Illyés stated in an interview in 1982 that "Hungary since the time of the holy king István always belonged to the West." Endre Bojtár, literary historian, declared "it is time to come back from Eastern Europe to Central Europe."

From 1988, when the transition arrived, to the historical turning point in Hungary, when János Kadár and his ruling Politburo were dismissed (in May) and a "peaceful revolution" (as Timothy Garton Ash called it) began, the new leading political slogan proclaimed "Back to Europe!" The dream and hope of integration into the European Community, of joining NATO and catching up with the West, was expressed through an effort to strengthen a European or Central European self-consciousness. The western rim of East-Central Europe has the opportunity (or at least feels it does) to be an economic and political part of Europe. Among the political parties there is a rivalry for the authentic representation of Western values. In 1991, Géza Jeszenszky, Minister of Foreign Affairs, in a heatedly debated interview followed by a speech in Parliament on behalf of the government coalition, sought to "monopolize" the representation of Christian-European values. Geographers published articles that Hungary is evidently a Central European country. In an oversensitive and difficult transformation process, both the traditional western term "Eastern Europe" and the historical concept of East-Central Europe became an irritating and often flatly rejected insult.

Parallel with all these political events and transformations, some historians challenged the historical concept of placing Hungary in East-Central Europe. From the older generation, Péter Hanák, in a joint publication (*Europe's Regions in History*) in 1986, wrote of a Central Europe which consists of "Switzerland, on the western side of it." In a newspaper article in October ("Central European Consciousness"), he wrote of a Central Europe consisting of "Czechoslovakia, Austria, Hungary, Transylvania and Slovenia and Croatia from the Yugoslav state." In 1990, as executive chairman of the newly formed Central Europe Association, he called for a historical debate and rejected the existence of a "huge Eastern European region," underlining the basic differences between the Central European countries and Russia. Péter Hanák criticized Pál Zigmond Pach's works of 1958 and

1963 and maintained that he requalified the Hungarian-Polish type of historical development from a near-Western *(nyugatias)* type to a East European type, though Hungary's history does not show similarities to Russia. In his argumentation Hungary represents a Central European type par excellence which, in his historical argumentation, was equated with the Hapsburg empire. In a very recent article, he ended with clear political reasoning: "In the present as in the past, many have denied the existence of Central Europe," and those who reject "the historical existence of Central Europe . . . are hindering not only its resurrection but also its exhumation from the dissolution of 1919 and from its burial of 1945."

From the younger generation Gábor Gyáni, in his article of 1988 ("Historian Debates About Hungary's Place in Europe"), accused those historians who described and analyzed the "East-Central European characteristics and structures" of Hungarian historical development of deliberately wanting to "shift Hungary into Eastern Europe" with their diabolical attempts to justify Yalta and the post–World War II division of Europe into East and West. He unsuccessfully tried to deny basic similarities between Hungary and other neighboring East-Central European countries and prove similarities between the British and Hungarian, Western and East-Central agricultural development. Pál Zigmond Pach's response was well argued and devastating. I am not going to cite and describe the arguments and counterarguments of their debate in the fall and spring 1992 issues of *Buksz* partly because the essence of the debate is rather old and well known (partly because it reminds me of a boxing match between a professional heavyweight champion and a paperweight amateur). The historians' debate regarding Hungary's place in Europe is starting all over again with a new-old vehemence. *Da capo al fine?* From beginning to end—all over again?

The outcome of the debate will be determined by the prospect and future of Hungary's integration into Europe. If the country becomes an integral, and thus equal, part of the old continent, successfully catching up and building its civil society and democratic structures, then the century-long debate will cease and nobody will argue over Hungary's place in Europe. It will be natural and organic, and nobody will question it. But if the integration process will lead, as it has in the past, to a position that is only peripheral, to a poor, early capitalism with a society and political structure befitting a backward state, then the debate about self-identification and Europe will continue. Both the uncritical and unrealistic emphasis of the Western or Central European character of Hungary's historical development and its angry rejection, the denial of Western values and the importance of autotelic, genuine Hungarianness will be present and confronted on board the "ferry-boat," which is sailing eastward.

Bibliography

Acsády, I. *A magyar jobbágyság története.* (A History of Hungarian Serfdom), (Budapest, 1906).

Ady, E. Morituri. *Figyelö* I. Vol. II Budapest, 1905.

Arató, E. *Kelet-Európa története a 19.század elsö felében.* (A history of Eastern Europe in the first half of the nineteenth century), (Budapest, 1971).

Baráth, T. "Kelet-Európa fogalma a modern történetírásban." (The concept of Eastern Europe in Modern Historiography), in *Emlékkönyv Domanovszky Sandor születese hatvanadik évfordulójának ünnepére.* (Festschrift to celebrate the sixtieth birthday of Sándor Domanovszky). (Budapest, 1937).

Bárdossy, L. Magyarország hivatása a Dunamedencében. *Uj Magyarság* August 26, 1941.

Barta, L. *Két szellemiségi forma.* (Magyrok és Csehek) (Two forms of mentality. Hungarians and Czechs) *Uj Szó.* Bratislava, November 3–4, 1929.

Berend, I.T. *Válságos évtizedek* (Decades of crisis) Third edition. (Budapest, 1986).

Berend, I.T., Ránki, Gy. *The Economic Development of East-Central Europe in the 19th and 20th Centuries.* (New York, 1974).

Berend, I.T., Ránki, Gy. *Industrialization and the European Periphery 1780–1914.* (Cambridge, 1982).

Bibó, I. *A keleteurópai kisnápek nyomorusága.* (The misery of the small nations in Eastern Europe). (Budapest, 1946).

Bogya, J. Magyarország és a világpolitika. (Hungary and world politics). *Nemzeti Ujság.* December 4, 1919.

Bojtár, E. A keleteuropéer pontossága. (The preciseness of a European) in Botjár, *A keleteuropéer as irodalomelméletben.* (An East European in the theory of literature). (Budapest, 1983).

Domanovszky, S. Zur Geschichte der Gutsherrschaft in Ungarn, in *Wirtschaft und Kultur. Festschrift zum 70. Geburstag von Alfons Dopsch.* (Baden bei Wien, Leipzig, 1938).

Ferdinándy, M. Középeurópai alakzatok, (Central European formations). *Az Ország Utja.* No. 10. 1938.

Ferdinándy, M. Kózép-Európa—Kárpát-Európa. (Central Europe—Carpathian Europe). *Magyar Nemzet* January 4, 1940.

Gál, I. A virtuális Középeurópa. (A virtual Central Europe). *Apollo.* December 8, 1934.

Gál, I. Közep-Európától Kárpát-Európaig. (From Central Europe to Carpathian Europe). *Magyar Nemzet* January 4, 1940.

Gál, I. Magyarország helye Európában. (Hungary's place in Europe). *Magyar Nemzet.* January 19, 1940.

Gunst, P. Kelet-Európa gazdasági-társadalmi fejlödésének néhány kérdése. (Some problems of the social-economic development of Eastern Europe). *Valóság.* No. 3. 1974.

Gyáni, G. Történészviták hazánk Európán belüli hovatartozásarol. (Debates of historians on the place of Hungary in Europe). *Valósag.* 1988. No. 4.

Hóman, B. -Szekfü, Gy. *Magyar történet,* Second edition Vol. III. (Budapest, 1935).

Horváth, M. XVII-dik század elsö felének jelleme Magyarországon. (The characteristics of the first half of the 17th century in Hungary) in Horváth, *Kisebb tórtáneti munkái. Vol. III.* Pest. 1868.

Imrédy, B. Asuj Európa irányitó eszméi (The leading ideas of the new Europe). *Uj Magyarság.* July 6, 7, 1940.

Kádár, J. Felszólalás az Európai Biztonsági és égyüttmüködési Ertekezlet záróülésén. (Statement at the closing session of Meeting on European Security and Cooperation) in *a szocializmusért-a békéért.* (Budapest, Kossuth Kiadó, 1978).

Kosáry, D. Közép-Európa vagy Kárpát-Európa. (Central Europe or Carpathian Europe). *Magyar Nemzet* January 9, 1940.

Künszeri, Gy. Balkán-Európa. (Balkan Europe). *Magyar Nemzet* January 26, 1940.

A Magyar Szocialista Munkápárt Központi Bizottsága mellett müködö Kulturpolitkai Munkaközösség állasfoglalása. A szocialista hazafiság és a proletár internacionalizmus idöszerü kérdései. (Statement of the Commission of Cultural Policy, Central Committee of the Hungarian Socialist Workers Party. Actual questions of socialist patriotism and proletarian internationalism). *Társadalmi Szemle.* October, 1974.

Makkai, L. Feudalizmus és az eredeti jellegzetességek Európában. (Feudalism and the genuine characteristics in Europe). *Történelmi Szemle,* No. 1, 1976.

Németh, L. Tejtestvárek (Milkbrothers), *Tanú.* I. November, 1932.

Niederhauser, E. Zur Frage der Osteuropäischen Entwicklung. *Studia Slavica.* IV. No. 3–4. 1958.

Pach, Zs. P. *Nyugat-európai és magyarországi agrárfejlidés a XV–XVII. században.* (Agragarian development in Western Europe and Hungary in the 15th–17th centuries). (Budapest, 1963).

Pach, Zs. P. Kózep-Kelet Európa és a világkereskedelem as ujkor hajnalán. (East-Central Europe and world trade in the dawn of the modern age), *Századok.* 1982.

Pach, Zs. P. A közep-kelet európai régió az ujkor kezdetén. (The East-Central European region at the beginning of the modern age). *Budapesti Könyvszemle (BUKSZ)* 1991. No. 3. (Fall).

Szabó, D. Magyarország helye Európában.-Keleteurópa (Hungary's place in Europe—Eastern Europe). *Az üt-elöre. Lúzetek, 9.,* (Budapest, 1935).

Szabó, D. A keleteurópai nemzetek egysége. (The unity of the nations of Eastern Europe). *Uj magyarság* September 1, 1933.

Szabó, Z. Magyarság és Közép-Európa. (The Hungarians and Central Europe). *Kelet Népe.* V. 1939. No. 7.

Széchenyi, I. *Kelet Népe* Pest, 1836.

Szekfü, Gy. A "turáni-szláv parasztállam" (The "Turan-Slavic peasant state"). *Magyar Szemle.* Vol. V.1.(17.) January 1929.

Szücs, J. Vázlat Európa háron történeti régiójáról. (A draft on the three historical regions of Europe). *Történelmi Szemle.* 1981.

Szücs, J.-Hanák, P. *Európa régiói a történelemben* (The regions of Europe in history). (Budapest, 1986).

Teleki, P. Magyarország és Európa. (Hungary and Europe). *Fiatal Magyarsác.* No. 2. 1935.

Váczy, P. A középkori Kelet-Európa. (Eastern Europe in the Middle Ages) in Hóman-Szekfü-Kerényi (ed.), *Egyetemes történet. Vol. II. A középkor története.* (European History. The history of the Middle Ages.) (Budapest, 1935).

Vass, Gy. *A Dunamedence ezer éve. Magyarország szerepe Kelet és Nyugat között.* (The thousand years of the Danubian Basin. Hungary between East and West). (Budapest, 1940).

Wellman, I. Mezögazdaságtörténetünk uj útjai. (New roads of our agrarian historiography) in *Emlékkönyv Domanovsky Sándor születése hatvanadik fordulójának ünnepére.* (Festschrift to celebrate the sixtieth birthday of Sándor Domanovszky). (Budapest, 1937).

The Idea and the Reality of Europe Among the Czechs

Jiří Kořalka

All Czech considerations and discussions about the phenomenon of Europe since the first half of the twentieth century include, explicitly or at least indirectly, two fundamental questions:

1. Can Europe be identified exclusively with the Christian West, or are Russia and the Balkans a part of Europe?
2. Is the concept of Europe sufficiently represented by the large nations, or do small nations have a special role in European diversity?

Bohemia as the Heart of Europe or as a Frontier Nation

The diffusion of pan-European ideas in the region of Bohemia and Moravia, as in all central Europe, depended on the teachings and untiring activities of the international "Republic of the Learned." Natural scientists, linguists, librarians and antique collectors, not only in Prague and Olmutz,[1] but also in Bohemian and Moravian castles, took up contact with those of a similar mind in other European nations. One read, wrote and spoke predominantly in French and German as the earlier importance of the Latin language lost significance in research and teaching. When Frantisek Palacky, the leading Czech historian and politician of the nineteenth century, looked back in February 1837 on the first ten annual volumes of the *Casopis Ceskeno museum*[2] (Journal of the Bohemiam Museum) scientific quarterly, he was pleased to note that the "new European culture" finally had reached Bohemia and that it made a new world of concepts, perceptions and thoughts accessible there, albeit in a foreign language, through the mediation of German-language literature.[3]

Palacky thereby scratched at an open wound of contemporary Czech national identity. Was the devoted battle for linguistic and national independence of such great value for the Czechs themselves and for Europe that it warranted harnessing all efforts in its fulfillment? Would it not be more appropriate to adopt the highly developed German language and culture and, within its framework, contribute immediately, without any detours, to the enrichment of European culture?[4] A good many educated people of ethnic Czech origin assimilated, in the course of the nineteenth century, into the predominantly German-speaking social and cultural milieu of the Austrian empire. But this was no solution for the five million Czechs in this densely populated area. "We are Czechs and intend to remain Czechs forever, and we want to be neither Germans, nor Magyars, nor Russians . . ."[5] Thus wrote Karel Havlicek, the influential Czech journalist in March 1846, in rebuttal to pan-Germanism, the pan-Slavism promoted by Russia and—here in the name of the Slovaks—against the attempted metamorphosis of Hungary into a Magyar national state. And for "his" Czechs, Havlicek demanded a position equal to that of every other European nation.

To perceive oneself simultaneously as a member of the Czech nation, the Austrian state (in the sense of a multinational monarchy), the European continent and of the entire human race ought not to be an irreconcilable contradiction. In the cited essay of 1837, Palacky declared the renewal of the modern Czech language to be an accomplished fact which was quite capable of cultivating its own scientific and fine arts literature on a contemporary European level. Or, as he put it figuratively: ". . . to introduce, as it were, the old Bohemia into the new Europe, and to naturalize the new Europe in Bohemia."[6] Palacky himself, in his view of the history of the nation of the Bohemians and Czechs, attested to the legitimacy of its equal status among contemporary European nations. According to the Czech historian, the Hussite reformation and revolution of the fifteenth century was not only a historical demonstration of Czech progressivism and love of freedom. It also as much as opened the way for a new age in Europe, when the Hussite Bohemians challenged the claims to universal authority of the Roman Catholic Church.[7] "This time, Bohemia was not limited as a state to its internal acts, but made its appearance on the world stage as a European power—albeit for the last time. Once again the full significance of the Bohemian peoples position in the middle of Europe became evident . . ." he wrote in 1860.[8]

This idea about the central position of Bohemia and the Czech settlements in the center of Europe—the very heart of Europe—was by no means in harmony with the view generally held in Europe and in part in Germany as well, which equated Europe with the Christian occident. Because the region of Czech settlements was almost completely surrounded by German-speaking peoples, nearly all Czech intellectuals who dealt with the European aspects of their national existence tried their best to find in Eastern and Southern Europe the necessary counterbalances to the West. In contrast to the Poles, who usually had to defend their identity and independence more strongly against Russia than against Germany, hopes that Russia would play a positive role in a European context were widely shared among Czechs until well into the middle of the twentieth century. Czech periodicals and the two large encyclopedias of the second half of the nineteenth century[9] were so well informed about Russian, Ukranian, Slovakian, Croatian, Serbian and Bulgarian conditions, principally in cultural affairs, that in some matters they were pioneering. The activities of many Czech high school teachers and other specialists in the southern Slavic territories and in Bulgaria after 1878 also confirmed the Czech public in its conviction that the non-Catholic Balkan peoples should be equal members of the European family of nations.[10]

After Bismarck fell from power, the "Young Czechs," a new generation of Czech liberal politicians, sought to oppose the feared predominance of the German Reich on the continent of Europe with the idea of an all-Europe accord. Gustav Eim, a "Young Czech" foreign policy expert, recommended in October 1892 an Austrian-Hungarian rapprochement with Russia and France, ". . . so that a large double barrier of peace lies across Europe, from the Atlantic ocean to the Urals and from the Adriatic sea to the Polar sea, which no disturber of the peace will find it easy to cross."[11] For the cosmopolitan, usually young group of professors at Prague University, a European orientation which helped overcome the almost exclusively German influence on Czech culture was a subject of vital importance beginning with 1882. The *Athenæum*, a scientific periodical edited by Professor T.G. Masaryk, provided extensive information about English, French and Russian professional literature in an evident desire to open the windows wide to Europe. Czech scientists, predominantly those who were independent of the Austrian civil service (e.g., chemists, physicians), appeared at European meetings as representatives of Bohemia or *pays tcheques*, not as Austrians.[12] Although early in the twentieth century few Czech political parties and newspaper editors dealt with international relations, those Czech politicians who were interested in the matter regarded Europe as a whole as far more acceptable than a Central Europe dominated by Germany.

Frequently Czech publications discussed the idea that Czechs in Europe play a mediating role between the Roman-Germanic West and the Slavic East. It was in large measure due to Masaryk's influence that an outstanding group of southern Slavic students at Prague's Czech University acquired a strong European persuasion before 1914,[13] or that West European public opinion gained more sympathy for the Croatian-Serbian opposition against the Hapsburg empire after two sensational trials.[14] It was this atmosphere of the era that produced the then most important Czech contribution to understanding of the European problem before 1914, T.G. Masaryk's two-volume work about Russia and Europe, published in Germany.[15] The Prague University professor, known internationally for his courageous opposition to anti-Semitism and for freedom of expression, attempted to explain the close relationship between Russian literature and the revolution in Russia.

Masaryk answered the fundamental question—whether, and to what extent, Russia is a component of Europe—largely positively, but he understood Russian reality at the start of the twentieth century as a colorful mixture of European and non-European elements. The effect of Europe on Russia appeared very large to him, just as the Russian revolution of 1905 had great effect on the rest of Europe. Masaryk placed the centuries-old humanistic and democratic traditions of Europe in the foreground, but these had to fight with absolute monarchism and militarism in Russia and in the remainder of Europe while finding compromises with them at the same time.

The Role of Smaller Nations in Europe

Beginning in the first decades of the nineteenth century, Czech poets, journalists and later politicians were likely to argue that the existence and independent development of the smaller European peoples had special value for the entire European continent. Looking back on 1848, the year of revolution, Frantisek Palacky perceived the now obvious nationalistic efforts of European peoples not as an artificially conceived agitation or aberration, but as being of "providential moment, as the natural and thus necessary reaction to a modern civilization of uniform sameness so that in uniting mankind its diversity would not disappear."[16] Palacky was convinced that only the next, i.e., the twentieth, century would see the large, hardly imaginable effects of advancing national differentiation in Europe and in the whole world. Palacky's contemporaries particularly stressed the spiritual and cultural values of the smaller European nations, to compensate for the disadvantages of their territorial insignificance and small population. The Greeks and the northern European nations, and Ireland since the 1840s, served as models for the Czechs.

In 1894, Jan Palacky, professor of geography at the Czech University of Prague and son of the renowned historian, wrote the article about "Europe" in the largest popular Czech encyclopedia. In his view, the significance of Europe to world history reflected the fact that no single power was able to exercise its hegemony across the entire European continent after the fall of the Roman empire. The Promethean spark of freedom was always able to find a safe haven somewhere among the manifold European islands and peninsulas, or in its hills. Among the various trends of European development Palacky included the remarkable fact that not only large nations such as Spain, France and England but also smaller ones like Portugal, the Netherlands and Sweden had their periods of fame and power in European history. "It was a kind of federation of nations that had made a relatively young Europe master of the world . . ."[17] He regarded the heterogeneity and peaceful competition in labor and education as the most worthwhile inheritance from Europe's past. Again he repeated the emphasis on the special role of the smaller European nations, noting that the younger members of the great family of nations could take the place of those larger ones that had become weary.

When Arnost Kraus, the leading Czech Germanist and expert in European languages and cultures, began publication of the monthly *Cechische Revue* (in German) in October 1906, he paid special attention in the first editorial to the general problem of the smaller nations of Europe. The journal published not only unprejudiced, though critical information about economic, cultural and scientific achievements of the Czechs, but also about the political and spiritual lives of those in similar circumstances and European nations that, owing to their small populations, experienced conditions like those of the Czechs. "Our occasional reports about foreign policy will have a peculiar coloration as a result," Kraus continued. "They will look at contemporary events precisely from the point of view of the usually ignored interests of the small nations. We hope with these reviews and individual reports about the role of the smaller nations, their relations with each other and with the dominating larger nations, to approach our goals more quickly, along a perhaps more indirect, rather than a straight path."[18] A special column, "Die Kleinen" (The Small Ones) in the *Revue* discussed news from the editor's special field of interest, i.e., Sweden, Norway, Denmark and Danish North Silesia. At the end of the *Revue*'s first year of publication Arnost Kraus had to admit that the varied small nations of Europe had few common interests, and those they shared dealt mainly with the fact that they could never count on the understanding of the major powers. In addition,

Kraus heard from friends in northern Europe and the Netherlands suggesting that he should have chosen English, rather than German, as the language for his publication. However, the efforts of the small Realist Party led by Masaryk, to which Arnost Kraus also belonged, were successful to the extent that they disseminated a broad, all-European viewpoint beyond Central Europe to part of the Czech intellectual class before the First World War.

Representatives of some smaller nations of Europe who had no nation state of their own could occupy almost equal positions in unofficial spheres of international relations, particularly in the socialist labor movement, in scientific organizations and in sports. Thus, they were able to prepare the way for the changes in Europe that were to come at the end of the war in 1918. Czech labor leaders, scientists and athletes at the turn of the century were among the most passionate supporters of international cooperation in Europe based not on the existing states but on national principles independent of them. The Czechs wanted to appear abroad as representatives of Bohemia, as representatives of their nation, rather than as Austrians. It was not a question of language because, like their Dutch, Scandinavian and Greek colleagues, they could not be successful abroad without knowledge of the world's languages. Instead, it was a matter of enforcing their own national identity with the goal of achieving an equal status as a European nation. In most instances, international recognition was achieved via the back door by nonofficial organizations of Poles, Finns and Czechs at the Congresses of the Socialist International or at the Olympic Games before 1914. Some attempts, such as for the cancelled 1916 Olympic Games in Berlin, were prevented by the outbreak of the war.[19]

The defense of their rights and the fight for freedom of the smaller nations, first the Serbians and then increasingly the subjugated peoples of Austria-Hungary, were among the official war aims of the Entente in World War I. At the same time, Germany sympathized with the fight for Irish independence from Great Britain and with the emancipation efforts of non-Russians in the czar's domain. On October 15, 1915, Masaryk gave the inaugural lecture at the newly founded School of Slavonic Studies of London University. His carefully selected title was "The Problem of the Small Nations in the European Crisis."[20] Masaryk took as his point of reference the fact that the Europe of the time included twenty-eight states but sixty-two nationalities. In contrast to the western part of Europe, where the existing nation-states of various sizes made for a kind of national balance, in the East he saw, aside from the great Russian nation, only small and smaller nations, among which only a few had their own independent states. According to Masaryk, the East and the West of Europe were not separated sharply or by a straight line. For example, Germany and Austria-Hungary were part of the West as well as of the East. It was precisely in this zone, comprising eastern Germany, the Balkans and western Russia, that Masaryk found the true center of national antagonisms: "Here is where the present war erupted, here is the region from which continuous uproar and tumult arises for all Europe. This zone is the true nucleus of the so-called Eastern Question; this zone provides the most urgent, most angry reason for transforming the political organization of Europe."[21]

Contrary to the assertion that the rules of history only favor the formation of large nations and states, Masaryk, agreeing with Frantisek Palacky, insisted that history was both an integrative and a disintegrative process. European development is not directed toward uniformity but to organized diversity. Centralist tendencies are balanced continually by the struggle for individualism, autonomy and federation. Masaryk was prepared to admit that small nations had to struggle with certain difficulties and disadvantages, that they could be impatient, and might seek to become larger at the expense of their neighbors. In view of the economic and cultural interdependence of European nations, he succumbed to the illusion that the liberated small nations in eastern central and southern Europe would be included in a new organization of Europe. As war aims on both sides became more defined, Masaryk's European program and the Czechoslovak position abroad became more overtly hostile to the Kaiser's empire. A free Poland, Bohemia (or Czechoslovakia) and a southern Slavonic state appeared to be the natural enemies of a German drive to the east.

Masaryk's summarized program of a "New Europe," completed toward the end of 1917, focused on concerted action of sovereign nations on the territory between Germany and Russia, most of all against a German Central Europe.[22] The symbolic high point of how inflated the role of small nations between the Baltic Sea, the Adriatic and the Black Sea had become was reached at a Congress held in October 1918 in Philadelphia under Masaryk's chairmanship. Here, Czechoslovaks, Poles, Southern Slavs, Ukrainians, Hungarian Ruthenians, Lithuanians, Rumanians, Italian irredentists, indentured Greeks, Albanians, Zionists and Armenians expressed their desire for a union which would then join a union of all the nations of the world.[23] Not represented, in keeping with the war psychosis, were the enemies of that time: the Germans, Hungarians, Bulgarians and Turks. What was more important was that the political developments in east central and southeastern Europe at the end of the war failed to reflect the wishes of the representatives of the enslaved nations gathered in Philadelphia. The new Europe experienced severe birth pangs. The realization of a democratic Central European Union as Masaryk had proposed in Philadelphia was totally inconceivable.

Europeanism and Democracy
in Czechoslovakia Between the Wars

The contradiction was so obvious that it could not escape notice by any careful observer. The conventional belief of a highly developed European civilization that also served as a shining model for other continents was destroyed in the trenches of World War I. The picture of reciprocal murder of members of the leading nations of Europe at battle sites was offset among the Czech public, however, by a general sense of happiness and satisfaction with the newly achieved national independence. The Czechoslovak Republic constituted itself as a parliamentary democracy. In the first ten years of its existence, it almost seemed to be an island of prosperity and internal political stability, particularly after some of the Sudeten-German parties took part in the government.[24] This impression was widespread in most European nations during the 1920s, although it did not correspond with the facts in every respect. Moreover, the founders of the Czechoslovak state made constant efforts to apply their moral-humanistic ideas whenever possible.

Never before — and never again until the middle of the 1980s — was there so much discussion and conversation about Europe in Czech politics and in print as there was between the world wars. Even before the founding of the republic, Masaryk, who was to be elected president four times, pointed out that Czech independence had to be a "part of the political and social organization of all Europe and humanity."[25] In a comprehensive account of his political activities during World War I, Masaryk expressed his belief that the defeat of triple theocratic absolutism (meaning the Russian, Prussian and Austrian) and the founding of new republics and democracies would also signify the acceptance of democratic principles in international affairs: "The United States of Europe ceases to be a utopia. The dominion of one great power over the continent of Europe, and the alliance of a number of states and nations against the other states and nations vanish before the peaceable society of all states and nations."[26]

This doubtless idealistic belief was refined, and in part corrected, by Masaryk's closest colleague, Edvard Beneš, the long-serving Czech foreign minister, in his unending diplomatic activity. From the very beginning, Beneš recognized the fateful position of Czechoslovakia as the point of intersection of the major streams of European great power politics. "Three great streams always will meet on our territory: Western influence, German influence, and Slavonic (Russian) influence," Beneš declared in June 1919 following the signing of the Versailles peace treaty. He understood that the all-European significance of Czech policies in the new state had to heed each of these three factors without ever being used as the tool of any of them.[27] As much as Czech foreign policy interested itself in the maintenance of the international system of the Versailles treaty, it nevertheless did not want to bind itself unilaterally to France. Instead, it tried to maintain good relations with Austria and Germany, and with the Soviet Union as well. Above all, Beneš worked with enormous personal effort in the League of Nations. As he recalled later, the days and weeks he spent each year in Geneva in which he acted on behalf of the League of Nations were among the happiest times of his political life.[28] Peaceful cooperation of all European states also appeared to serve the best interests of the Czechoslovak Republic.

Influential representatives of the Czech intellectual elite professed their belief in Europe and in the European idea of unity in plurality without reservation. The leading Social Democratic education expert and author, Frantisek Václav Krejci, who visited the Czechoslovak Legion in Siberia during the Russian civil war as leader of a government delegation in 1919–20, reported how Czech soldiers felt a European patriotism or European pride although they were then several thousand kilometers from Europe. Krejci characterized this Europeanism as clear awareness of belonging "to a joint cultural and moral whole."[29] A unified Europe was for him not something to be taken as a matter of course. It was not a given, but a higher goal. It was a lofty, desirable objective, for the achievement of which the victors and the vanquished of the world war would have to move away from some of their national maxims. He was convinced that the unity of Europe was destroyed by the Reformation and restored by the Age of Enlightenment; injured by the French revolution and renewed through European liberalism and democratic socialism; so badly shattered in its foundations by the world war that the non-European nations were confirmed in their aversion to Europe, but resurrected through the pan-European idea and with its proposals for a United States of Europe. The Czech public had shown such great interest for translations of foreign literature since the end of the nineteenth century that it even supplanted domestic production. In contrast to certain nationalist critics of the right, Krejci was not concerned by this development, seeing it as proof that "Europeanism was beginning to mean more than Czech nationalism on a cultural plane."[30]

No other Czech entered the fray for all-European understanding between the wars with more success than Karel Capek.[31] His personal friends included G.B. Shaw, and H.G. Wells; Romain Rolland and Paul Valéry, Gerhart Hauptmann and Thomas Mann, and authors of smaller nations as well. Capek was among the founders of the international PEN club, invited many authors to Prague and traveled frequently and with pleasure himself.

His loving travelogues from Italy, Great Britain, the Netherlands and Scandinavia provided his readers within Czechoslovakia and abroad with convincing views of European nations that were bound together by their differences.[32] At every opportunity, Capek noted not only the special characteristics of the various regions and peoples, but also the enviable evidence of the supranational and prenational past of Europe. When he found traces of the Hapsburg double eagle in the Netherlands with which he had become familiar in Prague, just as he had encountered them earlier in Italy, Spain and Hungary, he was deeply stirred by the thought of a dynastic pan-Europe of baroque times, some sort of league of submissive peoples. It had been a grand idea, one that was fumbled by the monarchs. Capek was convinced that in addition to the fight for national self-determination, the Czech tradition also included the will and the ability to join a supranational organization as a member just as it did in the Holy Roman Empire or the Hapsburg empire. "I repeat — we have in the history of our tradition a more or less broadly and deliberately defined political Europeanism. Perhaps this tradition should tell us something today."[33]

Karel Capek gave a subjective assessment of the phenomenon of Europe in May 1934. He was seriously disturbed by the resurgence of a political and economic nationalism that placed new barriers of mistrust and increased hatred between hope for human progress and the nations and states of Europe. At the same time, he noted a process of reducing all European civilization and culture to the same low level, without attention to some attempts to nationalize culture politically. "One may say," wrote Capek, "that the national differentiation of life slowly disappears; one lives more and more between constantly deepening trenches. That is the paradox of today's Europe."[34] In Capek's view, there were two possibilities for further development of Europe at a time when each nation was isolating itself and suffocating within its own borders. Either some European states will succumb to the notion of expanding their borders by force, which the nations whose territories are involved will oppose with all means at their disposal. In Capek's view, that would lead inevitably to war and a series of catastrophes; and no such war would provide the means to draw definitive borders. Secondly, he thought it plausible that the existing borders are made less limiting and to internationalize economies and policies. The sameness of everyday life in Europe could best be balanced by creative development of national cultures.

Following the assumption of power by the National Socialists in Germany in January 1933, and the defeat of the democratic Austrian opposition in February 1934, a large part of the Czech population was more than ever united in a European concept inspired by the ideals of political pluralism, parliamentary democracy and intellectual tolerance. With the exception of Switzerland, the Czechoslovak Republic remained the sole remnant of European freedom until the fall of 1938; German and Austrian political emigrants were very appreciative of this in 1933–35.[35] Traditional Czech efforts to integrate the eastern portion of the European continent into an all-European structure emerged once again in reaction to the new constellation of political power.

Before ratification of the Czechoslovak-Soviet alliance treaty of 1935, the old master of Czech literary criticism, Frantisek Salda, reflected on the belief that the political axis in Europe was moving steadily but imperceptibly from West to East: "Russian collectivism and western individualism will not be antagonist like fire and water forever, they will mix and permeate each other ever more in the future. A synthetic idea that anticipates this unification will not do badly. Could that not be a Central European, and particularly our idea? That is a cultural program not for a century, but for several centuries."[36] Jaroslav Durvich, the Czech Catholic author, supplemented these considerations with the note that the Czechs, through their thousand-year friendship as well as their peaceable contacts with the Germans, were able to adapt to the German lifestyle in thought and emotion and thus to fulfill an important European mission.[37]

Although many Czech newspapers published unsettling accounts of political persecution and disregard for human rights in the Soviet Union and in the German Reich from the middle 1930s, a society existing in orderly democratic circumstances could hardly imagine the true nature of the totalitarian system. The responsibility resting on the leadership of the Czech state was all the more critical as it watched with growing concern how the structures for peace and security built up with great effort by the League of Nations remained without influence against the violent appearance on the scene of certain powers. In view of the Italian war against Ethiopia, the occupation of the demilitarized Rhineland by Germany and the split between the great European powers in the League of Nations, Czech Foreign Minister Kamil Krofta declared to the Czech parliament, "All these happenings, combined with the economic crisis that has for a number of years weighed so heavily upon Europe, cloud the political horizon and the prospects for the future in dark gloom."[38]

Europe is at a turning point, repeated Edvard Beneš, elected president as successor to Masaryk in 1935, as he joined Foreign Minister Krofta in evaluating the international situation. Czechoslovakia continued to support the principles of European security and democracy, but at the same time it was impelled to seek accommodations both internally and in its relations with its neighbors. Foreign Minister Krofta told the Czech democratic press, in May 1937, "The complexity of our position at the crossroads and the center of Europe obliges us all to maintain the greatest possible impartiality, sobriety and discretion in our public statements about foreign policy in order to avoid influencing foreign policy decisions with domestic policy considerations, and so that attacks on the heads of state and on foreign leaders, regardless of their political orientation, are avoided."[39]

A pronounced European dimension characterized all contemporary political commentaries of the most important Czech writer of the period, Karel Capek. He watched developments in the neighboring German Reich with great concern, particularly after the annexation of Austria in March 1938, which was to unify the Germans, not only politically, but also spiritually (in terms of German Weltanschauung, education, culture and racial prejudice). "In other words, in the interest of its national unity, it (Germany) knowingly and deliberately turns its back on the European community, on the spiritual solidarity of the European nations." That could not be a matter of indifference for anyone to whom mankind, humanity and spirituality were not empty words, because the participation of a great nation in developing common European ideas would be sorely missing. This unification process had also been embraced by many Sudeten Germans, who now wanted to enjoy a peculiarly German right, the right to German national isolation. The Czech constitution and the good will of the Czech citizenry were obliged to give the Sudeten Germans all political and economic rights required by an educated citizen for a free and honorable life. But it was impossible to guarantee them the special German right they were now demanding. "To the extent that they want only to be German Germans, it seems to abjure the possibility of their being European Germans," complained Capek in April, 1938.[40]

Two months later, on the occasion of the Prague Congress of the International Federation of PEN Clubs at the end of June 1938, the Czech PEN Club published in English and in French an impressive declaration of allegiance to the idea of a democratic Europe.[41] Two renowned historians, a literary historian, an Evangelical theologian, a journalist and an author joined their talents in depicting Czechoslovakia as a small country with a great history. "It is Europe in miniature; it is the European West and the European East, as it were, in the palm of one hand . . ." wrote Karel Capek. "Imagine Czechoslovakia removed from the map of Europe. At once something like a North to South barrier emerges, going across Europe and dividing it both geographically and culturally into West and East. Let us not look at Europe from the viewpoint of whatever governments happen to be in power. For the future of mankind what unites Europe will be more important than what divides it. In the spiritual and political order of the world, Czechoslovakia will find its historical mission along the West to East line. It is called to this by its very position, its close ties to the culture of Western Europe and its kinship with the Slavonic East of our continent."[42] This idea of mediation permeated all chapters of the book, ending with a final contribution by Ferdinand Peroutka, containing a brilliantly witty homage to compromise and the golden mean as the sole alternative to death and destruction.

Compromises and negotiations, however, were of little value when the basic pillars of the idea of a democratic Europe — general civil and human rights, political pluralism and religious tolerance — were in question. On the Czech side, the hot summer of 1938 was filled with unceasing appeals to democratic Europe not to let the last bulwark of democracy in its center be destroyed. In vain. "The Moral Basis of Europe Shaken" headlined Karel Capek, October 2, 1938 commentary on the Munich agreement between Great Britain, France, Italy and Germany, in which Czech independence was sacrificed to National Socialist Germany. Not only the borders of the Czechoslovak Republic were now changed, but the internal configuration of Europe was altered in a manner most detrimental to smaller and mid-sized states and nations. "The means with which an acute European crisis was to be resolved at our expense is neither an enduring nor a final solution," wrote Capek. "Whether in months or years — this is not a prophecy, but a certain-ty — all of Europe will have to be recast. I do not mean only a displacement of borders, but an internal rearrangement because all of Europe is shaken in the foundations of morality and power . . ."[43] The Munich capitulation of the Western powers signified — far beyond the borders of Czechoslovakia — the collapse of the entire system of political principles ruling Europe.[44]

Czechs and Slovaks in the Shadow of Power Politics and the Ideological Chasm in Europe

The experience of Munich 1938 marked at least two generations of Czechs alive at the time. Young people obviously were more deeply affected than those who had experienced World War I and the prewar period. Along with the deep disappointment there was also a widespread abandonment of the distant ideal of a united Europe. A large part of the Czech population wanted to concentrate only on the internal problems of the now smaller nation and to live in agreement, if possible, with the new master of Central Europe. For Slovakia, the power political changes brought an easier realiza-tion of their desire for Slovakian autonomy; on March 14, 1939, an indepen-dent Slovak state was established, although at the cost of democracy and pluralism. The Slovak Republic was a willing vassal of National Socialist Germany and its expansionist policies from 1939 to 1945. The remaining Czech region was occupied by the German Wehrmacht on March 14–15 and transformed into the German Protectorate of Bohemia and Moravia. It was not subject to international law.[45] Deliberate assimilation of Czechs thought to be qualified for "Germanization" was to proceed hand in hand with forced liquidation of Czech intellectuals. All Czech universities were closed on November 17, 1939, bringing to an end the independence of the Czechs among European nations.

The second president of the Czechoslovak Republic, Edvard Beneš, who served in that office from December 1935 to October 1938, went into exile for the second time; for him it was the same old battle, interrupted by World War I, for democracy in Europe. In his lectures at the University of Chicago in April 1939, Beneš summarized the intellectual and political development of Europe from the feudalism of the Middle Ages to modern democracy. He dealt with the influence of World War I on the democratization of Europe and viewed the League of Nations, despite all its shortcomings and failures, as an expression of the democratization of Europe and the world. The fall of European democracy was the underlying cause of the failure of the League of Nations. For twenty years, he said, he had worked for a constructive peace policy; for twenty years he had fought tirelessly for peace at Geneva and had helped to organize the League of Nations. Finally, as Czech president, he had been only a few steps away from war, and only under pressure by two great allied powers had his country made a great but futile sacrifice, for this sacrifice was unable to resolve the issue of war and peace in Europe. Beneš was firmly convinced there would be war soon between democracy and dictatorship in Europe, and that democracy as the morally superior system would be the victor. "And the better, freer, and more democratic inner structure of the different European states will also bring a new and better external organization of Europe; a kind of federated Europe will be the final result of the present profound European crisis," Beneš concluded his Chicago lectures, with foresight but with many illusions as well.[46]

Aversion to the supposedly perfidious capitalistic West was widespread, if not general, in the Bohemian states, in part among political forces collaborating with the superior power of the Germans, but also among those resisting the German occupation. The director of propaganda of the Czech protectorate's government, Minister Emanuel Moravec, sought to rub salt into this open sore of Czech national and European consciousness by urging Czechs repeatedly in the widely-read Prague newspaper *Lidove Noviny* to reject corrupt capitalism. The 1938 Munich treaty was a more significant turning point in European history, he wrote, than the beginning of the

French revolution or the invention of the steam engine. "Only the discovery of America ranks with Munich," he wrote in February 1942. It had been a judgment over the decaying world of capitalism and democracy. "In 1938 began the great retreat of capitalism from the European continent. Europe has awakened to socialism."[47] Following the signing of the Hitler-Stalin pact in August 1939, the controlled Czech press for some months did not hesitate to point out the common features of the two socialist systems, but in fact there was only one alternative. "The ideas of German National Socialism became a common European property following the fall of France, for common hope and for the belief in Europe."[48] The inevitable German attack against the barbaric East brought the European community even closer together. Germany would be victorious for Europe on all fronts, as many posters and V-symbols dutifully proclaimed on public buildings, in newspapers and movie theaters. Using "New Europe" as a slogan, more than 400,000 young Czech men and women were put to work in Germany.[49] President Josef Tiso and his Slovakian government expected to be rewarded with a better position in the future Europe to be dominated by Germany because they had sent Slovak military forces to the eastern front. The independent Slovakian state served as a kind of showcase for smaller nations of southern Europe, to demonstrate how a small nation could thrive under the protection of the Greater German Reich. Direct contacts between Bratislava (Pressburg) and Bucharest and Zagreb (Agram) were viewed with displeasure in Berlin, however.[50] After June 22, 1941, the European concept played an important role in Germany's massive propaganda in Bohemia and Moravia against the growing influence of the Soviet Union and communism. It was claimed that the German soldier protected all Europeans, including the Czechs, against the Bolshevik threat. A poster showing sharp claws with hammer and sickle over Prague's Hradcany castle symbolized the danger said to threaten Czech culture. Forced mass visits to an exhibition of conditions in Soviet Russia and trips of prominent intellectuals to the excavations of graves in White Russian Katyn were related to the slogan of a joint defense of European values. The overwhelming majority of the population did not believe a single word of the German propaganda but Europe as an appeal was discredited significantly among Czechs under German occupation.

The Czechoslovak resistance domestically and abroad (including significant democratic groups among Slovaks) derived its hopes not from the concept of Europe, but from the active participation of the Soviet Union and the United States in the war against Hitler Germany. Edvard Beneš considered the idea of a democratic reorganization of postwar Europe and the world in London in the first half of 1942. He could not imagine it without the

Soviets. "Soviet Russia, in contrast to other plans (the so-called pan-Europe, for example) must be a component of this European organization and in the cooperation of the new European blocs."[51] Beneš believed that the wartime alliance of the Western democracies with the Soviet Union also would signify a closer approach domestically. As an alternative to the federalism and confederation plans considered by the British during World War II,[52] Czech foreign policy in exile held to the restoration of the European system of states as it had been before 1938, but with due consideration for Soviet political power interests. With the signing of the friendship and mutual assistance pact with the Soviet Union in December 1943, the Czechoslovak government in exile tacitly accepted its inclusion in the Soviet sphere of influence, with Beneš believing it would guarantee noninterference by the Soviet Union in Czech internal affairs after liberation. Not Europe, but the United Nations expressed the expectations of most politically interested persons—including the Czechs and the Slovaks—at the end of the Second World War.

The newly constituted Czechoslovak Republic of May 9, 1945, broke with the parliamentary democratic tradition of the period between the world wars not only in its foreign policy, but also in its domestic development. Only four Czech and originally two Slovakian political parties were admitted to the National Front (two additional Slovak parties were accepted shortly before the May 1946 elections) in the framework of a joint program. The former right wing of the political spectrum was excluded because it had collaborated with the Germans. The expulsion of the German population in 1945 and 1946, which was perceived as a security measure against possible repetition of the Sudeten-German irredentism, had even more serious consequences. Expulsion was not based on individual guilt. An entire population group was driven out or exiled because of German nationality. The wave of national vindictiveness was not unique to Czechoslovakia in the last phase of the war and immediately thereafter. The horrifying information from liberated concentration camps in Germany confirmed for many Europeans as well as the Czechs the skepticism, which had already existed in the resistance movements, about a possible democratic future for the German nation. Europe without Germany, in some sense Europe against Germany, existed for a time in 1945 as an independent and desirable phenomenon.

Two victorious superpowers, the United States and the Soviet Union, were more involved in Europe after the Second World War than ever before. After a few years, Europe found itself split into two parts, an event highlighted by the communist takeover of Czechoslovakia in February 1946 and the blockade of West Berlin in July 1948. Czechs and Slovaks henceforth were not to consider themselves as Europeans, but as members of a socialist world community stretching from the western border of Bohemia to Kamkatchka and to the 38th parallel in Korea. "It is not a problem for us (to decide) whether we will take the path of Western capitalism or that of Eastern socialism," claimed Zdenek Nejedly, the first president of the Czechoslovak Academy of Science, founded in 1952 in the pattern of the Soviet model. "And the problem for us is even smaller because the progressive world of socialism is represented today by Slavic and other closely related peoples."[53] A Western orientation of Czech culture and style of living was judged as unnatural, as a mentality inimical to the meaning of Czech history. The communist Czech view was a curious combination of outdated romantic nationalism and Russophilia in internationalist guise. The communists fought a never ending battle against the ineradicable Western influence in Czech society. In many instances, as in the campaign against cosmopolitanism, it took on almost grotesque forms.[54]

Return to Europe as a Slogan and a Political Goal

The national borders of the Czechoslovak Socialist Republic were protected with barbed wire, mine fields and watchtowers, but complete isolation was quite impossible. To the south, the Republic of Austria gained its neutrality in 1955 and started its rapid ascent to a welfare state. The western neighbor, the Federal Republic of Germany, condemned official Czech propaganda as revanchist and as the source of instability in Europe, but its successes in economic and social reconstruction could not remain hidden. Foreign Czech and Slovak language broadcasts were disrupted, but many people were able to hear Radio Vienna. While the first destalinization wave of 1956 had a far smaller impact on Czechoslovakia than on Poland and especially on Hungary, the second thaw after 1962 had deep and lasting effects on Czech intellectuals. The long years of interrupted contacts with the noncommunist free world were resumed with surprising speed, largely on the Czech side by the socially privileged group of critically disposed scientists, writers and artists. Among all the European nations, the Federal Republic of Germany displayed the greatest understanding by far in the 1960s for the slow disintegration process in the communist spiritual leadership, for the "reformation of communism," as a knowledgeable expert called it.[55]

It was a Germany different from the official image and what had been known about it before 1938–39. But more than anything it was a new Europe about which almost nothing whatsoever was known in communist Czechoslovakia — a Europe almost without national borders, where millions of people of all social classes could travel freely and convert their money freely. It was a Europe with a well-functioning social market economy where shops and department stores were not only full of goods, but also filled with shoppers; a Europe that (then still) loathed all forms of nationalism and fought against centuries-old prejudices. What did the Czechs do wrong to be excluded from this Europe? The western and northern small states and nations especially, their size and populations approximating that of the Bohemian lands, appeared to be particularly attractive examples. When I pleaded in 1968 for the development of Czech society as open, self-assured and tolerant to the outside world and as differentiated and structurally modern domestically at the time of the ratification of the Federation of Czechoslovakia, I was explicit about the model of the small- or medium-sized European states. "It should be a national society within our socialist conditions, similar to the present Swedish or Dutch society, much more a society than a nation, because the national in such a society is a matter of course."[56]

The European component played a significant, if not a decisive role in the Prague Spring of 1968. With few exceptions — and these were well outside the mainstream of reform communism — there was absolutely no talk of copying capitalist Western Europe. The aim was to form something new, something that had not been tried anywhere in the world. It was to be a "third way" between capitalism and communism, which would take over the best of both systems and overcome the worst. It turned out to be a fairy tale vision of Czech reformers of 1968 and of their numerous supporters everywhere in Europe and in other parts of the world. A form of socialism with a "human face" became a seductive hope for the European left, which had become bitterly disappointed with the so-called "real socialism" of the Soviet bloc. Thus the Czechoslovak reformist attempt helped Eurocommunism, which already existed in a nuclear form in Italy, Spain and France and in certain smaller communist parties of the West, to come out into the open on the European political stage.

However, the enthusiasm for the Prague Spring, and particularly for the resistance of Czechs and Slovaks to the assault by five armies of the Warsaw Pact, could not delay a more critical analysis for long. When, in exalted words, Czech author Milan Kundera wrote that the Czechs had moved to the center of the world stage for the first time since the Middle Ages because they sought a form of socialism without secret police and with freedom of speech and of the press, twenty-three-year-old dramatist Václav Havel responded. He rejected such ideas as narcissistic and laughable "provincial messianism." "Freedom and the rule of law are the first requirements for a normal, healthily functioning social organism and, when a state makes the effort to renew itself after these requirements had been absent for years, it is not doing something historically unique. Rather, it is only attempting to remove the aberrations, whether that state calls itself socialist or not."[57] For Václav Havel, the standard was not socialism as an allegedly higher form of social organization, but man and his rights. And those European states in which the social organism performed "healthily and well" could serve as models.

In the years following the suppression of the Prague Spring, the European components of the Czech spiritual resistance to communist controls were incomparably more strongly represented than before. The new German policy toward the East (Ostpolitik), symbolized by Willy Brandt, played a significant, usually positive role. Later, Václav Havel termed the Federal Republic of Germany's massive efforts for détente "an enormous contribution to modern European history,"[58] without ignoring some accompanying negative effects of this policy. It was possible then to undermine the apparently monolithic structure of communist domination in the nations of central Europe with officially sanctioned economic and cultural cooperation and to pull the rug out from under the campaigns against German revisionism and revanchism. Helsinki 1975 and the human rights accords signed there by the leading representatives of the Eastern bloc would have been unthinkable without the new German Ostpolitik. The joint responsibility for peace and multilateral cooperation of all European states including the Soviet Union — and the United States and Canada — as promulgated in Helsinki in 1975, sooner or later would have to come into conflict with the split caused by Cold War power politics in the middle of the European continent.

The European concept now established itself strongly in the official and in the opposition Czech press.[59] An appreciable number of outlawed and politically persecuted dissidents of various political views, most often after having been discharged from their employment, joined forces in the Charta 77 human rights organization. They initiated discussions about freedom and injustice, about human rights, democracy and political pluralism. "We were thinking, and therefore we dreamed as well," Václav Havel remembered later. "Whether in jail or outside, naturally we dreamed of a Europe without barbed wire, high walls, artificially separated peoples, and without gigantic munitions depots; a Europe freed of bloc systems, a European political system not subject to temporal or separatist interests."[60] More than forty years after Karel Capek's fundamental considerations in 1938, the European concept again moved into the foreground of Czech intellectual interests.

Pan-European associations also were clearly present in the passionate discussion about Central Europe that flared up following an essay by Milan Kundera.[61] Here Kundera dealt with the contradictory development of the western and eastern parts of Europe after 1945. He perceived the most complicated development "in that part of Europe which lies geographically in the center — culturally in the West and politically in the East," ascribing this characteristic specifically to three nations—the Hungarians, the Czechs, and the Poles. "For them, 'Europe' is not a geographic concept, but a spiritual one, equivalent to the word 'West.'"[62] Kundera believed the eastern border to have come about by the inclusion of Central Europe to the Roman-Latin cultural sphere in the course of a thousand years; the western border had been established only in the middle of the twentieth century by the political domination of the Soviet Union on this territory. Not only Lev Kopelev, the Russian author living in Germany, but also Czech critics led by Milan Simecka asked Kundera "not to exclude Russia from Europe."[63] How broad and varied Czech understanding of Europe was in the 1980s is demonstrated by the fact that *Stredni Evropa* (Central Europe), a mimeographed underground newspaper published since 1985, represented a pro-Hapsburg conservative point of view, while most experts on Central European history could not imagine a Central Europe without Germany.[64]

The dreams of the leading representatives of Charta 77 were defined in a samizdat manuscript by former radio correspondent Jiri Dienstbier, later Czech foreign minister from December 1989 to June 1992. The foreword to the manuscript is dated February 1986. While recognizing the existence of the U.S.-Soviet condominium over Europe, Dienstbier explored other ways for creating an enduring rapprochement of all European states and nations. German reunification, completely unlikely at the time, was a decisive lever for détente in Europe for Dienstbier and his friends.[65] Havel's fervent belief in the spiritual European tradition was the subject of an acceptance speech read when he was awarded the Erasmus Prize in Amsterdam in November 1986. The beautiful vision of a free, peace-loving, nonaligned Europe, he was convinced, could not be achieved by negotiations of presidents and governments. "The Europeans," said Havel in 1986, "obviously can dare to have their vision only if they have a sincere, serious inner reason for it, namely, if something I would call that European awareness connects and motivates them. A deep feeling of belonging together. A deep feeling of unity, even if it is the unity of difference. The deep awareness of the thousand-year-old common history and spiritual tradition provided by the confluence and interpretation of the elements of Judaeo-Christianity and antiquity. . . . Europe is composed predominantly of small nations whose spiritual and political histories interconnect them reciprocally with thousands of strands into a single fabric. Without the awareness and the experience of this reality, without a new understanding of its purpose and without pride in it, a European consciousness will not arise."[66]

In the stormy events in Central and Southeastern Europe in the fall of 1989, the striving for national emancipation was inseparably tied to a more or less clearly expressed feeling of pan-European togetherness. The revival of two key concepts of the nineteenth century, the bourgeois society and the nation, were certainly not in contradiction to the removal of barbed wire and the watchtowers at the borders and to the opening up of Europe. The majority of the hundreds of thousands of Czechs and Slovaks who were able for the first time in their lives to travel freely abroad, wanted their share of the prosperity of capitalist Europe as quickly as possible. The ideal of "the third way" of 1968 was forgotten or pushed aside. "We give the task facing Poles, Hungarians, Czechs and Slovaks today the working title 'Return to Europe,'"[67] declared Václav Havel as president of Czechoslovakia in April 1990 when the top political representatives of Poland, Czechoslovakia and Hungary met with the foreign ministers of Austria, Italy and Yugoslavia in Bratislava. The Czech and Slovak Federative Republic, as the state was designated officially in February 1990, was admitted to the Council of Europe and to its Parliamentary Assembly, concluded an associative agreement (like Poland and Hungary) with the European Community, and participated in several regional initiatives. The desired full membership in the European structures has no opposition in any Czech or Slovak political force.

It is not, however, only a matter of joining economically and politically to a European Community that has reached an advanced stage of development. There is much discussion of common European history and culture, and about how far the present state of Czech and Slovak societies, their education and effectiveness, correspond to the European standard. "'We and Europe' is beginning to be what the question 'We and Germany' was for our fathers and grandfathers," comments Czech historian Dusan Trestik appropriately.[68] Identification with Europe and contemporary European values clearly predominates in Czech society today. As the new Czech minister president, Václav Klaus, said, it would be superfluous to brood over problems of Czech identity because the Czechs belong to the average standard nations of Europe; they are neither large nor small, neither rich nor poor and, as Karel Capek stated sixty years ago, they have no reservations about participating as an independent member in a supranational organization. A strong tradition of local and regional self-government developed among the Czechs in the second half of the nineteenth century, promoting various active Euroregions beyond the national borders of Austria, Germany and Poland. In this atmosphere, it seems useful for some Czech historians and writers to warn of an "unfounded, proud Eurocentrism" and to point to the problems of the non-European world. Even West European integration is not what it was before the fall of 1989. "A real Europe of nations living harmoniously together, of pluralism and tolerance, has yet to be born," Czech historian Otto Urban concludes in discussing the promising ideal.[69]

In the unsettled postcommunist part of Europe, Czechoslovakia, with Václav Havel as its leader, for a time evoked the appearance of being an island of quiet and tolerance, an example of two nations with equal rights as the first step to admission into the federalized Europe. It was only a temporary stage, however. Following the pattern of the emancipated nations of the former Yugoslavia and the former Soviet Union, Slovak national society, freed from communist controls, also insists on establishing its separate identity as a state. In numerous discussions and negotiations with the Council of Europe and the European Community, Slovak politicians realized that a "Europe of Nations" in the West European sense really meant a Europe of national states, and that Slovakia's voice would be heard only at the secondary level, i.e., the "Europe of Regions."[70] Thus arose the graphic figure of speech, according to which Slovakia demands an independent seat in European institutions and its own star in the flag of Europe. Resistance to the belief that the Slovak nation was to be integrated into Europe only through Czech mediation strengthened the will for a declaration of Slovak national sovereignty proclaimed on July 17, 1992.[71] It will require enormous effort and much good will on the part of many not to let the forthcoming separation of Czechoslovakia become the occasion for a new partition of Europe according to economic systems and cultural orientation.

Notes

1. For a summary, see Walter Schamschula, *Von der Societas Incognitorum zur Böhmischen Gesellschaft der Wissenschaften* [From the Societas Incognitorum to the Bohemian Association for Science] in Ferdinand Seibt (ed.), *Vereinswesen und Geschichtspflege in den Böhmischen Ländern*, [Association activities and historical records in Bohemian states]. Bad Wiesseer Tagungen des Collegium Carolinum. (Munich, 1986), pp. 53–60.

2. Joseph F. Zacek, *Palacky: The Historian as Scholar and Nationalist. (Studies in European History 5).* (The Hague-Paris, 1970), pp. 19–20.

3. Frantisek Palacky, *Predmluva k vlastenskému ctenárstvu* [Foreword for patriotic readers] in *Casopis Ceskéno museum* 11(1837), pp. 3–8.

4. Similar thoughts were expressed by certain sensible Czech intellectuals (Hubert Gordon Schauer, Ladislav Karel Hofman) as late as the last decades of the nineteenth century.

5. Karl Havlicek Borovsky, "Slovan a Cech," in Karel Havlicek, *Politicke spisy* [Political Writings]. Vol. 1, Zdenek V. Tobolka (ed.), (Prague, 1900), p. 64.

6. *Casopis Palacky museum* II (1837), p. 7.

7. For broad relationships, see Jiří Kořalka: "Nationale und internationale Komponenten in der Rus- und Hussitentradition des 19. Jahrhunderts". [National and international components of the Russian and Hussite traditions of the 19th century] in *Jan Hus und die Hussiten in europäischen Aspekten* [Jan Hus and

the Hussites in European aspects]. Schriften aus dem Karl-Marx-Haus 56. (Trier, 1987), pp. 43–74.

8. Franz Palacky, *Geschichte von Böhmen* [History of Bohemia]. Vol. 4, sect. 2, (Prague, 1860).

9. See Stanley B. Winters, *Jan Otto, T.G. Masaryk and the Czech National Encyclopedia* in Jahrbücher für Geschichte Osteuropas 31 (1985), pp. 516–542.

10. See Václav Zacek (ed.), *Cesi a Jihoslovane v minulosti* [Czechs and southern Slovenes of the past] (Prague, 1975); Cesimir Asort (ed.) *Dejiny Ceskosloven-skobulharskych vztanu* [History of Czechoslovak-Bulgarian relations] (Prague, 1980).

11. Gustav Eim, [The Slovaks and the Triple Alliance. Remarks of the representative of the Kingdom of Bohemia]. (Vienna, 1892), p. 39.

12. See Jiří Kořalka, *Tschechen im Habsburgreich und in Europa 1815–1914. Sozialgeschichtliche Zusammenhänge der neuzeitlichen Nationsbildung und der Nationalitätenfrage in den böhmischen Ländern* [Czechs in the Hapsburg empire and in Europe, 1815–1914. Social historical relationships in recent nation formation and the question of nationality in the states of Bohemia]. Schriftenreihe des Österreichischen Ost- und Südosteuropa-Institut 18.(Vienna-Munich, 1991), pp. 283–288.

13. Arnold Suppen, "Bildungspolitische Emanzipation und gesellschaftliche Modernisierung. Die südslavischen Studenten an der Universität Prag um die Jahrhundertwende und der Einfluss Professor Masaryks" [Educational Policy emancipation and social modernization. South Slovenian students at the University of Prague at the turn of the century and the influence of Professor Masaryk] in Richard Georg Plaschka and Karlheinz Mack (eds.), *Wegenetz europäischen Geistes. Wissenschaftszentren und geistige Wechselbeziehungen zwischen Mittel- und Südeuropa vom Ende des 18. Jahrhundert bis zum Ersten Weltkrieg* [Pathway network of the European spirit. Centers of science and intellectual interrelationships between Central and Southern Europe from the end of the 18th century to the First World War]. Schriftenreihe des österreichischen Ost- und Südosteuropa Institut 8. (Vienna, 1983), pp. 283–288.

14. Arnold Suppan, "Grosserbische Propaganda und Agramer Hochverratsprozess," in Vasa Cubrilovic (ed.), *Velike sile i srbija pred Prvi svetski rat* [The Great Powers and Serbia before the First World War] (Belgrade, 1976).

15. Thomas G. Masaryk, "Russland und Europa. Zur russischen Geschichts und Religionsphilosophie." [Russia and Europe. Philosophy of Russian history and religion] *Soziologische Skizzen*. Vol. 1–2 (Jena, 1913).

16. Franz Palacky, *Gedenkblätter. Auswahl aus Denkschriften, Aufsätzen und Briefen aus den letzen fünfzig Jahren* [Commemorative papers. Selection of acknowledgments, essays and letters of the last 50 years] (Prague. 1874), p. 190.

17. Py. (Jan Palacky), "Evropa" [Europa] in *Ottuv slovnik naucny* [Otto's conversation lexicon], Vol. 8 (Prague, 1894), pp. 853–854; here p. 854.

18. Cechische Revue, Vol. 1, No. 1 October 1906, p. 3.

19. Jiří Kořalka, "Neue Nationalgesellschaften Mitteleuropas in den internationalen Beziehungen un 1900" [New national societies of Central Europe in

international relationships around 1900], in Fritz Klein and Karl Otmar von Aretin (eds.) *Europa um 1900. Texte eines Colloquiums* [Europe around 1900. Texts of a colloquium], (Berlin, 1989), pp. 235–247, here p. 246.

20. T.G. Masaryk, *Das Problem der kleinen Völker in der europäischen Krisis* [The problem of the small nations in the European crisis] (Prague-Leipzig, 1922).

21. Ibid, p. 18.

22. T.G. Masaryk, *Das neue Europa. Der slawische Standpunkt* [The new Europe. The Slavic perspective] (Berlin, 1922).

23. Karel Pichlik, *Zahranicni opdboj 1914–1918 bez legend* [Foreign resistance without legends, 1914–1918] (Prague, 1968), pp. 465–466.

24. Jan Kren drew an interesting parallel between the positive Czech policies in the former Austria and Sudeten-German activism in Czechoslovakia. See Jan Kren, "Nationale Selbstbehauptung im Vielvölkerstaat. Politische Konzeptionen des tschechischen Nationalismus 1890–1938" [National self-assertion in the multinational state. Political concepts of Czech nationalism] in Jan Kren, Václav Kural, Detlef Brandes, *Integration oder Ausgrenzung. Deutsche und Tschechen 1890–1945* [Integration or exclusion. Germans and Czechs, 1890–1945] Schriftenreihe Forschung zu Osteuropa (Bremen, 1986), pp. 15–65.

25. Jörg K. Hoensch, Die "Burg" und das aussenpolitische Kalkül [The "Burg" and foreign policy calculations] in Karl Bosl (ed.), *Die "Burg." Einflussreiche politische Kräfte um Masaryk und Beneš* [The "Burg." Influential political forces around Masaryk and Beneš] Vorträge der Tagung des Collegium Carolinum (Lectures at the meeting of the Collegium Carolinum) (Munich-Vienna, 1974), pp. 31–57, here p. 32.

26. T.G. Masaryk, *Die Weltrevolution. Erinnerungen und Betrachtungen 1914–1918* (Berlin, 1925), p. 376. The Making of a State. Memories and observations, 1914–1918. An English version, arranged and prepared with an introduction by Henry Wickham Steed. (London, 1927), p. 326.

27. Vera Olivova, *Ceskoslovensko v rozrisene Evrope* [Czechoslovakia in a disrupted Europe] (Prague, 1968), p. 109.

28. Peter Burian, Die Tschechoslowakei als Mitglied des Völkerbundes [Czechoslovakia as a member of the League of Nations] in Karl Bosl (ed.), *Gleichgewicht - Revision - Restauration. Die Aussenpolitik der Ersten Tschechoslowakischen Republik im Europasystem der Pariser Vorortverträge* [Equilibrium - revision - restoration. The foreign policy of the first Czechoslovakian Republic in the European system of the Versailles Treaty] Vorträge der Tagungen des Collegium Carolinum [Lectures at the meeting of the Collegium Carolinum] (Munich-Vienna, 1976), pp. 183–200, here p. 184.

29. F.V. Krejci, "Cesstvi a Ecropanstvi. Uvaha o nasi Kulturni orientaci" [Czechism and Europeanism. Thoughts about our cultural orientation] Politicka knihovna II-3 (Prague, 1931), p. 187.

30. Ibid. p. 208.

31. Various writings of Karel Capek have been translated into more than 50 languages. See Boris Medilek and others, *Bibliografie Karla Capka. Soupis jeho dila* [Bibliography of Karel Capek. List of his works] (Prague, 1990), pp. 459–552.

32. Published in German translation, among others, *Seltsames England* [Strange England] (Berlin, 1936; Oxford-Vienna-Zurich, 1947; Berlin-Munich 1953 and 1959); *Liebenswertes Holland* [Charming Holland] (Berlin, 1954; Munich, 1959]; *Ausflug nach Spanien* [Excursion to Spain] (Berlin, 1961).

33. Karel Capek, "Po stopach dvouhlaveho orla" [On the tracks of the double eagle] in Pritomnost, Vol. 8, No. 48 (Dec. 12, 1931), pp. 753–754.

34. Karel Capek, Evropa [Europe] in Zivot, Vol. 12, No. 7 (May 1934), pp. 106–109.

35. See: Vojtech Blodig: "Die tschechoslowakischen politischen Parteien und die Unterstützung der deutschen und österreichichen Emigration in den 30er Jahren." [The Czechoslovak political parties and the support of German and Austrian emigration in the 1930s] in Peter Glotz, Karl-Heinz Polick, Fürst Karl von Schwarzenberg and John van Nes Ziegler (eds.), *Das Ende des alten Europas*. [The end of the old Europe]. (Munich, 1938; Essen, 1990), pp. 251–270.

36. F.X. Salda, "Cesstvi v Evrop" [Czechism and Europe] in Salduv zapisnik 7 1935, pp. 226–231.

37. Jaroslav Durich, "Cesstvi v Evrop" [Czechism and Europe] in Listy pro umeni a kritiku 3, 1935, pp. 7–9.

38. Kamil Krofta, *Europa am Scheideweg. Expose des Ministers für Auswertige Angelegenheiten, gehalten in des Aussenausschüssen des Abgeordnetenhauses und des Senates am 28. Mai 1936* [Europe at the Crossroads. Speech of the Czechoslovak Minister of Foreign Affairs delivered before the foreign affairs committees of parliament and the senate on May 28, 1936] (Prague, 1936), p. 9.

39. Kamil Krofta, *Die Tschechoslowakei und die Kleine Entente in der heutigen europäischen Politik. Expose des Aussenministers, vorgetragen am 21. Mai 1937 in den Aussenausschüssen des Abgeordnetenhauses und des Senates der Nationalversammlung* [Czechoslovakia and the Minor Entente in contemporary European policies. Speech of the Czechoslovak Minister of Foreign Affairs delivered before the foreign affairs Committees of both houses of the national assembly May 21, 1936] (Prague, 1937), p. 72.

40. Karel Capek, "Lekce dejin" [A history lesson] in Pritomnost, Vol 15, No. 17, April 27, 1938, p. 257.

41. Karel Capek, Václav Chaloupecky, J.L. Hromadka, Frantisek Hruby, Albert Prazak and Ferdinand Peroutka, *At the Cross-Roads of Europe. A Historical Outline of the Democratic Idea in Czechoslovakia* (Prague, 1938). The French version was published with a different subtitle, Au carrefour de l'Europe. Essais sur la Tchecoslovaquie, place forte de l'esprit democratique (Prague, 1938).

42. Karel Capek "Introduction" in *At the Cross-Roads of Europe*, pp. 9–10.

43. Karel Capek, "Mravni zaklady Evropy otreseny" [Europe's moral foundations shattered] in Lidove noviny, Vol. 46, No. 495, October 2, 1938, p. 3.

44. Concerning the devastating effects of the Munich capitulation on internal conditions in Germany, see: Frank Boldt, "T.G. Masaryk und die europäische Friedenspolitik zwischen den Weltkriegen" [T.G. Masaryk and European peace policies between the world wars] in Glotz, Pollok, Schwarzenberg and Nes Ziegler (eds.) (Munich, 1938), pp. 97–114, here p. 111.

45. Detlef Brandes, *Die Tschechen unter deutschem Protektorat, Bd. 1. Besatzung-*

spolitik, Kollaboration und Widerstand im Protektorat Böhmen und Mähren bis zu Heydrichs Tod 1939–1942 [The Czechs under the German Protectorate. Vol. 1. Occupation policies, collaboration, resistance in the Protectorate of Bohemia and Moravia to Heydrich's death, 1939–1942.] (Munich-Vienna, 1969), p. 38.

46. Edvard Beneš, *Demokratie heute und morgen* [Democracy today and tomorrow] (Zurich-New York, 1944), p. 233.

47. Emanuel Moravec, *O cesky zitrek* [For a Czech future] (Prague, 1943), pp. 19–20.

48. Ibid., p. 21. Emanuel Moravec wrote three essays from a similar point of view for the *Europäische Revue* published in Berlin and Stuttgart: "Die Tschechen und das Reich" [The Czechs and the Reich], Vol. 15, No. 10, October 1939, pp. 303–314, "Die Tschechen und das neue Europa" [The Czechs and the new Europe], Vol. 17, No. 3, March 1941, pp. 149–154; "Die Tschechen und der gegenwärtige Krieg" [The Czechs and the current war], Vol. 18, No. 9, September 1942, pp. 439–447.

49. Václav Kural, "Valecna ekonomika a rezistence" [The war economy and the resistance] in *Odboj a revoluce 1938–1945* [Resistance and Revolution] (Prague, 1965), p. 231.

50. See Lubomir Liptak, *Slovensko v 20. storoci* [Slovakia in the 20th century] (Bratislava, 1968), pp. 178–179, 186.

51. Beneš, *Demokratie heute und morgen*, p. 242.

52. See Detlef Brandes, *Grossbritannien und seine osteuropäischen Alliierten 1939–1945. Die Regierungen Polens, der Tschechoslowakei und Jugoslawiens im Londoner Exil vom Kriegsausbruch bis zur Konferenz von Teheran.* [Great Britain and its eastern European allies 1939–1945. The governments of Poland, Czechoslovakia and Yugoslavia in London exile from the outbreak of war to the Teheran Conference] Publications of the Collegium Carolinium 59 (Munich, 1988), pp. 74–77, 134–142.

53. Zdenek Nejedly, "Za kulturu lidovou a narodni" [For a popular and national culture] *Sebrane spisy Zdenka Nejedleho* 36 (Prague, 1953), p. 32.

54. The editors of the newly founded official organ of Marxist historians promised at the beginning of 1953 that the journal would "reveal subversive, bourgeois tendencies and fight against the official historiography that serves capitalistic nations." See *Ceskoslovensky casopis historicky 1* (1953), p. 4.

55. Eugen Lemberg, *Reformation im Kommunismus? Ideologische Wandlungen im Marxismus-Leninismus Ostmitteleuropas* [Reformation in communism? Ideological changes in Marxism-Leninism of eastern central Europe] (Stuttgart, 1967).

56. Jiří Kořalka, *Co je narod?* [What is nationhood?] (Prague, 1969), p. 66.

57. Milan Kundera, "Cesky udel [The Czech destiny], in *Listy*, Vol. 1, Nos. 7–8, December 19, 1968, pp. 1 and 5; Václav Havel, "Cesky udel?" [The Czech destiny?] in *Tvar*, Vol. 4, No. 2, February 1969, pp. 30–33.

58. Václav Havel, "Über die Macht des Wortes" [About the power of words] in *Gewissen und Politik. Reden und Ansprachen 1984–1990*, Otfrid Pustejovsky und Franz Olbert, (eds.) [Conscience and politics. Speeches and addresses,

1984–1990] Kleine Reihe des Institutum Bohemicum 13 (Munich, 1990), pp. 40–51, here p. 47.

59. See Dietrich Beyrau and Ivo Bock, "Samisdat in Osteuropa und Tschechische Schreibmaschinenkultur" [Samisdat in eastern Europe and the Czech culture of the typewriter] in *Bohemia 29*, 1988, pp. 280–299.

60. Václav Havel, "'Europa'—eine reale Vision" ["Europe—a realistic vision] in Havel: Gewissen und Politik [Conscience and politics] op. cit. pp. 130–246, here p. 131.

61. See Rudolf Jaworski, "Die Aktuelle Mitteleuropadiskussion in historischer Perspektive" [The current debate about Central Europe in its historical perspective] in Historische Zeitschrift 247, 1988, pp. 529–550; Martin Schulze-Wessel, "Die Mitte liegt westwärts. Mitteleuropa in tschechischer Diskussion" [The center lies to the west. The Czech debate about Central Europe] in *Bohemia 29*, 1988, pp. 235–244.

62. Milan Kundera, "Die Tragödie Mitteleuropas" [The Tragedy of Central Europe] in Erhard Busek and Gerhard Wilfinger (eds.), *Aufbruch nach Mitteleuropa. Rekonstruktion eines versunkenen Kontinents* [Departure for Central Europe. Reconstruction of a lost continent] (Vienna, 1986) pp. 133–144, here, p. 133.

63. Milan Simeca. "Nach einer Zivilisation? Eine andere Zivilisation?" [After a civilization? Another civilization?] in Hans-Peter Burmeister, Frank Boldt and Gyorgy Meszaros, *Mitteleuropa, Traum oder Trauma? Überlegungen zum Selbstbild einer Region* [Central Europe, Dream or trauma? Thoughts about the self-portrait of a region] (Bremen, 1988), pp. 65–72, here p. 65.

64. See Jan Kren, "Historische Wandlungen des Tschechentums" [Historic transformations of Czechism] in ibid., pp. 191–232. About Germany's significance for the Czechs also see Jiří Kořalka, "Palacky a Frankfurt 1840–1860: husitske badani a politicka praxe" [Palacky and Frankfurt 1840–1860: Research about the Hussites and political practice] in *Husitsky Tabor 6–7*, 1983–1984, pp. 239–360, here pp. 284–286.

65. Jiri Dienstbier, *Träumen von Europa* [Dreaming about Europe] (Berlin, 1991).

66. Václav Havel, "Europäische geistige Tradition" [European intellectual tradition] in Havel, *Gewissen und Politik* [Conscience and politics] op. cit., pp. 33–39, here pp. 36–37.

67. Václav Havel, "Über ein erneuertes Mitteleuropa der kleinen Nationen" [About a renewed central Europe of small nations] in op. cit., pp. 110–118, here p. 112.

68. Dusan Trestik, "My v Europe" [We in Europe] in Pritomnost, Vol. 3, No. 1, January 1991, pp. 1–2.

69. Otto Urban, "Evropa a evropanstvy" [Europe and Europeanism] in Literarni noviny, Vol. 3, No. 21, May 28–June 3, 1992, p. 2.

70. Miroslav Kusy, "Slovensko a Evropa" [Slovakia and Europe] in Literarni noviny, Vol. 3, No. 21, May 28–June 3, 1992, p. 2.

71. "Deklarace Slovenske narodni rady o svrchovanosti" [Declaration of the Slovakian national assembly about sovereignty] in Lidove noviny, Vol. 5, No. 167, July 18, 1992, p. 3.

Europe from
the Polish Perspective

Andrzej Ajnenkiel

Until the present day, again and again Poland has been the object and the site of disputes between its neighbors in the East and the West. European agreement and cooperation provide the only hope for the Polish people one day to be able to determine their own fate in freedom. Just as the Franco-German reconciliation was — and is — the prerequisite for uniting the free West European nations, so a Polish-German reconciliation will be the prerequisite for a peaceful order in a united Europe; one that does not end at the iron curtain, but includes all mankind that believes in European tradition.[1]

For two years now Poland has been traveling on the path to its new place in Europe. Our strategic goal is integration into the European Community and membership in the new European security system as well. Our political path is defined by the agreements and treaties negotiated one after the other with France, Italy and Great Britain. Poland's political goals are determined by the development of regional relation with its immediate neighbors — the Czechs, Slovaks and Hungarians. We are building the relationship to the eastern neighboring states — Lithuania, Belorus, the Ukraine and Russia — on new foundations.

The 'post-Yalta order' is behind us, as is the strict division of the world, and the fiction of international military systems that served only the domination of one power. Behind the unreal political alliances were hidden obsolete rancor, mutual prejudices, and nationalistic stereotypes. What remain are painful experiences and the bitterness of the Second World War. It is not easy to forget them, but nor is it possible to live only in the past.[2]

Each nation on our continent has a different historical experience, a different past and, accordingly, a different vision of the future. For some, Europe is a foregone conclusion, particularly when the word means specific judicial and administrative institutions: human rights, social security systems and, not to be overlooked, the economic position and the conditions of life that result from it. For others Europe is a long-sought, and thus idealized, paradise. It should not be forgotten that the concept "Europe" in general is understood to include those states that form the economic nucleus of the European Common Market and the European Free Trade Association (EFTA). No one identifies the concept with the poor nations, although they are a part of the continent, too. Conversely, the slogan "Back to Europe" often reflects the desire to become part of the "Club of the Wealthy" as quickly as possible.

Europe. It is an opportunity, but at the same time a challenge as well. Fears and prejudices are a part of the challenge — are we able to keep in step? Does moving closer confirm, or even exacerbate our differences? Are we in danger, on the path to Europe, of becoming the permanent "poor cousins" or, even worse, of becoming a second class people? The iron curtain, lest we forget, was not only an instrument of separation and subjugation; its existence guaranteed for a period of time a sort of protection for an inefficient economy, for an artificially produced state of full employment. In consequence, it was able to deliver only a low and constantly worsening level of social services. At least two generations of East-Central Europeans accustomed themselves to these living conditions. Many of them came to fear the future following the initial period of euphoria after the fall of the communist regime. The path to Europe sometimes appears to them as the path to purgatory.

Another comment seems in order here. Not infrequently from the Polish perspective, the pro-European solutions are seen as more or less hidden slogans of our imperialist neighbors.

So much for the necessary preliminary remarks. It should not be forgotten that since the establishment of our state, we have been in our essence a part of Western Europe. This connection was shaped by the Church, which was ruled by Roman law; also significant were continental values, the judicial system and the institutions of the then existing medieval European *Communitas*, in which the attachment to a common culture and belief played a substantial role.

After entering the Christian sphere of influence, the Polish political elite classes showed themselves to be greatly receptive to Europe. The role of Polish political freedoms and religious tolerance that existed during the peaceful development of the Republic (known colloquially as the "Republic

of Two Peoples,") is worthy of note. The "Unia Lubelska" of 1569 contributed—despite the existence of separate institutions of the State—to the
formation of a class of nobles (Polish: Schlachta) through union of the Polish
crown with the Grand Duchy of Lithuania.

This class was very strong in comparison with prevailing European
conditions. It comprised 10 percent of the total population. By assuming
many privileges, the Schlachta formed the political basis of the state, the
backbone of the nation. Various languages and creeds were represented
within it well into the sixteenth century. Conversion to Catholicism and to
Polonization then began step by step.[3]

The age of reformation had great impact on Poland as well. Fear of religious
wars and the persecutions that would follow led to acceptance, in 1573, of
the "Warsaw Act of Confederation" by the Polish Sejm of the Republic. This
act guaranteed equality before the law of people in all the different strata of
society, regardless of religious adherence. Thus, the document recognized
the principles of freedom and provided them protection. Unfortunately, the
principles formulated in the agreement were ignored later. Nevertheless,
Poland remained a nation free of the inquisition and without its pyres.

From the point of view of Western Europe, Poland occupied a position on
the margin as a neighbor of the Ottoman empire and the Grand Duchy of
Moscow (later the empire of the Russian czar). The structure of the state, the
state's values and its religion all separated Poland clearly from the Weltanschauung of the Western part of the continent. That explains the conflicts
with its neighbors. Their motivation led to the development in Poland (as it
also did in Hungary) of a new "bulwark" ideology, defending not only
Poland, but other European states as well from the advance of the "infidels."
In addition to its function as a protective wall, Poland in fact also served as a
sort of bridge connecting the European East with the West.

The uneven political development, the unwillingness to surrender the
generously defined freedoms of noblemen, and the restricted economic
development (similar to that in Spain) arising from the destructive wars of
the second half of the seventeenth century were among the reasons for the
specific exclusivity of the Polish aristocracy and its xenophobia. This,
however, had no significant influence on cultural ties, nor did it lead to the
decline of Poland's legal rule or its association with common European
institutions. In fact, these connections emerged stronger during the era of
enlightenment, as evidenced by the reform undertaken during the reign of
King Stanislav August Poniatowski (1764–95), notably the laws adopted by
the Grand Sejm (Sejm Wielki) in the constitution in 1791.

The partition of Poland led to the destruction of a state which had
awarded its people freedoms that were incomparably greater (not only for

the aristocracy) than those enjoyed by the subjects of the powers responsible for the partition.

Before partition, the Republic of Poland was a very large land area. It was a sort of confederation with a variety of autonomy stages. Its contacts with other European states had come about naturally, and there was no further integration in the offing at that time. The period following partition of the Republic was characterized predominantly—as far as political action and political rethinking were concerned—by efforts to regain independence and to rebuild the lost structures of the state. At the same time, it was a period that strived to define a national self-consciousness, to be passed on to those strata of society where it had not been strong before. That was true especially of the peasants.

A clear conflict arose following the end of World War I, when Poland regained its independence. Josef Pilsudski proposed the concept for the Central-East European nations to form some sort of federation. This idea, however, found little acceptance among the populations involved, including Poland.[4] In any event, to use the formulation of the British diplomat Edgar Vincent d'Abernon, the "eighteenth decisive battle in the history of the world," the Polish victory over the Soviet army near Warsaw in August 1920 was important because it made it possible to establish an East-Central European order for twenty years after the war.[5] Today, after fundamental modifications, it is reborn.

For understandable reasons, Poles were rather inimical to the German concept of an East-Central Europe during World War I.[6] Nor did the plan for a pan-European community, hammered out at the end of the war, meet with much enthusiasm.[7] Poles feared correctly that such a plan would bring them loss of territory, or even loss of the entire nation. Polish diplomatic circles tried without success to form a local federation in the region of the Baltic Sea or beyond, in the so-called intersea region between the Baltic and the Black Seas. Poland's weakness prevented these plans. Unfortunately, the ghost of anti-Polish German-Soviet cooperation, which was portended in 1922 at Rapallo, now took on ever more palpable form. The Ribbentrop-Molotov pact of August 23, 1939, provided direct encouragement for Hitler's invasion of Poland.[8] At the same time, it signified the final destruction of the postwar order in Central Europe and its partition between the two totalitarian systems. It was preceded by the annexation of Austria and the Munich accords, which formulated the agreement of the Western powers for the occupation of a part of Czechoslovakia.

There was no room in the National Socialist "New Order for Europe" for a Polish state structure and the Polish people. The fate of the Poles and the Jews under Hitler's domination need not be explicitly recalled here.[9] It is worthy of note, however, that in the initial phase of the war, cooperation with the Reich brought about the fruition of earlier Soviet plans, destruction of the Polish state as an obstacle on the path to revolution that was to be carried on bayonets into the West. Sociologist Jan Gross characterized the effort to crush the organized national Polish folk structure with the term "Revolution from Abroad."[10]

The second phase of the war, when the Soviets found themselves in a forced coalition with Great Britain and the United States, brought the realization of another plan: the Soviets were to be awarded a much larger territorial share of Central Europe than had been agreed in the Hitler-Stalin pact. It was Stalin's conviction that the Western powers had accepted this plan at the Yalta Conference.

In the Shadow of Yalta

In the period between the wars, various ethnic groups lived together within the framework of a state structure (as they did, for example, in Czechoslovakia), despite differences, conflicts and sometimes even sharp disagreements. It was characteristic for the period. This type of coexistence of a variety of ethnic groups, cultures and religious groups was wiped out in a dramatic manner during World War II. The Jewish Holocaust during Hitler's time, together with ethnic antagonisms of peoples living on Polish territory, as encouraged by both the German and the Soviet totalitarian military powers, had the consequence of thoroughly unifying the populace by force. Poland was isolated from other nations and at the same time lost all benefits provided by exchanges with other cultural customs.

Other factors also played a role. The war and the postwar policies of the government imposed on the Poles almost caused the complete extinction of the cultural traditions that had existed before. Those traditions came, at least in part, from those of the Polish landed gentry stemming largely from Polish romanticism of the nineteenth century, a time of struggle for independence and the establishment of a national culture.

"The intelligentsia," with its typical characteristics derived from western culture—French, but also German in its Berlin and Munich variations, and partly Viennese as well—was fought bitterly as a relic of past epochs. The losses suffered during the war, together with wartime and postwar emigration, were aggravated by the elimination of the traditional intellectual occupations. At the same time, a new class, the bureaucrats (largely plebeian), emerged. The formerly prosperous class became impoverished. A new, so-called socialist intelligentsia emerged, differing significantly from the classic prewar intellectual class, at least initially. The new class, in contrast to its predecessors, had closer solidarity with the people in the sense of class origins and ethnic homogeneity. General education proceeded on a lower level, as did lifestyle and general attitudes. The group arose predominantly from poor peasant stock; at first it enjoyed satisfaction from the fact of its own social elevation. That satisfaction was not, however, denied to other groups stemming from the same milieu of prewar small towns and villages.

In full awareness of the fact that a large part of the population—approximately one-third of all those living in Poland—was forcibly resettled in the northwest regions assigned to Poland, the following needs to be noted: The feeling of uprootedness and loss of accustomed habits, together with the initially strong aversion to their new living conditions, had the consequence of forcing into the unconscious the fact that Poland and the Poles themselves were consistently isolated from association with the outside world. Compulsory evacuation of the Germans erected in effect a wall on the western border, separating a populace as different in mentality and language as nowhere else in Europe.

The war and the postwar period thus brought Poles isolation from the outside world. Travel outside Poland, and travel in general, became ever more complicated. The impenetrability of the iron curtain that separated the nation from the rest of Europe increased constantly; it was permeable only to transports of those who were to be resettled. From the beginning, only weak ties existed to institutions and persons which could bind Poles and Poland to Europe. UNRRA, the United Nations agency, was an exception to this rule. It provided real relief, particularly in terms of food, to the populace of the country. However, it ended its work in 1947.

The return of Stanislaw Mikolajczyk, former premier of the Polish government in exile in London, in the summer of 1945 prompted new hope that Poland would not be left to the mercy of the Soviets by the allied powers. When he joined the government—it was called the "temporary government of national unity"—he was greeted by a wave of hope among Poles in the West because of the short-lived activities of the Polish People's Party founded at the time. All the greater was the disappointment almost two years later. It played a significant part in the resignation of a large part of society, including the intelligentsia, which gave up resistance to the regime imposed upon Poland.

That is a complicated problem. Some of its aspects were described by Czeslaw Milosz in his book, *The Oppressed Spirit*. Other aspects have been analyzed by Jozef Mackiewicz.[11] Here we attempt a brief analysis of the attitude of Polish society after the Yalta order of Europe came into effect.

Polish resistance and the Polish government in exile in London sought an independent and sovereign Polish state after the war, one that would work closely with the Western democracies and with its immediate noncommunist neighbors. This model of an association with Western Europe had no chance of realization because of the Soviet position. The politicians who promoted the plan remained in the West after the war as political exiles. (The "West" was understood as a political concept in Poland, as a part of the world not subject to Soviet influence.) The exile government residing in London until 1990 was a kind of symbol of continuity of a legal government and the struggle for independence.

The forces fighting for independence, now living under Soviet influence, were compelled to engage in conspiratorial activities subject to severe retaliation, including physical removal. These forces represented several political persuasions, from the extreme nationalist right to adherents of the Christian Democrats who were in power before the war, to the socialist movement fighting for national independence. An armed resistance movement of various political groups also existed. All of these forces were ruthlessly eliminated; in practice, they were banned from the political scene within a short period of time.

Stanislaw Mikolajczyk made an attempt to find a *modus vivendi* with Moscow while simultaneously attempting to check the constantly growing strength of the communists. His efforts to preserve the domestic independence of the state and its democratic institutions were without success. Mikolajczyk's adherents either had to accede to the constantly increasing dominance of the communists or they were eliminated from public life in sometimes brutal ways. The conditions in the country, the ever greater isolation of the iron curtain by the Soviets, the fraudulent elections of the communists in January 1947 (reenacting the 1946 referendum)—all this influenced the attitudes and later events in society. Increasingly, it became clear that any resistance to the regime imposed by the Soviets had no chance of success. Weariness, and, not surprisingly under these conditions, opportunism were the guiding motives controlling the attitudes of the people. Other important factors played a part as well. After the war, the Soviets promoted an aura of triumph throughout the continent. One might have thought the Soviet ideology was the solution to all of the problems of Poland and the other states of Central and Eastern Europe. After all, before the war Poland had been among the poorest nations of Europe. It had serious social problems: unemployment and poverty in the rural regions. It was weakened by national conflicts. Because of the tragedy of the Polish Jews and the horror of the Holocaust, many Poles saw anti-Semitism as a sad and shameful matter fanned by the Right before the war. The war years caused attitudes in many strata of society to become radicalized. The necessity for extensive social reforms and democratization of society seemed self-evident.

The communists, who took power in Poland under the protection of the Soviets, used these conditions to their advantage. They talked about establishing a just social system, restitution for wrongful injustices, and the elimination of obstacles that stood in the way of raising some social groups who had been disadvantaged before. In doing this, they used the slogan of building Poland into a democratic state that would afford the broad masses a chance for rapid advancement and access to culture and education. At the same time, their actions seemed to suggest that their slogans would indeed become realized. They called for active participation in rebuilding the state and emphasized that Poland had been abandoned by the Western allies and terribly devastated by the Germans; only the Soviets could supply the necessary help. Having to relinquish some regions (largely inhabited by non-Poles) that had been part of Poland before World War II was the sole threat and at the same time a reactionary factor in the state, according to communist propaganda. The communist rulers would not permit public reminders of the close relationship between these regions and the rest of Poland, nor of the numbers of Poles who had lived there for hundreds of years. Mention of Soviet crimes in these regions in speech or in writing was strictly forbidden and subject to severe penalties.

In addition, there was another significant problem. The government imposed by the Soviets turned out to be the only power that could guarantee Poland those territories promised it by the agreements reached in Yalta and later in Potsdam. The assignment to Poland of former German territory was treated as a kind of restitution for the regions it lost in the East and compensation for suffering sustained at the hands of the Germans in the war. At the same time, it was a necessary step to make resettlement in the new areas possible for the millions of Poles who were driven out of the eastern regions and for those who, with central Poland destroyed, were in need of a new livelihood.

The Western powers took no clear position on this issue. This explains the argument that only the Soviets and communist rule could guarantee the new Polish territorial arrangements, something which seriously influenced the Poles. Another important aspect must not be overlooked; the Hitler system and its ethnic policies, along with the antagonisms of all population groups that had lived in the prewar regions of the Republic in the end destroyed the existing bonds and interpersonal relationships. The government imposed on the Polish people exploited this circumstance uncompromisingly and fanned the anti-German feelings of the Polish people as a result of the war. Communist propaganda not only kept alive the recent tragic memories of World

War II, but also appealed to resentments from earlier days — the division of Poland with the aid of Prussia, or the Polish battles with the crusaders. The centuries-old varied and peaceful, almost exemplary relations of Poland with its western neighbors took on the guise of a hundred-year bloody German-Polish struggle in Polish society as a result of the regime's propaganda, a struggle that was finally won thanks to the help of the great Soviet neighbor, who brought forth a new, progressive form of statehood. This version of the past totally supported the Polish-Russian conflicts, and the crimes inflicted on Polish victims, particularly during the years of World War II.

The depiction of the murders at Katyn were a kind of "propaganda model." The campaign moved along two tracks. First, it suppressed all mention of the massacre of Polish officers and second, it blamed the Germans for the crime.[12] In addition, there was still another aspect. In the Polish tradition of national-democratic thought the belief predominates that of the two big neighbors, Germany and Russia, the former was the more dangerous. Poles assumed that because of their higher civilization they were not endangered by cultural Russification; Germany, in contrast, at a higher level of civilization could more readily germanize Poland. Moreover, given the generally accepted traditional expansion drive to the East of the Germans, the possibility of peaceful neighborly relations between the two peoples was unlikely. The experiences of the war strongly reinforced such ideas. Now the communists exploited them.

Step by step it became increasingly evident that the nation was being isolated from Western Europe. This view was voiced among others, by *Kuznica*, a periodical with ideological ties to the Polish Workers' Party: "We do not applaud those of us who snobbishly hold on to values long obsolete abroad; nevertheless we feel bound to these values because they had their origins in the Polish tradition and because they provided a contribution to the creation of European values with their true humanism."[13]

These very unclear formulations meant, as was soon to be learned, only one thing — the party declared it alone would decide what was to be published and promoted in Poland. The decree of November 16, 1945, "Concerning particularly dangerous offenses during the time of reconstruction of the State," was symbolic of this position. It provided, in addition to the threat of the death sentence, long-term incarceration for contacts with persons working for foreign governments or foreign organizations against the state.[14] This decree served for many years as a means of isolating Polish society from all foreign contacts.

The iron curtain served in a similar way to separate the People's Republic — since its inception — from the external world. The function of a barrier was provided by the Soviet zone of occupation (German Democratic Republic since 1949) in Germany. The Czech border played a similar role.

In its early days, the official government emphasized that it wanted to maintain friendly relations with the Soviet Union and the great Western democracies as well. These declarations echoed the position of the rulers in the Kremlin who, for economic reasons, had no desire to aggravate the situation. A significant change followed the elections of January 1947, which were accompanied by massive vote fraud. Following the election many voters protested, as did, officially, the ambassadors of Great Britain and the U.S. Governments of both nations, however, believed diplomatic relations should not be broken off despite the voting violations of the communists, as that would only serve to strengthen the iron curtain.

In June 1947, George Marshall formulated the basic principles of the U.S. aid plan. Initially, the Warsaw government accepted the proposal for Polish participation in the Marshall Plan, but then, under pressure from Moscow, the American offer was officially rejected.

Until 1947, the communists stressed that they wanted to create a combination of capitalist economy and a "liberal" governmental system in the Soviet pattern. In the field of economics, "three economic zones" were established. The most important of these belonged to the state and the second to the cooperative societies. The third zone was the private economy, including most importantly ownership of land by small farmers. Large and medium-sized land holdings had been expropriated after the war; the land was parcelled out in a compulsory land reform. The second group included private property other than farm land. These were the trades people, small and medium-sized industrial firms, retail and wholesale establishments, pharmacies, etc. The so-called industry nationalization, i.e., takeover of businesses by the state, affected those with more than fifty employees and those that were or had been under German ownership; in fact, these guidelines were not honored even then. Official propaganda proclaimed that the Soviet system would not be imitated. Those who pointed out that the real goal of the regime was the sovietization of Poland were punished for disseminating "enemy propaganda." Furthermore, steps that could create the impression that Soviet solutions were being copied were halted from time to time. This was intended to accustom Poles to the new regime, in which the majority had no trust. At the same time, at least some of the communist leaders, with Wladyslaw Gomulka at the top, hoped to retain the three-sector model under Soviet protection, while building a totalitarian system. In this model communist power held the sole decision-making authority in all areas of life, regardless of formal ownership titles.

The Beginning of Official Sovietization

Step by step, far-reaching changes were undertaken at all levels. First the opposition represented in the Sejm was reduced by manipulating the results of voting, then it was eliminated entirely. Similar procedures were used at the time in Bulgaria, Hungary and Rumania. One method was the physical elimination of people who took an independent political position, by a variety of political trials that terrorized the populace. Draconian verdicts were handed down, many with death sentences among them. To avoid such a trial, the leader of the Polish People's Party, Stanislaw Mikolajczyk, fled Poland with the aid of the U.S. embassy. Almost simultaneously, the leadership of the Polish Workers' Party launched the so-called "Struggle over Commerce." Its purpose was to limit private and cooperative trade. A special commission was set up with power to indict people for alleged economic crimes, to take away their property without a trial and to lock them up in prison camps. Thousands were removed from the commercial world in this way, people who were difficult for political or other reasons.

At the initiative of the Soviet Party, a meeting was held in September 1947 of nine communist Workers' Parties in Szklarska Poreba, in the Sudetic Mountains. The presentation made by Andrei Zhdanov, number two in the Soviet hierarchy, made it quite clear that the world was divided into two blocs: an "imperialist anti-democratic" bloc with the United States in the leading role, and an "anti-imperialist/democratic" bloc led by the Soviet Union. That democratic bloc had the duty to stop war preparations of the imperialists and to plan for the victory of democracy.

The meeting in Szklarska Poreba, announced to the public after a week's delay, meant the end of the verbal assurances that the Western powers would continue to be allies of Poland. Now the way was clear to denounce "American imperialism and its vassals" publicly.

The result of this meeting was the formation of an information bureau of the Communist Workers' Parties, the abbreviated designation of which was Cominform. This signified a return to practices that had already been used by the Communist International (Comintern), with which the Soviet Party exercized exclusive control over the activities of the other communist parties. Now word went out again that only the Soviet Party held leadership in the international communist movement. The capitalist world was said to find itself in the second profound phase of a crisis, with reactionary and aggressive components; its internal contradictions were said to become deeper.

In answer to the "aggressive activities of the imperialists" (according to communist propaganda), the "democratic forces," as they called themselves, were to close their ranks. That was to hold, of course, for states governed by communists. At the same time, these states were instructed of their "historic task" of building socialism. In this process general rules, discovered and applied creatively in the Soviet Union, had to be followed. "National characteristics" also were to be given due attention. These characteristics were to provide a kind of intermediate phase, i.e., to have second-rate significance. Much more important was the condition that Moscow retain for itself sole freedom to make decisions about what these national characteristics were. Everything included in the definition of these concepts was disapproved as a deviation from the general basis of socialist reform. This formed the basis of the subjugation process of the satellite states to Moscow as well as to its unabashed sovietization.

The changes agreed at the Szklarska Poreba meeting strongly affected the situation in Poland. The new line found its first echo in the October 11, 1947, decision of the Central Committee of the Polish Workers' Party, in which the need to fight the "American lifestyle" was announced. It was important that active steps be taken against American influence on schools, the press, in literature, etc.[15]

Events followed each other. Czechoslovakia, until then in control of some meaningful freedoms in its domestic affairs, took a leading role in the sovietization process after the February 1948 putsch and the subsequent purge. In Poland, Gomulka was relieved of his power and imprisoned shortly thereafter accused of "tendencies toward right-wing nationalist deviations." He was charged with wanting to retain "the Polish path to socialism" and Polish characteristics. Leading the party, as he had led the state since 1944, was the previously unaffiliated Boleslaw Bierut, an official of the communist Internationale before the war and, as many signs indicated, the NKVD as well. He was the man personally responsible for the death sentence imposed on many opponents of the regime.

In this atmosphere of struggle against "deviation to the right" and "American imperialism," the Polish United Workers' Party was founded in December 1948. This party declared its ideological base to be Marxism-Leninism and its model the Soviet state. It announced its intent to build the foundations for a socialist order in Poland. Defining itself as the guiding coordinating organ of the working class of the Polish people, it introduced a system giving the party complete power over all spheres of society.

It is not the intent here to describe the totalitarian model of government in Poland as it was built up consistently since the end of the 1940s. The main elements and the goals of this model were terror and intimidation, and isolation of Polish society from all contacts with nations on the other side of the iron curtain. Anyone with relatives or contacts abroad had to expect trouble. This became progressively worse the closer the Cold War came to erupting in open armed conflict. The Soviets reacted to the increasing integration in Western Europe with extraordinary militancy. This became visible in various activities and in the language of propaganda as well.

A resolution adopted at the August 1948 World Congress of Intellectuals for the Defense of Freedom in Wroclaw was prototypical. The resolution, among other things, indicted the governments of the noncommunist nations. Without discussing the totalitarian methods of the Soviets, the congress called for "elimination of the barriers to freedom of movement of persons campaigning for peace and progress . . ." In translation, this definition meant a demand for unimpeded communist actions, not infrequently conspiratorial in character. This language used by Soviet propaganda reached its peak in the attack by the Soviet delegate on Jean-Paul Sartre, who was decried as a "typewriting hyena."[16]

The increasingly severe, ruthless subordination of Central Europe by the Soviets led to closer cooperation in defense and in political and economic matters by West European nations who felt threatened. March 1948 saw the signing of the Brussels pact and the formation of the Organization of the European Economic Community (OEEC). Work began toward the formation of the Council of Europe, founded a year later, eventually leading to the transformation of the Brussels pact into NATO.

The blockade of West Berlin was meant to intimidate the West and test its reactions. At the same time, the Council for Mutual Economic Assistance (COMECON) was established as Moscow's answer to growing integration in Western Europe.

The practical goal of COMECON was to form close economic ties between the satellite nations and the Soviet Union. These nations, already characterized before the war by different stages of economic development, now were to assume uniformity in accordance with the Soviet model and Moscow's decisions. The result was a model of totally centralized state economy, with heavy industry at its center and the production of weapons predominating. Simultaneously, efforts were made to form within the Soviet sphere of influence an autonomous, self-contained economic model independent of Western imports. This corresponded to an arbitrarily determined price structure imposed administratively, which was independent of world market prices. The theoretical basis of the plan, when COMECON came into existence, was derived from a pseudo-theory postulating the development of a separate socialist market, which was regulated by its own rules. The economic relations between member states were defined by treaties between governments; these included guidelines for single-year and long-term economic plans. This led to enormous bureaucratization of the entire economy. Artificial price fixing, decision making under Soviet pressure and the incredibly complicated and bureaucratic processes of implementation were fundamental elements of a system later characterized by J. Kornai as the "economy of shortages."

The iron curtain separated the socialist bloc from its Western neighbors, but because of efforts toward self-sufficiency within the socialist bloc, tendencies to go separate ways began to arise among nations within the bloc. As a consequence of the drive toward self-sufficiency throughout the bloc, analogous reflexes were seen in the various states, and even to a large degree within the internal structure of the economic institutions. This situation had the consequence that the economy's "instinct" for self-sufficiency, if it can be expressed in this way, also included the basic production sectors of the economy. Two important additional details. First, the well-developed concentration in decision making. A short time ago I studied some documents of the actual leadership of Poland, the secretariat of the Politburo of the Polish United Workers' Party. This was the forum in which decisions were made which, in a free market economy, are left to top management of a firm or, sometimes, to a lower level. Decisions for changes in the plans were made at the highest level of the executive, the presidium of the government. Second, autarkic tendencies within the bloc states also led to the final elimination of those economic relations with Central Europe that had existed before the war with Western European nations.

"Cosmopolitanism," which was understood to mean all contacts with the free world, was challenged strongly at the end of the 1940s. The fight's objectives were not only to limit extensively artistic and cultural contacts, but also to rail against many ordinary customs in daily life which follow the Western pattern. This was expressed clearly in the officially required ignorance of Western technological advances. According to communist propaganda, only the Soviets could be leaders in this field.

The isolation of Poland and the other so-called people's democracies from the outside world came hand in hand with the process of adaptation to solutions valid for the Soviet Union. A fundamental reorganization of the administrative system was carried out in 1950. The office of public prosecutor and the courts were restructured in the Soviet pattern. New laws legalized use of repressive measures; among other things, for example, it became possible to jail workers for being tardy in arriving at their jobs. The new Polish constitution, effective in July 1952, was modeled after the Stalinist pattern. The result was an end to separation of powers and other structures typical of democratic states. The state in the constitution was given a class character which had the goal of "building a socialist society." The officially declared model and pattern for the purpose was the Soviet Union. Poland was officially named People's Republic of Poland.

Totalitarianism and sovietization extended to all areas of life; only the Church was able to protect its independence, although it was subject to persecution and repression as well; many members of religious orders were arrested and convicted. In this sense, the conditions in Poland, of which the predominant portion of the populace was Roman Catholic, differed from those in other socialist states. Even during the period of the worst Stalinist terror—a time during which a popular anecdote noted that the population was divided into three classes: those who had been in jail, those who were in jail, and those who would be there—all steps undertaken by the government against the Church and religion met with resistance, sometimes massive in nature. Steps taken to turn society against the West, in contrast, more frequently met only passive resistance. Some aspects of the religious resistance have already been mentioned. Polish religion in a broader sense is closely related to Latin cultures. Polish society, unlike Czech or Bulgarian societies, for example, had a traditional position inimical to Russia. Too many Poles had personal experience of the real conditions in Russia to believe the official propaganda. The economic inefficiency already apparent at the beginning of the 1950s had the consequence that skepticism, at least with respect to the Soviets and the imposed government, became a general phenomenon.

We come now to an additional problem. The tight seal of the iron curtain was made more porous by the millions of Polish emigrants, particularly in the United States. These emigrants desired to help their countrymen at home. The government was forced to tolerate this, at least in part, for economic reasons. As a consequence, hard currency, a variety of goods and countless private gift packages flowed into Poland. Possession of such articles led to a kind of snobbism and increased prejudice against the government. This explains the propaganda war and punishment of people who were termed "fashion freaks" (Polish: Bikiniarstwo) and who were accused of having become enslaved by the American lifestyle. Despite the official edict against having or dealing in hard currency, such practices in fact became the rule, although severe punishments could be expected upon discovery. Thus, just as the continued postwar existence of armed partisan groups and the political underground was typical of Poland for several years, so too the development of a black market ("secondary commercial relations") became typical of the country. Forced collectivization of private farmers in the past several years was the underlying cause for such black markets; they flourished despite several sanctions against the semilegal and illegal bazaars. These existed in many places throughout the land, most of all in Warsaw.

Another means to pierce the iron curtain was the radio. Even during the war, the BBC Polish-language broadcasts had enjoyed great popularity; they were a source of information although the occupiers did not permit Poles to possess radios. Later, the Voice of America, Radio Madrid and Vatican broadcasts were added. They became a significant means of mutual communication although interference with these broadcasts began in 1951 and threats of punishment existed for listening to them. The Polish program of Radio Free Europe began to play a special role. Its all-day broadcasts, beginning on May 3, 1952, provided information about events in the free world. Government propaganda, which tried to portray conditions in the capitalist nations in a bad light, was countered successfully. These broadcasts had wide popularity and Radio Free Europe was not infrequently called "Warsaw West" by the populace.

Peregrinations of the Thaw

The Thaw—the term is that of the Russian writer Ilya Ehrenburg. Following Stalin's death, brutal totalitarian terror began to ease. This facilitated contacts outside the iron curtain, particularly on the cultural level. The previously practiced formula of "socialist realism" as method and technique of contemporary arts became more elastic, step by step.

From the middle of the 1950s, after a long period of dogmatic enforcement of the so-called Marxist principles in science and art, people began to turn away from the guidelines valid until then. Those in power were required, despite the various limitations and repressive measures they imposed, to tolerate the open existence of human spirit and thought, and particularly the work of the Catholic Church. Nevertheless, no stone was left unturned in the effort to weaken the position of the Church and to destroy the bonds to the Vatican and Christian thought in the free world. Stalin's death did not change any of this. Sensational evidence of this was provided by the arrest of Stefan Wyszynski, primate of Poland. He was interned in complete isolation and under strict political control for more than three years, until October 1956.

Before the so-called "Polish October" of 1956 a phenomenon occurred that would become typical of the Poland of later years. The widespread efforts of many humanistic artists developed into a "window to the world," making the iron curtain even more porous. For years, the literature published in Poland, films and theatrical productions and the artistic and musical life played significant roles in openings to the outside world. Of course, freedom of expression in these fields was relative. Topics and names that were taboo for political reasons and relative freedom in one area were balanced by a need for compromise in others. It must be added, however, that an "honest Marxist infection" (about which Milosz has written) was present and that a belief of the historic mission of the Soviets remained in many people despite the numerous, widely known crimes.

Another important international aspect is noted here. Following the Cold War (and sometimes the "hot war" as well), there was a phase of détente between the Soviets and the nations of the West. Moscow's military might was not in question, nor had its general concepts changed. This was expressed in the Warsaw Pact of May 1955. It was simultaneously a political demonstration and an answer to the continuously expanding militarization and political integration of Western Europe, whatever the difficulties.

Under these conditions, the Western nations accepted the conditions existing east of the Elbe River. The Polish centers of independence in the free world, particularly the legally existing Polish government in exile (with its program rejecting the Yalta agreement), had no influence on the policies of the West. The political centers which expressed the desire, in the name of the people living behind the iron curtain, to integrate with a European institution were treated in an analogous manner. In 1953, for example, an International Democratic Congress for Central Europe took place in New York. The Polish, Hungarian and Czech politicians living in exile founded a group, the Christian Democratic Central European Union. Its purpose was to have the states of Central Europe become a part of the European Community. But no one believed in a realistic resolution of the conflict without a military effort. Dramatic proof of this was demonstrated in the suppression of the Hungarian uprising by the Soviet army in 1956.

A kind of consolation was provided for the nations independent of the Soviets by the development of the "convergence theory" by Western political scientists.[17] It predicted advancing adaptation of both systems — that of the free world and that of the Soviet bloc. The Soviets and their client states were to devolve via a slow democratization process and technological advances were expected to make conditions of life on both sides of the iron curtain similar.

In Poland, on the contrary, a very different view was promulgated. The unification process of the nations behind the iron curtain was to make them an intrinsic part of the Soviet system. Tendencies in this direction were seen in Soviet policies. They found expression, if mildly, in the so-called Brezhnev doctrine of limited sovereignty of socialist nations. For a long-term prognosis, therefore, people tended to believe that Poland could expect at best a kind of "Finlandization." That is, Poland would have a certain amount of autonomy in regulating internal affairs, but in military matters and foreign affairs it would be completely dependent on Moscow. This belief had the consequence that, for example, during the October 1956 period there was no effort for radical separation of the nation from Soviet dominance. Poles sought only to reduce dependence on the Soviets somewhat by limiting their intervention in the security services and by relieving Soviet generals from the top of the military hierarchy.

During this period mass repression and lawlessness were stopped. More freedom of expression was achieved and cultural policies were given clearly liberal impulses. Contacts with artistic circles of the free world were strengthened.

Wladyslaw Gomulka resumed leadership of the party following his release from prison. He was fully aware of how limited maneuverability was vis-à-vis Moscow and, not unimportantly, he remained an orthodox communist who sought to translate the concept of a "Polish path to socialism" (within the framework of the general Soviet doctrine) into reality. In consequence, after a few months of "honeymoon," the cooperation with the intellectuals who had supported him initially came to an end. Some artists and scientists once again returned to the so-called internal emigration, others, in contrast, formed a more or less open opposition.

The grand hopes for extensive changes in Poland, including those involving Gomulka, found expression, if only temporarily, in the monthly journal *Kultura*, published in Paris since 1948. This periodical and the associated literary institute played a significant role in formulating Polish and European political thought free of suppression. It was a "window to the world" for at least two generations of the Polish intelligentsia. Thanks to this periodical (and other spiritual centers abroad) Poles became aware of their true history and learned of the various social manifestations of life in the West. These centers, often working under very poor conditions, also helped to showcase what was most valuable in our culture and our spiritual lives. And they represented our rights as well, which must not be forgotten.

The Roman accords, signed on March 25, 1957, laid the cornerstone for the European Community. The Soviets, together with their communist-led satellite states, described this event as practically insignificant in their propaganda, as a political deception of imperialism. Since the second half of the 1950s, Poland had become the most comfortable or, as suggested by some, the "most cheerful barracks" in the Socialist world—even in the face of the more orthodox course pursued by the Gomulka team. Despite political governmental maneuvers, despite the (no longer quite so comprehensive) political repression, the process of isolation from the "free world" was slowed and, in some areas, even stopped. The Polish film school, Polish theater, the literary works of Slavomir Mrozek, Josef Mackiewicz, Czeslaw Milosz and Witold Gombrowicz—these are only a few examples of Poland's lively presence in European culture.

Official Poland—without changing the prevailing propaganda line signif-icantly—attempted diffidently to move closer to the capitalist world. A first step in this direction was its move in 1959 to join the General Agreement on Trade and Tariffs (GATT); eight years later, it achieved full membership.

Awareness of our ties to Great Britain, France or the United States, even on an emotional basis, was very strong despite governmental propaganda; for reasons already noted, it was nonetheless not easy to discard the prevailing negative attitude toward the Federal Republic of Germany. There was no way to imagine how democratic the character of this nation had become, the extent to which it had undertaken to deal with the past, and to overcome its totalitarian inheritance. So much the greater, therefore, was the significance of the first independent church activities. Contacts were initiated in 1958 by independent Catholic envoy Stanislav Stomma. On the German side, at the beginning there was a memorandum of the Evangelical Church of Germany: it dealt with the problem of Poland's western border and with overcoming mutual antagonisms as well. A letter of November 1965, from the Polish bishops to the German bishops, was widely noted. It recalled the suffering of millions of German refugees and emigrants displaced by "order of the conquering powers . . ." The bishops pointed out that Poland had fallen victim to destructive waves of war several times since 1914, leaving ruin, rubble, poverty, disease, tears and death, but also increasing the desire for "revenge and hate" in the land. In addition, the bishops wrote, "We forgive and beg for forgiveness."[18]

While this document was received in a very friendly way in Germany, the Polish government started a hate campaign against it. Five years later, the agreement on normalization of relations between Poland and Germany was signed, in which Germany recognized Poland's western border.

Unleashing of the campaign of anti-Semitism in 1968, under the direction of the leadership of the People's Republic of Poland, surely did not serve our return to Europe. We need not recall here the sad and for us shameful course of this campaign. It should be noted that the event was condemned by many parts of Polish society. The year 1968 brought the "Prague Spring" in Czechoslovakia, a test of "Socialism with a human face" that foundered only upon military intervention by the "fraternal armies." Two years later came the bloody battles with striking workers along the Polish coast.

Limited Attempts at Openings to the West

In the 1970s, a new government, with Edward Gierek at its head, undertook the attempt to reduce accumulated conflicts. There was some liberalization of "passport politics"; the border to the German Democratic Republic (GDR) was opened. Poland received significant foreign credits. The attempt was made to modernize the Polish economy. The results, alas, did not come up to expectations. The first symptoms of an economic crisis became visible in the middle of the decade.

The period of Gierek's rule was perceived as a time of Polish attempts to find openings to the West. But the reality was not quite so unequivocal. Modernization and liberalization were governed by the guidelines of communist doctrine. Steps were undertaken still with the aim of, for example, limiting private farm ownership. Greater integration with the Soviet economy, which was very disadvantageous for the nation, followed. This close connection of the state with the Soviets in line with the "Brezhnev doctrine" found its expression in a planned amendment to the constitution then in effect. These efforts, for the first time in a quarter century, unleashed public protests in the nation. The text that was finally accepted for the constitution was forced to pay heed to these protests.

Negotiations began in 1973 for a Conference on Security and Cooperation in Europe (CSCE). The Soviets and the communist governments were very anxious to convene this conference. It provided a form of acceptance of the status quo of European territoriality and its systems. In addition, it offered the chance to intensify economic cooperation, in which the Soviets were obviously very much interested. The Final Accord, including the "third basket" that included broadly defined human rights, was signed in Helsinki in 1975. The communist states were forced to agree to the human rights accords, with the Gierek team being most concerned about receiving additional credits from the West, and therefore anxious to present a good image in Europe for the state and the government. As a result, a tolerance previously unknown in a totalitarian system to persons critical of the system began to develop. Of course, this tolerance had its limits. For example, loud public criticism of the fundamentals of socialism, of the party, of the Communist Party leadership, of membership in the socialist alliance, or of the leading role of the Soviets was not permitted. Organizations independent of the government similarly were not accepted. To the contrary, control of already existing organizations tended to increase. Nevertheless, the clearly milder methods and much greater freedoms led people in Poland to speak of that period as a post-totalitarian regime.

In the middle of the 1970s, it became increasingly obvious that the socialist economic model was no longer able to fulfill its responsibilities despite financial assistance from the West. A crisis with unpredictable consequences began. The traditional solution to such crises was to cut consumption. Its consequences were workers' strikes and mass protests in

June 1976. The subsequent repressions, although weaker than those of December 1970, led to a new Worker Protection Committee, an organization never before known in the socialist nations.[19] The same year also saw the establishment of the underground Polish League for Independence. It called not only for Polish independence, but also sought closer ties between Poland and Western Europe. Like the Ruch organization founded years earlier, or the somewhat later Movement for the Protection of Human and Civil Rights, which later became the Confederation of Independent Poland, these movements (regardless of their differences) were convinced that now a chance existed for Poland to break away from Soviet domination and to regain independence.

So much for the (preliminarily only theoretical) description of the position taken by Poland in Europe and its relation to its neighbors, particularly to Germany.

The Twilight of Yalta

Finally we come to the most recent decade, beginning with the conclusions of the Conclave of October 16, 1978. The election of Cardinal Karol Wojtyla as Pope signified, in the perspective of time, that the Roman Catholic Church had broken through the barriers erected at Yalta. Regardless of the realities (i.e., the iron curtain and the Berlin Wall) the Church turned to its own agenda. John Paul II preached in his apostolic mission that there could be only a single Christian Europe in diversity, that it could not close itself off to the inclusion and presence of East-Central Europe as a part of the spiritual and cultural life of Europe. Thus, Sts. Kyril and Metodi were recognized in the encyclical "Slavorum Apostili" as among the patrons of Europe.

The role of *Solidarnosc*, the largest mass movement in the history of Poland, need not be examined here; all of Poland was involved in the peaceful effort to eliminate communist power and to carry out a "soft revolution."[20] Before martial law, during the period in which it was legal, the working methods of *Solidarnosc* can be described in the famous words of Jacek Kuron as "a self-limiting revolution." Its goal was to bring about far-reaching changes, initially within the framework of the existing system. It did not doubt Poland's position in the Soviet system and the at least theoretical political foundations of the People's Republic of Poland. Other views were voiced by forces, not very significant at the time, who sought independence.

The position changed after imposition of martial law. It became clear that this system was not capable of reform. Polish society, as a structure independent of the power apparatus (with a flourishing underground press and many other initiatives as well), with increasing frequency began to pose the question of what would happen after the downfall of communism. No one, it must be emphasized, was aware of how close to reality Andrei Amalrik had come in his famous essay: "Whether the Soviet Union will reach the year 1984."

The aid received from the West by Polish society and *Solidarnosc* following the imposition of martial law had very great material and moral significance. It made better survival possible and displaced the feeling of being alone and dependent only on oneself. But it cannot be ignored that Poland was perceived in the West, before and after martial law, as a nation that still remained in the Soviet sphere of influence. The same is true of other socialist states. This opinion was not altered after the assumption of power by Mikhail Gorbachev.

The Fall of the Wall

Three years passed after the Polish "roundtable" discussions. Not infrequently the impression arose that the world, Europe and even Poland had forgotten what had happened during that time. Without a world conflict, without spilling any blood, a miracle, if I may use that word, occurred. The satellite states of the Soviet empire regained their independence again. The totalitarian Stalinist bastion, the GDR, ceased to exist. Germany was reunified. Furthermore, we became eyewitnesses to the gradual disappearance of the Molotov-Ribbentrop and Yalta agreements. As if that were not enough, communism and the internal structure of the Soviet empire fell apart.

It is not surprising, then, that the changes and their tempo exceeded our imagination. Poles had lived for almost a half century under conditions imposed by others and had been forced to adapt to them. From time to time, one had been able to criticize the ruling regime, sometimes softly, at other times more loudly, (if one wanted to avoid greater reprisals). A minority took such risks at various times and with varying intensity. The great majority of the populace resisted sometimes, unconsciously or passively, the fulfillment of obligations by pretending to fulfill them. As pressure from the regime diminished perceptibly, it appeared to many people that it had never existed. Forgotten was the fear and terror of the 1940s and 1950s. The youngest did not even know of them. For psychological reasons it is quite normal that only pleasant events are remembered. For that reason, a kind of idealization of the past occurs. It is also necessary to consider that whole groups who had been "down" before the war could not forget their postwar social, economic and cultural rise. The previously existing system offered the opportunity to adapt; it permitted an existence on a very modest, but stable level. Many people had the desire for far-reaching changes but thought only in terms of socialistic reform, particularly because they were familiar with "real socialism" in the communities, in the small towns and in the villages, and had learned to live with it. This group today forms a populist stream of post-communist power. Its members voted in 1991 for the previously unknown presidential candidate Stanislaw Tyminski, who promised in his election campaign to combine the positive elements of communism and capitalism. These people were not then and are not now aware of the fact that what they remember from the epoch of "real socialism" is an idealized picture of the system of economic policy, a system that functions only on credits and, with increasing difficulties, found itself one day on the brink of catastrophe. The growing problems of the transition period—long lines in front of stores, rationing—were visible external symptoms of advancing deterioration. However, economic deterioration of the system was overtaken by political deterioration. At least that is the way it happened in Poland. The matter appears different from the perspective of Rumania and the Soviet Union. The speed of the changes even overtook the oppositional elite. The period of martial law was accompanied by an enormous increase in the number of publications outside censorship (the so-called second circulation). People began to think about various future options. It was unbelievably difficult to break through deeply rooted stereotypes; but the question of a practical rapprochement to the states of the West had to be considered. On this topic, an important text appeared by Jan Jozef Lipski. Entitled *Two Homelands, Two Patriotisms*, it discussed the necessity of rapprochement to the neighboring nations, eliciting very lively discussion. Independent circles slowly developed the idea that the reunification of Germany was also in Poland's best interests, because only then would the wall that separated us from a free Europe fall.

If we speak of the activities undertaken by the now free government of Poland, we must point to the great importance of the joint Polish-German declaration of November 14, 1989. It is well known that during Chancellor Helmut Kohl's visit to Poland the Berlin Wall fell. Almost simultaneously, the "velvet revolution" took place in Czechoslovakia and changes occurred in Hungary.

At the beginning of 1990, one still believed, however, that the structure called the German Democratic Republic would continue to exist. It appeared that the relics of the past (or, more precisely, the realities of Yalta)—Soviet army garrisons in Poland, the GDR, Hungary and Czechoslovakia—would remain. One assumed that the Warsaw Pact and COMECON would still exist, only in a form with more equal rights. That is all part of the past today. The Soviet empire also is a thing of the past. Recent events in our part of Europe have a greater significance than those that occurred after World War I. The First World War caused the fall of the Austro-Hungarian empire and the Hohenzollern Reich and the defeat of the Russian Romanovs, but also the founding of independent national states in Central Europe. The disintegration of the Russian empire and the founding of an independent Ukraine means, from the Russian point of view, return to the seventeenth century, to the time of the Perejeslawska accord of 1654. At that time, the Cossack political elite joined with Russia because it was unable to find a compromise with the Polish-Lithuanian state, as that state was unwilling to accept the autonomy of the hetmans in the Ukraine. The result was subjugation of the Ukraine by the czars.

The independence of Belorus signifies for Russia a return to the time before the partition of Poland and Lithuania, that is, to the position before 1772. Even worse, today the western border of Russia, crudely described, runs like the western border of the Grand Duchy of Moscow under the rule of Ivan the Terrible in the sixteenth century.

These highly abbreviated reminders indicate the gigantic territorial revisions which are taking place in Central Europe today. To them is added another great problem—the political, economic and social consequences related to the disintegration of "real socialism." This "real socialism" has died with all its consequences. The next question is, what should be created to take its place, and when will that happen?

Let us attempt here to put together, in far from complete form, a catalog of Polish problems. We must begin with the reminder of a simple fact: never, during the entire period of communist rule, did we stop thinking of ourselves as a part of Europe. This is true generally as well for Hungarians and Czechs. For that reason, restoration of traditional relations with Great Britain, France, Italy or the United States was easiest. As the structures, Warsaw Pact and COMECON, imposed by the Soviets began to disintegrate and the initiatives for cooperation with immediately neighboring states which Moscow had blocked were resumed, a community of cooperation began to form, not without encouragement from the states of the West, in the Visegrad triangle. The purpose of that effort is the reconciliation of Poland, Czechoslovakia and Hungary on political, military and economic levels. Preparations are going forward to establish a free trade zone between these states. Importantly, Poland has no quarrels with its neighbors. A second very important factor for cooperation by the Visegrad States was their desire to find connections to West European structures, particularly the European Community, and security guarantees through close contacts with NATO.

The politically most complicated task facing Poland was its relations with Germany. As Germany was reunified, the process of improving of mutual relations accelerated. Furthermore, and just as important for us, was the final acceptance of the existing borders as described in the German-Polish treaty of November 14, 1990, an agreement of historic importance for good neighborly relations and friendly cooperation. Speaking during the ratification debate in the Polish Parliament, Jan Krzysztof Bielecki, then prime minister, noted: "Not for a long time in their centuries-old history as neighbors have Poland and Germany been so close, and looked with so much hope to the future. This arises from the deep understanding that a united Europe is unimaginable without good Polish-German neighborliness and without a close community of interests. The Polish path to integration with the European community leads through Germany. That is the European character of this treaty in which the Federal Republic of Germany feels committed to the strategic goals of our policy, which is entry into the European Community."[21]

Relations between Germany and France today could serve as a model for neighborly relations between two erstwhile enemies. Perhaps that would influence the rapprochement between Paris, Berlin and Warsaw. Negotiations are taking place at present between the states of the Visegrad triangle and the European Community. Mutual cooperation is being increased. The May 1992 meeting of Presidents Walesa, Havel and Hungarian Prime Minister Antal strengthens this bond. Assistance in overcoming difficulties when joining the Community was promised by British Prime Minister John Major during his visits to the capitals of the triangle states in May 1992.

Poland sees its traditional role as a bridge between East and West Europe. That explains our support for the independence of Lithuania and other Baltic states and the effort to improve relations with Belorus and especially the Ukraine. It is not a coincidence that Poland was the first country to recognize the independence of the Ukraine. Our policies also must take into account the actual position of Russia in the new European constellation. President Walesa's visit to Russia, which culminated in the signing of an agreement between both states on May 22, 1992, was a demonstration of that.

Mutual relations between Poland and Russia have a troubled history. The fear remains that Russia might return to its policies of imperialism. Thus the great significance of the treaty as a factor repudiating such historic experiences of our nations and creating new relationships on a mutual and friendly basis.

The new international conditions resulting from the disappearance of the Soviet empire have influenced other events as well. In the past the integration process in Eastern Europe was marked by fear of Soviet aggression. Today, in the Maastricht ratification, other previously unconsidered factors have an influence. Nationalistic tendencies are beginning to appear. In Germany, they are a negative product of reunification. These tendencies may also become a danger to the postcommunist states. The tragic example of Yugoslavia forces us to see the problem of European security in a new light. Against the background of this tragedy, the victims of which are now the populations of Bosnia, Croatia and Serbia, and with a similar threat hovering over the population of Kosovo, the Visegrad Triangle states appear as a haven of peace and stability. In each of our nations, we can point to visible successes as we transform the previous economic model. The price for this, however, is very high. In Poland, for example, the living standard has fallen markedly over the past several years. Unemployment has reached 10 percent of the work force. At the same time, it should be noted that the overwhelming part of the working population has no savings. They live, as the saying goes, from one payday to the next. Under these conditions, the position of the unemployed, particularly in smaller towns (where there was often only a single employer) is very difficult. The example of the GDR demonstrates how difficult the true market chances are for even well known businesses. Because of the disappearance of the chief market, the Soviet Union, for many Polish products, the prospects for many factories are very poor. Large financial resources are required for modernization of these factories, but they are difficult to find internally in Poland. Financial aid from abroad is understandably slow to arrive. Financial aid from elsewhere, e.g., the International Monetary Fund, requires certain conditions, which would reduce the living conditions in Poland if they are met. Nor is it clear that measures taken in that direction would bring the desired success. Thus it is understandable that the mood in many population groups tends toward disappointment, even toward rejection of the West. That could lead to increased nationalistic feelings and to greater hostility to foreigners, although these have been marginal until now. The financial means that have flowed into Poland up to now have not been very large. At the same time, because the Polish government's position is not always consistent, being swayed by the mood of the population, Western readiness to invest in Poland is not very strong. Given this background, the recent contract with Fiat deserves special notice.

President Walesa, describing the nation's disappointment during his February 4, 1992, visit to the meeting of the Council of Europe, of which Poland has been a member since October 1991, said, "Reality mocks those who believe that the downfall of communism allows the Eastern world to come closer to the Western world. . . . In fact, unity lies in the distant future. . . . Europe is partitioned by economic differences. . . . We citizens of the poorer Europe have the feeling that the rich, well-to-do Europe is closing itself off to us."[22]

Dramatically, the Polish president pointed out to Western governments and the societies of Western Europe that an excessive difference — if not an abyss — between the two parts of the continent could have serious consequences by destabilizing not only our continent. Perhaps a new Marshall Plan for economic problems as well as social problems would be helpful. The tasks we face in the process of restructuring society are enormous. Nevertheless, and I would close with this thought, our generation is among those who are fortunate to be able to truly experience history and help to shape it, the restoration of sovereignty by a people who have had to dispense with it for years; and the active participation in fashioning our joint European future.

Notes

1. From a letter of the German "Europa-Union" to the Society of Polish Federalists, 1959, in *Wiadomosci Zwiozku Poiskich Federalistow* (Paris, 1959), p. 6.

2. From the address of Polish Minister President Jan Krzystof Bielecki during the German-Polish treaty ratification debate in 1991, in *Polska v Evropie*, Warsaw, Nr. 7/1992, p. 29.

3. See also N. Davies, *Heart of Europe. A Short History of Poland* (Oxford/New York 1987), O. Halecki, *Borderlands of Western Civilization. A History of East-Central Europe* (New York, 1952); A. Zamoyski, *Polish Way. A Thousand-Year History of the Poles and their Culture.* (New York/Toronto, 1988). The last contains an extensive bibliography on the subject.

4. M.K. Dziewanowski, *Josef Pilsudski. A European Federalist 1918–1922* (Stanford, 1969).

5. Viscount d'Albernon, *The Eighteenth Decisive Battle of the World* (London, 1931).

6. See also: *Das Mitteleuropabild Friedrich Naumanns und seine Vorgeschichte* (Marburg, 1941); F. Fischer, *Griff nach der Weltmacht. Die Kriegspolitik des Kaiserlichen Deutschland 1914–1918* (Düsseldorf, 1971).

7. The concept was made particularly popular by R. Coudenhove-Kalergi, *Pan-Europa* (Vienna, 1923).

8. See also *Nazi-Soviet Relations 1939–1941.* Documents from the Archives of the German Foreign Office, Washington, 1948; N. Davies, *Heart of Europe, op.cit.*; E. Oberländer (ed.) *Hitler-Stalin Pakt 1939. Das Ende Ostmitteleuropas?* (Frankfurt/M., 1989).

9. For Polish literature about the period of the occupation, see C. Madejczyk: *Die Okupationspolitik Nazideutschlands in Polen, 1939–1945* (East Berlin, 1987), also Menetekel, *Das Gesicht des Zweiten Weltkriegs. Nürnberger Gespräch zum 50. Jahrestag d. Entfesselung d. Zweiten Weltkriegs* (Krakow/Nuremberg, 1991). My discussion included here deals with social changes in Poland during the war.

10. J. Gross, *Revolution from Abroad* (Princeton, 1986).

11. See also, J. Mackiewicz, *Sieg d. Provokation* (Frankfurt/M. 1987); *Der Weg ins Nirgendwo* (Munich, 1957).

12. See, J. Mackiewicz, *Katyn — Ungesühntes Verbrechen* (Frankfurt/M, 1983); J.K. Zawodny, *Death in the Forest. The Story of the Katyn Forest Massacre* (Cambridge, 1980).

13. *Kuznica*, No. 1/1945, June 1.

14. Register of the Republic of Poland, No. 53, 1945.

15. Cited in M. Fik, *Kultura polska po Jalcie. Kronika lat 1944–1981*, (London, 1989), p. 87.

16. Ibid., p. 105.

17. See E. Brzezinski, *The Soviet Bloc. Unity and Conflict* (Cambridge, 1971).

18. Cited in J. Karpinski, *Portrety lat. Poslka w odcinkach 1944–1988* (London, 1989), p. 140.

19. Cited in J.J. Lipski, *KOR. A History of the Worker's Defense Committee in Poland 1976–1981* (Berkeley, 1985).

20. See, J. Holzer, *"Solidarnosc" 1980–1991* (Paris, 1984).

21. See note 2.

22. Cited in *Zycie Warszawy*, (February 5, 1992).

The Path to Europe from Moscow's Perspective

Alexander O. Chubarian

Between Europe and Asia

Russia and Europe. For decades and even centuries, the relationship has been central to social and political discussions in Russia and abroad. It is talked about in politics, philosophy, historical writings, literature, and art, and as a result has been a constant source of inspiration for public opinion.

For many reasons, the topic has elicited various reactions in Russia. Extreme right monarchist circles and organizations have declared their interest and used it for their own ends. It also was very popular with Russian liberals. Time and again since the end of the nineteenth century, it had been taken up by leftist circles—Russian social democrats, anarchists, social revolutionaries and the Bolsheviks. For the official circles, the politicians and the diplomats, Russia's relations with the European nations have played a decisive role in defining and pursuing domestic policy and the foreign political course.

The juxtaposition of "Russia and Europe" was regarded very differently in Russia than in all other European countries, which helped create a particular complexion and a specific mentality of the Russian consciousness. This idea found its expression among the intellectual elite and in dominant general views and ideas. How is this to be explained?

The first consideration is the geographical location of Russia. Russian and Western chroniclers who have argued endlessly over where Europe ends in the East, generally considered Russian territory as part of Europe, but at the same time saw it in its relation to the nomadic peoples and the Asian continent. Russia's affiliation to Europe was increasingly put into question when the Russian central state arose—a power whose influence extended beyond the Urals, the Volga region, and the vastness of Siberia. Geographically, Russia lay both in Europe and in Asia.

For centuries Russia was an ethnic conglomerate of different European and Asian elements. Dozens, even hundreds, of tribes and peoples, each with their own languages, customs and specific culture, settled in this immense area in which it was extremely difficult to create a unified culture, generally acceptable beliefs, and a type of human being with more or less the same mentality.

The Russian empire emerged from this situation. From its inception, the empire was forced to use power and violence to create a complicated mechanism to subordinate this huge assembly of peoples and tribes to a unified will and an organized leadership, under the direction of a central power.

The difficulties of the situation also were intensified by religious factors. The Greek Orthodox Church, Islam, Buddhism and the Roman Catholic Church coexisted with each other on the same Russian territory. This religious pluralism made the creation of common Russian characteristics even more difficult, as it did in establishing unified Russian policies and a common Russian economy and culture.

In contrast to the states that had formed in Western Europe, whose people had reached a similar level of social development, considerable differences always existed in the educational and cultural niveau and economic development between the people of central Russia, the Ukraine, and the Balkan region on the one hand and the people of Siberia, the Volga region, and central Asia on the other. This made it all the more difficult to work out common principles, unified guidelines, and rules for integrating the various regions into the system of the Russian empire. Multiplicity and diversity in Russia was reflected in the social thought, consciousness, culture, art, and literature of the country.

Since antiquity, reference has been made in Russian chronicles and historical writings, and later in literary works and philosophical treatises, to Russia's relationship to Europe and Asia and to its unique position between the two continents.

Over the course of world history, contradictions between Russia and Europe arose constantly in their relationships and contacts. Historians can cite many facts and furnish proof for the organic and far-reaching connection between Russia and Europe's development. Trade and economic relations between Kiev, Moscow, Novgorod, and Petersburg with western and northern Europe increased and became more complex. The reciprocal cultural influences and the connections of the czarist dynasties with European nobility contributed to the incorporation of Russia in the European political and cultural process.

Russia, however, was always regarded as a special case on the periphery of Europe. For the Europeans, Russia was and remained an unknown and mysterious land that resembled the classical European prototype in certain ways, but which also differed in many respects. The terrible blow Russia suffered under Tatar and Mongolian domination set it back and widened the existing chasm between it and Europe. The contradictory nature of the situation becomes evident here as well. On the one hand, Russia threw itself into the breach and protected Europe by holding the Tartars and Mongols in check and then finally conquering them. On the other hand, it was devastated and ruined as a result. Because the nomadic tribes became assimilated, a peculiar synthesis arose out of European and Asian traditions.

The Tatar and Mongolian oppression had long been an inhibitor and barrier to Russian development. This is also the reason for Russia's backwardness and alienation. The schism in Christianity was a factor as well; the Greek Orthodox and the Russian churches developed each according to its own rules, traditions, and laws, which differed from European models.

Considered within the context of the development of a civilization, it is clear that Russia's unique halfway position, its place in European as well as in Asian civilization, was decisive. A special synthesis arose out of this position—the mixture of two great civilizations and cultures that included a multiplicity of diverse trends, movements, and characteristics. Many other countries and peoples that lived in areas bordering other civilizations met with a similar fate; witness the history of southern Europe and Asia Minor, and that of North and South America. But usually such zones of contact between civilizations only had local effects, which no doubt significantly influenced the development of the people in question (though this was by no means the only influence).

For Russia, however, this contact between civilizations was of existential significance. The huge Russian empire arose in the middle of different types and zones of civilizations. It succeeded in becoming strong and powerful as a result of its vast territorial expanse and the size of its population and its enormous economic and natural resources. Petroleum and ore deposits, vast, still undeveloped regions, and millions of inhabitants formed the basis of the economic strength of the state. But the empire was seriously backward compared to other European countries. Under these conditions, Russia constantly had to pursue greater consolidation and develop principles, methods, and organizational and administrative mechanisms to bring together the various regions and give the inhabitants a common ideal. From the beginning, it was obvious that the idea of Russian patriotism, the idea of a united, strong state on Russian soil, harbored profound contradictions, as it also set free centripetal and centrifugal tendencies at the same time. The empire developed into a powerful and strong state, yet suffered under the contradictions unique to such a diverse multinational population living in different regions and cultures. That was the logical consequence and the contradictory nature of Russian history.

With Peter the Great began Russia's actual movement toward Europe. The czar won access to the Baltic Sea, the Black Sea, and the North Sea. He began to bring foreigners to Russia, visited several European countries, and established active trade relations with England and Holland, the countries that had the most influence on European life at the time. Russia appropriated much of the European lifestyle for the development of its government and civil service and borrowed habits and customs as well.

Peter I founded the new capital of the Russian Empire, St. Petersburg, which developed into an important trade center and port that connected Russia with the West. By suppressing rising resistance through force, the czar and his government introduced order and a way of life comparable to European standards of the time. The process of Europeanizing Russia continued after Peter I. Catherine II did not want to trail behind the enlightened monarchs of Europe and, therefore, patronized the arts and sciences. In addition, eighteenth-century Russia increasingly became a component of European politics, a very important element in the system of the European balance of power. Russia had connections with the leading European powers, France, England, Sweden, Holland, Spain, and others. The issue of "Russia and Europe" was the most discussed topic in Russian intellectual circles.

The ideas of the French Revolution, embraced by all of Europe, had also reached Russia. The problems of independence and freedom, monarchies and republics were debated in the salons of St. Petersburg and Moscow. For the first time in history, the Russian officer corps and the aristocratic elite had set foot in Europe's heart by way of its victorious army. The returning officers brought the spirit of European life and ideas of freedom back to their homeland.

It was as if Russia had rediscovered Europe and proclaimed its intent to take part in shaping Europe's future. Many Russian officers, who became acquainted with Europe while fighting Napoleon, protested on the Senate Square in December 1825 against autocracy. For the first time in history, Russia became familiar with the new European values: the principles of freedom, democracy, and the republic. The issue was no longer the geographical interpretation of European integration, but rather matters of substance related to ideas of freedom and human rights, as well as the principles of liberalism. Discussion in Russian social circles during the nineteenth century focused on this problem.

The very widespread and somewhat relative classification of the representatives of society into followers of the West ("Westerners") and Slavophiles ("Friends of the Slavs") indicates the intensity of the debate and the polemics. Many Russian politicians, writers, and philosophers advanced the position that Russia and the West belonged together, that Russia should and must follow the European path. Alexander Herzen, Piotr Chaadaev, and Ivan Turgenev advocated the "Europeanization of Russia." For them, the issue was not the direct appropriation of European models. The Russian liberal "Westerners" wrote and spoke much about the contradictions and the negative aspects of European life and saw the future of Russia mostly in its participation in European traditions. They did not ignore what was specific to Russia, but rather saw this in context with the entire European process, in which Russia must claim its place.

The desired "Europeanization of Russia" in the nineteenth century was connected to a large extent with the views of the European liberation movement. In reaction to this orientation to the West, a tendency to introduce theoretical justifications for a specific Russian path became increasingly more intense. Russia's position between Europe and Asia provided the basis and argumentation for this movement. The spectrum of these Slavophile, or Russophile, ideas and views was very broad. The advocates of these ideas focused mainly on the theory of a special path and the particular fate of Russia. They were also concerned with the negative effects of Western culture and European traditions on Russia. Naturally, there were nuances in this perspective. The open chauvinists and pan-Slavs stood opposed to the more "honest" Slavophiles in the middle of the 1860s. The dividing line between these opposing social forces was clearly drawn.

Nikolai Danilevski's book *Russia and Europe* and the writings of the Russian philosopher Nikolai Berdiaev lent expression to these views. They also inspired the theory of a united European and Asian realm: Eurasia. These views resulted in attempts to establish the existence of a European civilization with Russia at center and having its own independent development and worldwide mission.

The concept of Eurasia found strong support later in the 1920s. The groundwork, however, was laid in the nineteenth-century discussions about the various views concerning the potential for Russian development. The debates in Russia in the last century about the problem of Russia and Europe went far beyond geographical questions. They centered on the analysis and understanding of European integration and Western liberalism, of Slavic unity and Russian elitism, which was compared to Western European standards. In discussions in the second half of the nineteenth century, advocates of Russia's special mission appealed to the old Russian traditions and experiences. They idealized the Russian community and other traditional forms of Russian life.

The situation was also intensified by the fact that Russia continued to remain behind the level of economic and political development of Europe. Russian reforms of the 1860s to the 1880s certainly influenced the development of the country; however they were not sufficiently far-reaching to bring about a vigorous economic boom or a fundamental reorganization of social life and the state. At the beginning of the twentieth century, social life in Russia was still somewhat archaic, democratic institutions were still underdeveloped, and not much more than the beginnings of a multiparty system existed. Nevertheless, Russia had considerably increased its political power, its weight, and its influence in solving European and world problems.

The czars took part in the battle for influence in Europe and in Asia at the same level as the other European nations. Conservative Europe saw a bastion of the old order in Russia—a strong factor in the battle against the liberation and growing revolutionary movements.

This situation was one of the factors that contributed to the strengthened position of those Russian social circles that believed in a development unique to Russia not only in cultural, historical, and religious realms, but also as a major world power. The members of these circles also dreamed of Russian domination of the Balkans, the channels of the Black Sea, Eastern Europe, and Asia. The invigoration of the reactionaries inspired a rebirth of the tendencies toward liberation—a rebirth in the struggle of liberal and leftist circles against autocracy and extreme reaction.

Bolshevism and Proletarian Europe

Bolshevik victory in October 1917, and their ascent to power, changed the map of Europe and, in many regards, determined the fate of Russia in the twentieth century.

Lenin and his followers thought in terms of a world revolution. Their view of the problems of Russia and Europe can be understood and assessed only in the context of their concept of a world revolution. The notion of the revolutionary explosion in Europe permeated the theoretical work of Lenin, Trotsky, Bukharin, and their adherents. The Bolshevik leaders, the educated Marxists, were brought up under the influence of Western traditions. They supported the idea of Russian affiliation with Europe and its development according to Western models and traditions. However, the entire problem lay in their preconceived notion of Europe and which European values they held to be most important for the new revolutionary Europe they wanted to create.

They consistently represented the theory of the class conflict and negated the ideas of the bourgeois liberalism and the bourgeois democracy. They made an appeal to the traditions of revolutionary solidarity and to the proletarian stage in the development of Europe. For Lenin, the uprisings in Russia in the nineteenth century were only paving the way for a proletarian revolution, and socialism and communism.

Bolshevik writings and the party platform always revolved around forthcoming revolution in the West—the revolutionary potential in Germany, England, France, the United States, etc. In accordance with their ideas, Russia would join in the revolutionary wave, and in doing so, connect its fate with the realization of the proletarian world revolution, and most importantly, with the realization of the revolution in Europe. In their opinion, the experiences of the Marxist Internationale showed that an international organization that organized and directed the actions of the revolutionary forces was necessary and unavoidable.

However, there was no complete theoretical and organizational unanimity among the Bolsheviks. The same ideas that had already divided Russian social circles in the previous century also arose in their discussions.

In both his writings and practical activities, Lenin tried to combine the pro-Western view as it related to the European revolution and the notion of Russia's special mission and role in the world. However, the Bolsheviks had their own ideas about Russia's mission. While paying special attention to the Russian anarchist movement's experience with revolutionary violence, traditions, and strategies, they chose to prepare the Russian proletariat for armed mass struggle and revolutionary uprising instead of advocating terror on an individual level.

The Bolsheviks saw Russia's specific historical mission as the center of the revolutionary movement, which would be the source of the revolutionary impulses in Europe and the rest of the world. From this arose the idea of Russia's revolutionary calling, reviving in a new and peculiar form the old notion of Russia as a chosen people. While the Slavophiles and their followers had appealed in the past to Russian historical and cultural traditions, the Russian soul, and the Russian psychology, Bolshevism developed a new concept of the Russian revolutionary elite and Russia's historical mission, which was to lead humanity on the path toward socialism and communism.

At the same time, there was another movement within the Russian Social Democrats, represented by the Mensheviks and the followers of Trotsky. They attempted to bring the Russian revolution closer to the Western revolutionary movement and international social democracy. However, they too believed Russia was called to fulfill a historical mission, which would make use of the experiences of the international and European Social Democrats.

Lenin also expressed his opinions regarding a united Europe in a treatise on the subject in 1915 discussing "The United States of Europe." He reiterated his view that the realization of this concept could occur only through a unification of the revolutionary powers in Europe. Otherwise, the idea was either reactionary, because it would mean, in effect, an alliance of reactionary Europe to divide up the world, or it was absolutely unrealistic.

Immediately after the revolution, Soviet Russia began actively to turn into reality its agenda of a world revolution. In its very first appeal, in the "Decree of Peace," ratified two days after the revolutionary seizure of power, Lenin called on the workers of Germany, England, and the other European nations to engage in revolutionary struggle and to support Soviet power. In the period that followed, Soviet Russia actively supported the November revolution of 1918 in Germany, the revolution of 1919 in Hungary, and other revolutionary activity in Europe.

The main task of the Comintern, which was founded to coordinate the revolutionary movement, was to support the European revolution by all possible means; thus Russia had turned toward Europe once again, however this time in the form of a revolutionary messiah who wanted to fundamentally change Europe and the rest of the world.

This resulted in a fundamental change in the European attitude toward Russia. For the leftists and the emerging communist movement, Soviet Russia became the ideological center they supported in their activities and struggle. To the European governments and to the entire continent, Russia became a constant threat to Europe's stability and its institutions. The old ideas excluding Russia from the classical notion of Europe were revived and won a new popularity. But while before the threat of the big power ambitions had come from the czarist empire, in the eyes of the West, Russia had now become a breeding ground for revolutionary viruses that threatened to destroy the European political and social systems.

But the real situation weakened the rigid position of the Soviet leadership. As the planned world revolution failed to occur and the revolutionary wave in Europe subsided, Lenin and his comrades found themselves forced to change their strategy and to establish normal relations with the capitalist world and, most importantly, with the European countries. In principle, Lenin had already foreseen this possibility in his foreign policy strategy.

The dualism of the Soviet foreign policy was also expressed in the attempt to reconcile the declared objective of a world revolution with the need for peaceful coexistence with capitalism. By 1918 Moscow already had tried to initiate relations with the West. Such efforts were especially intense by 1920. Trade agreements were signed with England, Italy, and Germany, and diplomatic relations were established with practically all of the European countries by 1924; thus, Soviet Russia was incorporated into the European political world with the approval of Western Europe.

At the Genoa Conference in 1922, Soviet Russia announced its intention to join the European economic system. The Soviet agenda in Genoa had a very broad, all-encompassing character. The Bolsheviks declared their position in favor of the establishment of a uniform gold standard with the West, common measures for solving fuel and energy problems, the construction of a transatlantic railway between London and Vladivostok, and, naturally, comprehensive economic and commercial relations with the West.

The Soviet leadership, however, was not in complete agreement. A faction of the pragmatists (Litvinov, Krassin, Chicherin, and others) insisted on making certain ideological compromises in order to secure Western credit and loans. Trotsky, Rakovsky, and others wanted to follow the ideological and revolutionary principles as before. On the governmental level, Russia returned from revolutionary rhetoric to the international (European) arena, although it retained its ideological persuasion, which was seen in its support of the Comintern, in the emphasis on world revolution, and in the harsh criticism of capitalism as an antagonistic social order.

Propaganda against Western values was launched immediately following the revolution in the Soviet Union. Russia was prepared to work with Europe on an official level; however, it continued dogmatically to oppose the values and principles of the European democracies. Its integration into the European order was, as a result, very one-sided and limited. It had more to do with Soviet Russia's admission into a system of governments than with a structural integration. This was also the reason for the constant contradiction and the continued tension and hostility between Europe and Soviet Russia.

As for the West, it accepted Russia as a geopolitical partner and a member of the European system of nations, but at the same time made it clear that it rejected the Soviet form of government, its principles, and its direction. The West limited itself to only the most necessary contacts and agreements.

Stalinism and Europe

Under Stalinist rule, Russia in its relations with Europe continued to pursue the plans and strategies developed earlier by Lenin. Stalin actively persisted, indeed in a considerably more cynical fashion than Lenin, to plan for a world revolution. Certain points of the plan had already been modified while Lenin was still alive, with the focus of revolution shifting to the East. Following the failure of the initial revolutionary turbulence immediately after the October Revolution, Europe had lost its position as the only center of Moscow's plans.

This development was recognized by Stalin and the Comintern, which now paid a great deal of attention to China, Latin America, and even Africa. But revolution of the European countries and the attention of the Soviet leadership to leftist and communist forces in Europe remained on the agenda. The European social democracies were also considered an important target in the work of the Comintern. Stalin's definition of "social fascism" in effect characterized social democrats as the main enemy. This position led to a shift in the Soviet Union away from leftist social democratic circles in Europe, with the communists remaining the sole hope.

Stalin's attitude toward the pacifist movement in Europe and pacifism in general followed a similar direction. Fierce criticism of the so-called abstract pacifists was the reason the powerful union of European pacifists and the Soviets failed to reach an accord.

Stalin's view of abstract humanism had a similar effect. Soviet propaganda continued to criticize bourgeois liberalism harshly because of its "class limitations" and its hostility to the Marxist-Leninist ideology. Indeed, it was typical of the communist regime to oppose vehemently all different manifestations of the liberal ideology and liberal thinking.

When the confrontation between fascism and democracy in Europe became critical, the position of the leadership under Stalin, although opposed to fascism at first, did nothing to help in bringing together Europe's social groups in the fight against fascism.

The European agenda of the Soviet Union, however, was not only characterized by social intolerance, bias based on class conflict and ideological confrontation with capitalism. During the late 1930s, Stalin went back to the old big power concept of Russia and played with the idea of expanding the area of Russian influence in Europe. The symbiosis of revolutionary ideology and a big power ambition resulted in a very specific form of policy and a unique mentality. This big power agenda increasingly destroyed the ideals of socialism that had predominated for decades and had been the inspiration for communist supporters the world over in October 1917.

In the late 1930s the Soviet Union thus distanced itself even farther from Europe and its democratic and liberal values and institutions. Moreover, another factor contributing greatly to Russia's isolation was the reign of mass terror, which was strongly condemned by large parts of the European public.

On the other hand, the Soviet Union still played an active role in Europe as it worked together with nations of Western Europe on an official governmental level. Around the mid-1930s, the creation of a system of collective defense was often discussed. This project was fervently supported by French Foreign Minister Louis Barthou, Soviet Foreign Minister Maxim Litvinov, Yugoslav King Alexander, and others.

The idea of collective security, however, was not to be realized. After the assassination of Barthou, France gradually started to change its policy. The policy of appeasement, supported especially by the leadership of Great Britain, was increasingly adopted by the Western countries. It reached its climax in the Munich treaty in September 1938, which gave Hitler permission to annex Czechoslovakia. This set a precedent: from now on an aggressor would not have to fear resistance, but could count on being rewarded with concessions.

After Munich, the outlines of Soviet policy became increasingly clear. The Soviet big power ambitions were evident in the Soviet-German treaty of August 1939, which included a secret protocol of the areas of interest to be divided between Germany and the Soviet Union. Contrary to all principles of international law and all moral norms and ethics, the Soviet and German leaders made arrangements deciding the fate of European countries and its peoples.

With the Hitler-Stalin pact of 1939 the Soviet Union found itself in conflict with the European democracies and the European public, especially after World War II had broken out and Great Britain and France had declared war against fascist Germany.

As historical facts show, during the dramatic 1938–39 period, neither the leaders of the Western democracies nor Soviet leaders succeeded in overcoming their prejudices and ideological intolerance in order to form an anti-Hitler coalition. This coalition first came about only after the German surprise attack on the Soviet Union. From 1941–45, it seemed as if all the prerequisites for an all-encompassing, long-term cooperative effort between the USSR and the Western countries were being established. The idea of a world revolution obviously was put on hold, and the Comintern was dissolved. The central focus of Soviet policy became national defense and the defeat of the common enemy.

The victory over fascism in 1945 was met with an atmosphere of euphoria by the Allies. However, the illusions evaporated quickly and hope was destroyed. The Cold War, a long period of embittered confrontation, had begun for Europe and the entire world. It was a conflict that impaired international relations, froze the rigid principles and rules, and coined a new, unique mythology, psychology, and way of thinking.

I do not want to go into the general questions surrounding the inception and development of the Cold War, but only address the problem of the Soviet Union and Europe and the special features of Soviet domestic and international policies.

As a result of the war, the country had been devastated and had suffered enormous losses. It was, however, aware of its great victory, its increase in world recognition and authority. For the first time in his political career, Stalin saw the chance not only to proclaim his international political goals and ambitions, but also to realize them. Soviet troops were stationed in practically every country of Eastern Europe and in Berlin.

Stalin's big power plans, which stretched well beyond the Soviet border, were now stimulated afresh. New documents from Soviet archives show that serious consideration was given in political and military circles to a possible advance into Western Europe. It must have been known, however, that this would mean the beginning of a new war. At the same time, an embittered political and diplomatic battle began between the USSR and its allies over the future of Germany and Eastern Europe.

The Stalinist totalitarian regime managed to widen the chasm between it and Europe's democratic values even more. It had violated the principles of freedom, independence, and human rights and isolated the Soviet Union from a democratic Europe. Stalinism in the USSR and National Socialism in Germany embodied the totalitarian European systems. However, while National Socialism was prepared to accept the ideas of European integration in order to subjugate Europe, the Stalinist leadership wanted to continue to export Stalinism to other European countries and realize its big power ambitions by dividing Europe into spheres of influence. Neither regime concealed its intentions to put an end to the liberal values and experiences of the European democracies.

The Soviet Model and Eastern Europe

From 1945 to 1948, the nations of Eastern and Southeastern Europe were at the center of general interest. These nations differed not only among themselves, but also had great differences in their historical connections and relations to Russia. Poland once had been part of the Russian empire. For that reason, anti-Russian sentiment had always been strong among Poles. Czechoslovakia, the most developed nation of Eastern Europe in terms of its economy and democracy, wanted to resume its former position and sought new forms and variations of its relations with the West. In the Balkans, Russian influence traditionally was strong. The Balkan people had not forgotten that they had been able to shake off Ottoman rule with Russia's assistance and support. The Soviet Union now attempted to find a common denominator for this conglomerate of forces and peoples by exploring the Soviet model of social development in their national reconstruction.

The old traditional parties of the Eastern European nations slowly lost their influence. Communist single-party regimes established themselves behind a spurious multiparty system. The Soviet Union imposed uniform social structures and institutions of power on the nations, introduced political prosecution, consolidated ideological conformity and unanimity, and prevailed in its claim to leadership.

In this, Stalin not only permitted himself to be led by the guidelines of the 1930s, but he also translated new forms of his big power policies into reality. Once again, there was a synthesis of the idea of world revolution, documented in the formation and consolidation of the Soviet world system, together with the big power ambitions of the Soviet Union, which continued the traditions of the former Russian empire. But while Lenin proclaimed the unification of proletarian Europe as a strategic goal during the first years of Soviet power, Stalin now wanted unity of some Eastern European states and the Soviet Union based on common ideological, economic, and social policies. Although the independence and autonomy of the states was retained, their dependence on Moscow was great. Because the path of joint socialist development and the relations between states were closely connected, the prerequisites for integration of Eastern Europe under the leadership of the Soviet Union were achieved.

At the same time, the nations of Eastern Europe adapted their historical traditions to the new circumstances, the interests and requirements of socialism. This process took place differently in the various nations. East Germany invented the formula of two Germanies; in Bulgaria and in some other nations, only those traditions that were related to the socialist and revolutionary movement and to class struggle were permitted to be retained. As in the 1920s and 1930s in the Soviet Union, liberal ideas and movements and all appearances of middle class ideology and dissent were vigorously opposed.

This imposition of discipline was not limited only to the national framework. Economic (COMECON) and military policy (Warsaw Treaty) institutions of the "socialist community of states" were organized. Thus a new concept of "Europeanization" arose: Eastern European integration within the confines of socialism and under the leadership of the Soviet Union. The USSR, in a sense, had returned to Eastern Europe as the protector and leader of the socialist group. A new political elite, dedicated to socialist convictions and oriented to the Soviet Union, arose in the Eastern nations. In their enthusiasm for the successes of socialism, the leaders of the Soviet Union and the East European nations neither saw nor perceived how unstable and contradictory the new states were, nor how crises were ripening.

The various measures and transformations initiated by the Soviets in Eastern Europe led to a new and quite contradictory view of the Soviet Union that had become the heir of the former Russian empire. In official propaganda, the Soviet Union was described as the protective patron and "big brother," and characterized as an example to be copied. But other voices and tendencies formed within society as a whole and in the personal belief of individuals. National self-assurance grew and became stronger, frequently on an anti-Soviet basis; it found expression in the pursuit of independence from the Soviets. The tragic events in Poland and Germany in 1953, in Hungary in 1956, and finally in Czechoslovakia in 1968 demonstrated clearly that the Soviet Union was prepared to use its military to subdue the people's striving for freedom and independence.

These crises only sharpened the tensions in the nations of the "socialist community," undermined the stature of the Soviet Union, and fomented anti-Russian and anti-Soviet perceptions in large groups of the populations of these states.

In terms of public opinion in the Soviet Union itself, it must be said that many who were unaware of the true conditions of the nations of Eastern Europe spoke of the successful development of world socialism. They were very pleased to note that the ideas and standards prevailing in the USSR had been adopted by other nations, thus strengthening the international position of the Soviet Union.

Nor should it be ignored that just at this period, international relations were worsening, and the Cold War had already begun.

The Cold War

The history of the Cold War is often perceived only as a confrontation between the Soviet Union and the United States. However, it must be noted that the struggle between the systems was played out in Central Europe and, in many ways, determined the fate of that region.

Historians continue to discuss the reasons for the Cold War and why the time-tested cooperation during World War II could be transformed so quickly into enormous rivalry and global confrontation in all matters of international relations.

To answer these questions it must be remembered that cooperation of the nations of the anti-Hitler coalition was devoted to a single principal purpose, victory over fascism. The closer the victory became, the more obvious it was that the glaring contradictions that separated Russia and the West continued to exist, becoming evident on political, military, and ideological planes.

The war had taught the allies to depend on power as the most important factor in international relations. This power syndrome also played a decisive role in the postwar period for the allies. The Americans depended particularly on the monopoly of the atom, while the Soviets placed bets on their strong land-based military forces in the European nations.

The Yalta decisions dividing the world into spheres of influence also contributed to this confrontation, because both sides watched with great mistrust to make sure the agreements were kept and the balance maintained. Serious strains in their relations followed the events in Eastern Europe, which were perceived in the West as expansion of communism.

On the other hand, Soviet leadership and ordinary people in the Soviet Union perceived the "Pax Americana" doctrine as a threat to the development of the USSR and the entire socialist community.

Stalin found himself at the zenith of his power and might. His imagination was fired by the great victory, and he attempted not only to secure his gains, but to extend them. The experiences of the twentieth century have shown that the principal dangers to Russian national interests threaten from Europe. Thus Stalin concentrated his attention in the first instance on Europe. As he extended the Soviet model of socialism to the nations of Eastern Europe, it became clear to him that the German question had become a keystone in the struggle between the systems. Partitioned Germany became a symbol of the partition of Europe and of the military zone where East and West deployed their forces.

Stalin wanted to apply constant pressure to Western Europe with the aid of the socialist states of Eastern Europe and the German Democratic Republic (GDR). Soviet leadership was convinced that significant upheavals were coming to a head and that communists and other forces of the left were gaining in influence. Stalin was ready to set Russia in motion in the direction of Europe. However, he perceived this as the dissemination of communist theory and practice and the expansion of Soviet influence on the European continent. The contradiction here was that Soviet leadership imputed to its European policies far greater significance, while simultaneously it took great pains to keep the Soviet populace as far away from Europe as possible.

The situation was reminiscent of events following the victory of Russian troops over Napoleon in 1812. Again this time, many thousands of young Soviet officers had been in Europe and had come into contact with the local population and allied troops. They, and several million Soviet citizens, saw representatives of the West as something other than enemies. In fact, interest increased in Western concepts, literature and art, and lifestyles as well.

The Soviet leadership recognized a danger in this, and, as early as 1946, initiated a counter-campaign. Ideology was the principal means selected to combat Western influence and to prevent the incursion of middle-class concepts into the socialist nations. Special resolutions, requiring greater adherence to ideological purity and allegiance to the principles of Marxism-Leninism in literature, art, and music were adopted. The anti-West campaign clearly was heating up. From 1949 to 1952, a large-scale campaign took place against "cosmopolitanism," and against the inroads made by Western ideology and lifestyles. In this campaign, the concept "West" was, in fact, identical with the U.S. and Europe, where, according to Soviet ideologues, Americans dominated anyway.

The ideological actions soon were backed up by a new wave of repressive measures, among which were the dissolution of European antifascist committees and the imprisonment of their leaders, and the so-called "case of the physicians." As in earlier years, "unscientific" work of Western scientists was "exposed" in science and ideology and all modernistic developments in art and literature were strongly criticized. Political liberalism was explained as the principal danger to Soviet citizens; it was said to undermine the "progressive ideology" of the workers of the Soviet Union and of the Western nations. All this led to Russia being isolated from the external world like a beleaguered fortress. The renewed isolation from the West resulted from the existence of this iron curtain.

The European values of the past, together with contemporary social and political accomplishments in European science, art, and literature, remained closed to the Soviet populace. It seems appropriate to conclude that Russia had not returned to Europe, rather the contrary was true.

Furthermore, as in the past, nationalistic ideology gained renewed influence in the Soviet Union; the special role and mission of Russia, and its exclusivity, were emphasized. This absurdity reached its peak when, in the course of general policies of prohibitions and the struggle for purity of ideological principles in the Soviet Union, the works of turn-of-the-century Russian thinkers were put on the index, allegedly because they advocated religious views and opinions.

The West did its own part to isolate the Soviet Union from Europe. The Soviet Union and Russia were depicted as the "chief enemy and principal opponent" in anti-Soviet campaigns in the U.S. and in some European nations. Contacts of Western intellectuals and public representatives with the Soviet population also were reduced to a minimum.

The increase in international tensions, the arms buildup, and the construction of dozens of military bases by the U.S. and NATO encircling the Soviet Union was accompanied by loud propaganda campaigns that furthered alienation and confrontation between the West and the Soviet Union. The foreign policy of the Soviet Union, as in the 1920s and 1930s, was characterized by contradictory tendencies. While confrontations were increased on an ideological level, Soviet leadership launched foreign policy initiatives and deemed the USSR an important, decisive factor in world politics. Increasing contacts between Soviet diplomats and the West clearly showed the crass differences that were made between the Soviet elite and the "common man," for whom any contact with the West was seen as a sign of poor patriotism and deficient loyalty to the Soviet lifestyle and to Marxism-Leninism. This situation only served to aggravate the differences within Soviet society and produced privileged classes separate from the broad mass of the Soviet populace.

Discussions about and confrontations over the Marshall Plan played an important role in the Cold War. How this plan arose is widely understood, but little is known about the point of view of the Soviet Union and the nations of Eastern Europe. The Americans, who had offered their assistance in the economic reconstruction of Europe, formally did not exclude anyone, so initially there was discussion about including the Soviet Union in the Marshall Plan. The Soviet leadership signalled readiness to consider the question and worked out proposals for the conditions that would make possible participation of the nation in the American aid program. The Americans knew that the USSR, devastated by the war, desperately needed loans and credits. Therefore they assumed that the Soviet Union had some interest in the plan. Documents from the archives of the Foreign Ministry of the USSR indicate that Soviet diplomacy had prepared itself for participation in the negotiations concerning the plan and for participation in the 1947 Paris conference at which the modalities and the realization of the plan were to be discussed. But a change in course came rather quickly in Moscow. Arguments against Soviet participation in the Marshall Plan were formulated. Obviously of decisive importance were the conditions in the East European nations and the course of confrontation against the West.

One of the political goals of the plan (and the Americans did not deny this) was to include the Eastern European nations in the aid program in order to keep them in the Western sphere of influence and to prevent their drift into the sphere of power and influence of the Soviet Union. Documents in the archives of the Foreign Ministry of the USSR explain rejection of the Marshall Plan. In their reports and position papers, experts—economists and others—listed various arguments against Soviet participation. Among other things, strategic questions were raised about international developments. A position paper written in the style then traditional noted, for example, that the economy of the U.S. was facing an imminent crisis and that Soviet participation in the plan would only open new markets for the

Americans, thus helping them to overcome the effects of the predicted crisis.

Other documents focused on the danger implicit in acceptance of the plan: separation of the Eastern European nations from the Soviet Union. The new leaders of these countries already closely allied to the Soviets waited for Moscow's decision, with the documents indicating that the position of Czechoslovakia was especially important. The Czechoslovak leaders, including those of the Communist Party, advocated participation in the American aid program, pointing to previous long-term cooperation with the West and good experience at that time. But just a few days before the Paris conference, the Czech leaders were ordered to Moscow and required, in an ultimatum, to renounce participation in the Marshall Plan. Under pressure they agreed. In the final analysis, the Soviet Union, the East European, and Southeast European nations, together with Finland, all rejected the aid offered by the American Marshall Plan.

The question also had its purely diplomatic side. How wrong the Soviet decision had been became apparent soon afterward, when the question of Soviet responsibility for the partition of Europe arose. Documents prove that Soviet agreement to participation in the Marshall Plan would not have altered anything. Many American documents, reminiscences of participants, and the works of historians demonstrate that the Marshall Plan would hardly have been ratified by Congress if the Soviet Union had decided to participate. We must not forget that the Cold War had already escalated and that it would have been very difficult for Americans to translate their Eastern European policies into reality in the event of Soviet acceptance.

In any case, Soviet rejection of participation in the Marshall Plan was the decisive event in the deepening split in Europe, and it led to global effects.

The relations between the USSR and the Western nations changed radically in the post-Stalin era. If confrontation and hostility remained symptomatic at the end of the 1950s and the beginning of the 1960s, nevertheless a dialogue about many international matters began, slowly. Both sides obviously were interested in reducing international tension. The contacts and exchange of opinions also increased on unofficial levels.

In Europe, recognition that relations to the Soviet Union had to change became increasingly pervasive. Western politicians became oriented to a more flexible course toward the Soviet Union. That was related as well to internal events in the USSR; Khrushchev's "thaw" had its effects. Although neo-Stalinist tendencies gained the upper hand again toward the end of the 1960s, as was expressed most clearly by the occupation of Czechoslovakia by Soviet and other Warsaw Pact troops, nevertheless the idea that changes were unavoidable permeated the opinion of the Soviet public.

The position of the Soviet leadership was characterized on the one hand by becoming more insistent with its socialist allies to preserve the "unity of the socialist camp at all costs," while it was ready, on the other hand, for far-reaching compromises with the West. Thus, already at the end of the 1960s, vigorous economic and political cooperation had developed between the Soviet Union and the nations of Western Europe and the U.S., reflecting changes in the policies of leading Western nations toward the East.

The USSR and the CSCE Process

The process associated with the Conference on Security and Cooperation in Europe (CSCE, Helsinki Conference) opened a new stage in East-West relations, particularly in terms of cooperation between the Soviet Union and Western Europe and in the all-European movement toward unity and identity.

Western European integration of economies and policies increased continuously during this period. From the very beginning, the Soviet Union assumed a position of skepticism and rejection toward European integration. This had both ideological and class-related causes because integration was classified as a middle-class and imperialistic process directed "against the interests of the workers." In this, the centripetal European tendencies were underestimated and the role and significance of "interparliamentary contradictions" overestimated.

This negative attitude toward integration had the consequence that Soviet relations with the EEC were rejected and bilateral relations with individual European nations were preferred. The West adjusted to this, so at the end of the 1960s and the beginning of the 1970s important agreements and treaties were reached between the Soviet Union and France, the Federal Republic of Germany, Great Britain, Italy, and other West European nations.

In relation to these treaties, in Moscow and in the European capitals the talk was of historical traditions and experiences in the relations between Russia and the nations of Western Europe, of the changes needed in the general political climate of Europe, and the desirability of the development of comprehensive commercial and economic relations. In time, attitudes of the peoples and the nations of Europe toward each other began to change. Most important, however, was the fact that there was talk, for the first time in many years, of a Europe stretching from the Atlantic to the Urals. Until then, the thought had been suggested in many nations of Western Europe, and in the minds of the European public, that Russia should be excluded from classical Europe and the concept of pan-European realities.

General de Gaulle's thesis that Europe extends from the Atlantic to the Urals in a certain sense brought the Soviet Union back into greater Europe and supplanted the notion of a Europe within borders stretching "from Brest to Brest." This was also the basis for the German policies toward the East, which led to ratification of important treaties between the Federal Republic of Germany and the USSR, Poland, and Czechoslovakia. These signals were read with satisfaction in Moscow. Cooperation between the USSR and the nations of Western Europe was activated. All these activities prepared the ground for far-reaching initiatives that launched the all-Europe process and reached its peak in the Final Accords of the CSCE.

Without going into detail about the various aspects of this problem, I want to emphasize that the Soviet Union was drawn comprehensively into the political aspects of a unified Europe by the CSCE process. Quite possibly this led, for the first time in the twentieth century, to a completely different set of problems in the controversial relation between Russia and Europe.

Many all-European projects of the twentieth century excluded Russia and the Soviet Union from plans of European integration and perceived them as foreign bodies. But now it was confirmed, both in Moscow and in other European capitals, that the USSR was a component of European history and the all-European process.

Questions of economic and political cooperation, as well as the formation of a European security system were posed among the first to be addressed in this process. The political situation at the time made these matters of equal interest to Moscow and Western Europe. With the signing of the Final Accords of Helsinki, the Soviet Union accepted several fundamental principles of European life.

It must be emphasized that this was largely a matter of international policies. Both sides had come to the recognition that nuclear confrontation was hopeless and dangerous, and that parity of rockets and nuclear weapons potential simply had to be acknowledged. That was the basis for Willy Brandt's thesis of new European thinking in the era of missiles and atomic weapons.

The new European thinking was based on the political realities at the end of the 1960s and the beginning of the 1970s. But at its very inception, the CSCE process was understood and appraised differently in the West and in Eastern Europe. That is particularly true of the so-called humanitarian questions—human rights, expression of opinions, and freedom of movement. The West wanted to include these matters in the total package of the Accords by making a link between acceptance of the agreed political questions and agreements on humanitarian matters. In Moscow, in contrast, efforts were made to limit, to the extent possible, commitments in matters of human rights and other "delicate" problems.

In the end, agreement was reached with a compromise that forced Moscow to accept this side of the all-European process. The compromise consisted of a concession wrung from the West permitting the Soviet Union to deal with matters in this sphere in accordance with laws and regulations in force in the USSR.

Thus the Soviet Union also participated in these aspects of the formation and development of Europe, even if it did so in a limited way and with restrictions. For the first time in the history of Soviet power, Moscow's leaders in general had recognized such European values as freedom of movement and human rights, although they interpreted these rights from the point of view of Marxist-Leninist ideology. This demonstrates the significance and contradictions of the Helsinki Accords. These contradictions had very strong effects during the following period. For that reason, reduction of tension in Europe was not at all without strains; successes alternated with reverses. At the end of the 1970s and the beginning of the 1980s, the process of détente moved very slowly. Among the reasons cited for this are Soviet intervention in Afghanistan and repressive measures against dissidents and the human rights movement in the Soviet Union and some Eastern European nations.

Détente elicited significant changes in Europe. It did not lead, however, to a breakthrough in principle in the relations between Europe and the USSR.

As in the past, there was a deep gap between the economies, the politics and the intellectual sphere, and in the understanding and interpretation of the values of European history and democracy. The old regime, which resisted the values of European history and democracy, continued to rule in the Soviet Union.

Infractions of human rights and persecution of those who thought differently remained a part of the everyday agenda. History and traditions were treated from an ideological point of view. Despite apparent lip service, Western values, such as that of Europe being a "common European house," were rejected. Despite expanded contacts and the political adjustment in Europe confrontation continued between Soviet socialist theory and practice and European democracy.

Soviet society recognized that changes were absolutely necessary because the inheritance of totalitarianism and stagnation otherwise would lead the nation into a blind alley and place it into stark contrast with the entire civilized world.

The Long Way to Europe

For the Soviet Union, Perestroika did not lead only to fundamental changes in the nation, in its social life, and in its social order. Indeed, it led to decisive advances in its foreign policies and in its international relations.

In the nation itself it led to painfully overcoming old dogmas and rules, to the transition from a totalitarian system to a civilized lifestyle, to a civilian society, and to a nation of laws. The transition was characterized by dramatic successes and reverses, positive and negative events, and conflict between opposing forces and movements. But the historical role of Perestroika was that it initiated changes and that it produced significant alterations in the lives of people and in their mentalities and ideas. Developments in Europe and elsewhere have demonstrated how difficult and complicated transition is from a totalitarian system to democracy, and the variety of historical changes that can occur on this road.

This process is more difficult in a nation that had nearly no experience in dealing with democracy and a multiparty system; in a society in which the totalitarian state and totalitarian thought were deeply rooted; where for seventy years a single party had ruled without limits and where now fundamental transformations were required in the economy and in society to overcome the low income level and poverty among millions.

Perestroika took place in a multinational state in which centrifugal forces already had developed behind a facade of well-sounding and grandiloquent words about "staunch unity" of all ethnic groups. An apparently unshakable social order was undermined by the Perestroika initiated in the middle of the 1980s.

It remains for history to summarize all these developments and to evaluate the various stages of Perestroika, particularly as completely unexpected and serious events may still occur. But even today it can be said that the system that ruled for seventy years in the Soviet Union has been shattered and destroyed in its fundamentals. As a first step, the Communist Party lost its monopolistic position in society, and then formally left the political scene entirely. Similarly, the socialist and communist ideals lost their attractiveness and discredited themselves in the eyes of millions of people.

At the beginning the leaders of Perestroika sought to reform communism, to give it a new "human face" and to breathe new life into it. Then they set the goal for themselves of changing the Communist Party into an organization that would approximate the social democratic parties of Europe in its ideological fundamentals and its internal organization. But the process went out of control so that the single-party system no longer found support in the nation and in society. The first free elections with several alternative candidates took place in the USSR for the soviets (parliaments) at all levels. Then the first president to receive a mandate from the people was elected.

The formation of a civil society and a nation of laws in our country proceeded with great difficulty and contradictions. Fundamental changes were initiated in the economy with the painful and difficult conversion to a market economy experienced by millions. The former centralized system was destroyed; the military-industrial complex lost its power.

New priorities also were established in spiritual and ideological realms. Recognized, generally accepted values and human rights replaced the concept of the class struggle and the ideological purity of Marxism-Leninism. The rigid theory of socio-economic formations as the main driving force for the development of humanity was valid no longer and was replaced by the thesis of a world civilization. The view of the world that had dominated the past and the very recent present had lost its fundamental basis.

Currently, these trends and changes provide direction and form the condition of the society and its perspectives. We recognize, however, that the new ideas and views will prevail only slowly, particularly as a bitter conflict continues in Russian society. In their arguments, conservative forces exploit the dissatisfaction of many groups with the deteriorating material conditions that were caused by the transition to a free market economy. But decisive steps have already been taken. Society has begun on a new path and is developing new values and new concepts.

The collapse of the old ideas and values is inevitably accompanied by negative effects. Some have become apathetic and no longer have any faith in values and ideas. Consumerism has triumphed, criminal behavior has increased and drug addiction has spread. Yet all in all, Russia moves slowly and with much effort in the direction of those ideals and lifestyles, those democratic structures, social organizational forms, and values that, in the end, lead to closer ties with European nations and the principles and standards of Europeanism. This decisive step fulfills the chief requirement for the actual, honest return of the former Soviet Union to Europe.

But these prerequisites and requirements, it should be noted, include another very important aspect, that of foreign policy revision. Seeing the world through a prism of class struggle must be relinquished in foreign policy guidelines, nor can the chief purpose and most important instrument of Soviet foreign policies be the support of all revolutionary forces. The new Soviet leadership began along this path, for Gorbachev declared publicly that all relevant values have precedence over ideological and class-related principles. The Soviet Union also renounced superpower goals in its foreign policy and declared itself ready to have normal relations on an equal basis with all nations, as is customary in the civilized world. The right of each nation and of all peoples to determine their own development was stated explicitly.

Soviet leaders undertook definitive steps in their European policies. In agreement with their declared principles, they proclaimed that they would not interfere in the turbulent processes that had begun in the socialist nations. This led to the fall of the communist regimes in the former Soviet client states within a matter of weeks; the socialist community no longer existed. At the same time, they gave a green light to the reunification of Germany, the rapid realization of which astounded the rest of the world. The Soviet Union withdrew its troops from Afghanistan and condemned its actions in Hungary in 1956 and in Czechoslovakia in 1968.

This brought an end to the theoretical and political division of Europe into blocs of opposing military policies and social systems.

The new leaders of the Soviet Union accepted the all-European values and ideals as equally valid for all nations and peoples of Europe and thus opened the way to reconciliation of all Europeans on the platform of democracy, pluralism, freedom, and human rights. The Soviet Union also declared that its previous position rejecting the executive institutions of West European integration would be revised. At the same time, the former allies of the Soviet Union in Eastern Europe were rushing to establish closer ties with other European countries. In Poland, Czechoslovakia, Hungary, Rumania, and finally in Albania, pluralism and liberalism prevailed at last, while the previously ruling communists were driven into the background. Mikhail Gorbachev defined the principles of the Soviet position toward Europe in his speech to the Council of Europe in July 1989. He expressed the desire of the Soviet leadership that, following its renewal, the nation be readmitted to the family of nations as part of Europe. The Soviet leader spoke repeatedly of human rights, the values of democracy, and a democratic society, appealing to the best traditions of Europe's political and social legacy and the achievements of European democracy.

While in the first stage of Perestroika foreign policy was reformed, with the relations to the U.S. and Western Europe reaching a fundamentally new stage, the European integration process gained a new impulse and a new dimension, and a basic change began in government relations of state between the Soviet Union and the European nations, signalling Soviet readiness to participate in the integration of democratic, civilized Europe.

The Western partners indicated their readiness as well. The end of the Cold War changed Western policies and Western patterns of thought. Russia was no longer the constant enemy and eternal threat. West European politicians finally abandoned their old stereotyped notions and previous pan-European concepts, according to which Russia was excluded from classical Europe. As a consequence, an important step was taken at the end of the 1980s and the beginning of the 1990s to achieving the principles of Europeanism, the ideals of democracy and of human rights, market economy and a civil society in the entire European region from the Atlantic to the Urals. This provided the chance to overcome the division of the continent and to begin to establish a greater Europe.

In this new stage of Europe's development, the European Community itself faces a complicated task. As they did twenty or thirty years ago, the twelve nations still continue to debate how the national interests can be brought into harmony with European unity, how the transition to a new phase of unification can be set into motion while national sovereignties, cultures, and traditions are preserved. It has been extraordinarily difficult for Europe to accept the nations of Eastern Europe and to cope with them, just as the unification of Germany causes problems for the Federal Republic. For these reasons, the unification of all Europe is not on the agenda for now or for the near future. In the interest of Russia and of Europe, it will be essential to form a common democratic region in which the principles of freedom, market economics, and human rights become reality.

Russia and Europe

The events in the Soviet Union developed precipitously. After the failed putsch of August 1991, the once monolithic structure of the state fell apart. All the national republics declared their independence and the end of the Soviet Union. Diplomatic recognition of the former Soviet republics and their entry into the United Nations followed.

At present, fifteen independent states exist on the territory of the former Soviet Union; their relation to Europe had to be renegotiated. In recognition of the role of the USSR in the Conference on Security and Cooperation in Europe (CSCE, Helsinki Conference), all former Soviet Republics were accepted as participants in the CSCE.

Important geopolitical changes occurred. The Baltic republics (Latvia, Lithuania and Estonia) are coordinating their domestic and foreign policies and seek ties especially with northern Europe. Belorus and the Ukraine orient their relations primarily to their neighbors on the western borders and seek a dialogue with Western Europe. Russia remains as the chief partner of Europe. It has assumed the responsibilities of the former Soviet Union and is extending its cooperation with Germany, France, Italy, Great Britain, and Spain. Russia intends to become a member of the Council of Europe and to insist on forming ties to the European Community. In this way it proclaims its commitment to the establishment of a greater Europe.

Now that reciprocal relations between Europe and the Soviet Union are no more, the old question of "Russia and Europe" arises again, albeit with new aspects and nuances. As in the nineteenth century, the historical role of Russia and its place in the history of the world of today is once again a topic of discussion in today's Russia. Interest in what is specifically Russian in nature has grown with the new geopolitical situation. Russia is a part of Europe and Asia; its culture and civilization developed from a synthesis of two great civilizations. The old and apparently long forgotten theories of Eurasia and Eurasians have been picked up again.

New editions of the works of defenders of Russian Slavophiles, the works of Danilevski and Berdiaev, and collected writings of Eurasians of the 1920s are finding Russian readers today as if they had been written specifically for them. The place of Russia in history and its historic mission are the subject of articles and lively discussions. The once popular idea of the "Russian soul" finds great resonance among experts and common people as well.

If not as vehemently as in the past, discussions are once again examining the extent to which Russia is a part of Europe and the character its relations and attitudes to the West should take. Ideological aspects still play a role in these debates. Former apologists of socialism warn against adoption of Western values and transforming the nation to capitalism. Their appeals are not directed specifically against Europe, but they warn of an "excessive and exaggerated" shift to the values of Europe.

In addition to the ideological aspect, the "Russian idea," which revives the earlier concept of the special position of Russia and interprets it under the new conditions and in new forms, finds increasing acceptance. As in the past this can lead to a revival of chauvinistic ideas and illusions. These tendencies are promoted by nostalgia for the former power of the nation, the painful loss of access to the Baltic Sea and the tense relations with the Ukraine because of the Crimea and the Black Sea coast.

Voices are even being heard demanding that the priorities of foreign policy be shifted and that principal attention now be given to the East—Asia, the Far East, and the Pacific region. But all of these currents are only expressions of a growing self-consciousness and the new geopolitical position of Russia and appear to be temporary in nature.

Through its history and its geopolitical position, its traditions and its civilization, Russia has belonged to and continues to be a part of Europe. That assessment, however, does not alter the fact that the Russian path is a special one. Russia is not only a part of European, but also a part of Asian civilization, not only bridging, but also integrating two important cultures and civilizations.

If we speak of the long road of Russia to Europe and attempt to illuminate the future hopes of the nation, we must pay special attention to the incorporation of Russia into a democratic Europe.

The present and the future of Russia depend on how rapidly and thoroughly we proceed with rebuilding a civil society and the rule of law and accomplish its consolidation, and how the market economy, human rights, freedom of information, freedom of thought, and freedom of movement are realized. These cornerstones of European democracy, which developed in Europe in a difficult and weary process, must be the major forces that bind Russia to Europe. These principles, more than anything else, will determine the affiliation of Russia to Europe.

When we speak of Russia and Europe, we must acknowledge its century-old relationships and the mutual intertwining of the destiny of their peoples. Russia also was involved inevitably in the numerous conflicts of the past and in both world wars, which began on European territory. The peace of today and of the future depends decisively on how stable and successful the new architecture of Europe and the new European security system—which is expected to assure the security and peaceful development of all nations and peoples of Europe—turn out to be.

The final years of the twentieth century will be characterized by sharply worsening national problems, including some on the European continent. National conflicts are shaking many nations and regions of Europe; Russia has its own share of these. Europe is interested in resolving these conflicts in Yugoslavia, in Russia, and in other European regions. The future of Europe depends in many ways on jointly overcoming such conflicts once and for all.

Russia today is increasingly involved in the European integration process. For Russia it is above all else an economic question; it must overcome its backwardness with respect to the West and reach the West European standard of living. Poland, Czechoslovakia, Bulgaria, the Ukraine, Belorus, Latvia, Lithuania, and Estonia are equally facing this same problem.

But the problem of European unity and European identity also depends on the question of whether we are dealing with a "Europe of the Fatherlands" or a joint European fatherland. The most recent debates related to the ratification of the Maastricht agreements have demonstrated that there is in Europe as well a strong lobby for preserving national sovereignty, for national traditions, history, and culture. That applies even more to Eastern Europe, and especially to Russia, with its own characteristics and peculiarities. From this point of view, Russia can make an incalculable contribution to the all-European process shaping the interrelationship between what is national and what is common to all, to the preservation and consolidation of national statehood and particularity in the development of a unified Europe with its economic integration, lifestyle, and political order.

Russia has a long, difficult, and contradictory road to travel before it takes part in this process. Nevertheless, it is important that it take this road and that this movement become irreversible.

Russia and Europe can, in the end, look back on a culture and civilization common to both. The centuries-old interweaving of history, culture, literature, art, science, and education has produced strong traditions of mutual relations.

The future heirs of European civilization will inherit the historical legacies of all the nations and peoples of Europe. Russia has played a worthy role in the development of European civilization in the past. The Russia of today and tomorrow must be integrated into this all-European process.

Bibliography

(All published in the Russian language)

N. Berdiaev, *The Fate of Russia* (Moscow, 1918).

N.J. Danilevski, *Russia and Europe* (Moscow, 1901).

A.I. Klibanov, *The Social Utopia of the Peoples in Russia. Period of Feudalism* (Moscow, 1977).
The Slavs and the West (Moscow, 1975).

M.W. Netshkina, *When Two Generations Meet* (Moscow, 1980).

N.W. Novoselzev, W.T. Pashuto, L.J. Cherepin, *Paths of Development of Feudalism* (Moscow, 1972).
The Cultural Connections of the Peoples of Eastern Europe in the 16th Century (Moscow, 1976).

D.M. Projektor, *Europe in the 20th Century: War. Its Lessons. The Will to Freedom* (Moscow, 1987).
The USSR and Western Europe. Problems of Trade and Economic Relations (Moscow, 1986).

N.A. Yerofeiev, *Cloudy Albion. England and the English from the Point of View of the Russians (1775 to 1853)* (Moscow, 1952).

About the Authors

Andrzej Ajnenkiel

Born in 1931 in Warsaw. Studied history and law in Warsaw. Professor at the Institute for History of the Polish Academy of Science. 1988–91 President of the Polish Historical Society; member of the scientific advisory staff of the President of the Polish Republic.

Important book publications: *Model of Polish Parliamentarianism to 1926* (1972), *The Political History of Poland 1926–1939* (1980), *History of the Polish Sejm During the Second Republic* (1989), and *The Polish Constitution* (1992).

François Bédarida

Born 1926 in Lyon, France. Studied history at the Paris Sorbonne. 1979–84 Director of Paris L'Ecole des Hautes Etudes en Sciences Sociales; 1978–90 Director of Institute of Contemporary History of CPW, Paris; since 1991 Director of Research at Centre National de la Recherche Scientifique, Paris. Since 1990 General Secretary of the International Committee for Historical Science.

Important book publications: *English Society from the Middle of the 19th Century to Today* (1976), *The Victorian Era* (1974), *The Secret Strategy of the Drole du Guerre* (1979), *Nazism and Genocide* (1989), *The Vichy Regime and the French* (1992).

Ivan T. Berend

Born 1930 in Budapest. Studied history and economy in Budapest. Professor of history at the University of Budapest and at the University of California, Los Angeles. First Vice President of the International Historians Association; member (former president) of the Hungarian Academy of Sciences; corresponding member of the British Academy and the Austrian Academy of Sciences.

Important book publications: *The Economic Development of East Central Europe in the 19th and 20th Century* (1974), *The European Periphery and Industrialization* (1982), *Underdevelopment and Economic Growth* (1979 — these three titles together with G. Ranki), *The Crisis Zones of Europe* (1986), *Economic Reforms in Hungary* (1990).

Valerio Castronovo

Born in 1935 in Vercelli, Italy. Studied history in Rome. Professor of contemporary history at the University of Milan; since 1972 full professor of contemporary history at the University of Turin. Corresponding member of the Turin Academy of Economics, member of the Italian Central Commission for Social Sciences, editor of the periodical for science and history *Promoteo*.

Important book publications: *The Italian Press from the Founding of the Italian State to the Fascist Era* (1979), *The Industrial Revolution* (1972), *History of Italy — Volume 4: Economic History* (1975), *Italian Industry from the 19th Century to Today* (1981), *The Upper Middle Class and the Middle Class. The Italian Road to Capitalism* (1988).

Alexander O. Chubarian

Born 1931 in Moscow. Studied history at the Moscow Lomonossov University. Scientific collaborator at the Institute for History of the Academy of Sciences of the USSR; 1965–87 professor of history at the Moscow Diplomatic Academy; 1977–87 scientific collaborator at the Institute for World History at the Academy of Sciences of the USSR. Since 1988 Director of the Institute (today Russian Academy of Sciences). Vice President of the International Association for Contemporary History. Since 1990 member of the Bureau of the International Committee for Historical Sciences.

Important book publications: *The European Idea in History* (1987), *Concepts of Europe from Napoleon to Now* (1992).

Jiří Kořalka

Born in 1931 in Sternberk, Czechoslovakia. Studied history at the Charles University in Prague. 1955–74 scientific associate at the Institute of History of the Czechoslovak Academy of Science, discharged for political reasons (1975–91 at the Hussite Museum in Tabor) end of 1991 rehabilitation and returned to work at the Academy. Member of the International Commission for the History of Social Movements, honorary member of Società di Studi Trentini di Scienze Storiche.

Important book publications: *The Origin of the Socialist Workers Movement in the Area of Reichenberg* (1956), *The All-German League and the Czech Question at the End of the 19th Century* (1963), *What Is a Nation?* (1969), *The Czech Research of Citizenship* (1989), *Czechs in the Hapsburg Empire and in Europe 1815–1914* (1991).

Wilfried Loth

Born in 1948 in Wadern, Germany. Professor of Contemporary History at the University of Essen. Member of the Liaison Group of Historians of the Commission of the EC.

Important book publications: *Socialism and Internationalism. French Socialists and the Postwar Order of Europe 1940–1950* (1977), *The Partition of the World. A History of the Cold War 1941–1955* (1980), *Catholics in the Empire. Political Catholicism in the Crisis in Wilheminian Germany* (1984), *History of France in the 20th Century* (1987), *The Road to Europe. A History of European Integration 1939–1957* (1990).

Wolfgang J. Mommsen

Born in 1930 in Marburg, Germany. Since 1968 professor for contemporary history at the Heinrich-Heine University in Düsseldorf. 1977–85 Director of the German Historical Institute in London. Chairman of the Historians Association of Germany, President of the International Committee for the History of Historiography in the International Committee for Historical Sciences.

Numerous books about the history of the nineteenth and twentieth centuries, about problems of European imperialism, about the theory of history as well as about Max Weber.

William Wallace

Born 1941 in Leicester, England. Studied at Cambridge University. Taught at Cornell University (1962–66) and the University of Manchester (1967–77). Director of the Royal Institute of International Affairs (1978–90), and Senior Research Fellow in European Studies at St. Anthony's College, Oxford, since 1991. Member of the Council in the Great Britain–East Europe Centre, board member of the Institute of European Politics, Bonn.

Important book publications: *The Foreign Political Process in Great Britain* (1976), *Policy Making in the European Community* (1983, together with H. Wallace), *Options for the Transformation of Western Europe* (1990), *The Dynamics of European Integration* (1990, together with other authors).